Mindfulness-Based C Living

Mindfulness involves learning to be more aware of life as it unfolds moment by moment, even if these moments bring us difficulty, pain or suffering. This is a challenge we will all face at some time in our lives, and which health professionals face every day in their work. The Mindfulness-Based Compassionate Living programme presents a new way of learning how to face the pressures of modern living by providing an antidote which teaches us how to cultivate kindness and compassion – starting with being kind to ourselves.

Compassion involves both sensitivity to our own and others' suffering and the courage to deal with it. Integrating the work of experts in the field such as Paul Gilbert, Kristin Neff, Christopher Germer and Tara Brach, **Erik van den Brink** and **Frits Koster** have established an eight stage step-by-step compassion training programme, supported by practical exercises and **free audio downloads**, which builds on basic mindfulness skills. Grounded in ancient wisdom and modern science, they demonstrate how being compassionate shapes our minds and brains, and benefits our health and relationships. The programme will be helpful to many, including people with various types of chronic or recurring mental health problems, and can be an effective means of coping better with low self-esteem, self-reproach or shame, enabling participants to experience more warmth, safeness, acceptance and connection with themselves and others.

Mindfulness-Based Compassionate Living will be an invaluable manual for mindfulness teachers, therapists and counsellors wishing to bring the 'care' back into healthcare, both for their clients and themselves. It can also be used as a self-help guide for personal practice.

Erik van den Brink studied medicine in Amsterdam and trained to become a psychiatrist in the UK. He has extensive experience in meditation and specialised in mindfulness-based and compassion focussed approaches to mental health. He currently works at the Center for Integrative Psychiatry in the Dutch city of Groningen and is a frequently asked guest-teacher at training institutes across Europe. Website: www.mbcl.org.

Frits Koster is a vipassana meditation teacher and certified mindfulness teacher and healthcare professional. He has taught mindfulness and compassion in healthcare settings for many years. He studied Buddhist psychology for six years as a monk in Southeast Asia. The author of several books, he trains mindfulness teachers across Europe at the Institute for Mindfulness-Based Approaches (IMA). See www.fritskoster.com or www.compassionateliving.info.

Mindfulness-Based Compassionate Living

A New Training Programme to Deepen
Mindfulness With Heartfulness

Erik van den Brink and Frits Koster

To Joanne,

For wisdom.

Happiness and

(Self) Compassion

15/6/15

Routledge
Taylor & Francis Group

LONDON AND NEW YORK

First published 2015
by Routledge
27 Church Road, Hove, East Sussex, BN3 2FA

And by Routledge
711 Third Avenue, New York, NY 10017

*Routledge is an imprint of the Taylor & Francis Group,
an informa business*

Previously published in Dutch as 'Compassievol leven', Boom, the
Netherlands, 2012. This edition translated by Marjo Oosterhoff and
updated.

British Library Cataloguing in Publication Data
A catalogue record for this book is available from the British Library

Library of Congress Cataloging-in-Publication Data
Brink, Erik van den.
[Compassievol leven. English]
  Mindfulness-based compassionate living : a new training programme to
deepen mindfulness with heartfulness / Erik van den Brink, Frits Koster.
— Dual Edition.
    pages cm
 1. Attention.   2. Self-esteem.   3. Mindfulness-based cognitive
therapy.   I. Koster, Frits.   II. Title.
  BF321.B825 2015
  616.89'1425—dc23
  2014040496

ISBN: 978-1-138-02214-0 (hbk)
ISBN: 978-1-138-02215-7 (pbk)
ISBN: 978-1-315-76418-4 (ebk)

Typeset in Times New Roman
by Apex CoVantage, LLC

Paperback cover photograph courtesy of Joanna Clegg,
www.abstractnature.co.uk

Audio-downloads: Victoria Norton. See www.mindfulness-in-bremen.de

MIX
Paper from
responsible sources
FSC
www.fsc.org   FSC® C013604

PRINTED AND BOUND BY CPI GROUP (UK) LTD, CROYDON, CR0 4YY

To all who seek alleviation from suffering
There is a crack in everything
That's how the light gets in
(Leonard Cohen)

Contents

Endorsements

'There is no way we can truly heal and free ourselves without self-compassion. *Mindfulness-Based Compassionate Living* offers clear, practical guidance in cultivating a mindful and kind relationship with our inner life. This creates the grounds for relating to our world with a wise and caring heart.'

Tara Brach, PhD, clinical psychologist, meditation teacher
and author of Radical Acceptance (Bantam, 2003)
and True Refuge (Bantam, 2013).

'*Mindfulness-Based Compassionate Living* is an important and beautiful book. Decades ago, when I learned to meditate, I was taught to practice mindfulness and compassion practices equally. I have always felt grateful for that training and have come to understand why mindfulness and compassion are seen as two wings of a bird—they offer balanced and essential qualities on our journey towards wholeness. Both are necessary.

As mindfulness becomes increasingly popular, it is equally important to develop specific ways to cultivate "heartfulness", kindness and connectedness. In developing the Mindfulness-Based Compassionate Living programme Frits and Erik have done just that. With intelligence and skill they have created a rich and powerful course that will surely be of benefit to many.'

Vidyamala Burch, co-founder of Breathworks—mindfulness- and
compassion-based approaches to pain, stress and illness, author of
Living Well With Pain and Illness (Piatkus, 2008) and coauthor
(with Danny Penman) of Mindfulness for Health (Piatkus, 2013).

'With tremendous wisdom and skill this book offers a way to deepen and develop the learning that has started in an 8-week course of Mindfulness-Based Stress Reduction or Mindfulness-Based Cognitive Therapy. Here participants learn some of the building blocks that enable compassion to flourish—the possibility of stepping aside from the battleground of thoughts, and of gently and tenderly allowing experience to be as it is. This book and the programme that it describes bring these compassionate responses to the fore and offer systematic methods to explicitly develop them, so that mindful compassion can become a natural and accessible part of our being. A wonderful contribution.'

Rebecca Crane, director of the Centre for Mindfulness Research
and Practice, Bangor University, U.K., and author of
Mindfulness-Based Cognitive Therapy (Routledge, 2009).

'This new volume by Van den Brink and Koster speaks to the pressing need to bring more care and warmth into daily life, particularly for those in the health-care professions. Drawing on the latest theory and evidence from contemplative science and positive psychology, it presents a range of helpful practices for cultivating compassion, even in the most difficult of circumstances. This book is destined to be of great value not only to readers but also to those whose lives they touch.'

Barbara Fredrickson, PhD, professor of psychology at the
University of North Carolina, author of *Positivity* (Three Rivers
Press, 2009) and *Love 2.0* (Penguin Books, 2013).

'This innovative book brings the ancient, healing wisdom of compassion training to a modern audience. Based on solid research, contemplative experience and clinical practice, this eight-session training programme strengthens our natural instinct for compassion and provides important tools for managing emotional pain in a healthy, radically new way.'

Christopher K. Germer, PhD, clinical psychologist, Harvard
Medical School, and author of *The Mindful Path to
Self-Compassion* (Guilford Press, 2009).

'This book is a treasure, full of insight and wisdom. It brings together in a very effective way ancient wisdom and modern science, the ethical and cognitive, the theory and practice and the mind and heart. It recognises that compassion is an essential part of mindfulness and that mindfulness training is only true mindfulness training when it is compassion training as well. The book gets better as you read it as the chapters build on one another. It is not only an invaluable resource for professional teachers and trainers, it is also a wonderful guide for anyone who wishes to live authentically with courage and compassion. The authors are not only consummate professionals and teachers but also committed practitioners.'

Sr. Stanislaus Kennedy, social campaigner and author of *Day by Day*
(Transworld, 2013) and *Moments of Stillness* (Transworld, 2011).

'Every major contemplative tradition, evolutionary biology and a growing body of science emphasise the importance of compassion. *Mindfulness-Based Compassionate Living* is a compelling guide, skilfully conveying how compassion can be cultivated in the service of relieving suffering. Through their extensive personal experience, deep knowledge and a rich collaboration Frits Koster and Erik van den Brink embody what they teach. They generously offer teachings that have been transformational for the authors and have the potential to be transformational both for therapists and their clients.'

Willem Kuyken, PhD, professor of clinical psychology at the University of Exeter. His work with people with mood disorders spans 20 years and is focussed on mindfulness mechanisms, clinical trials and implementation. He is author (with Christine A. Padesky and Robert Dudley) of *Collaborative Case Conceptualization* (Guilford Press, 2011).

'This book, which presents in detail a training programme known as Mindfulness-Based Compassionate Living (MBCL), nourishes the brain and the heart. Erik van den Brink and Frits Koster present a solid review of the scientific basis of compassion training. They also show the value in human terms of how opening our hearts to ourselves and to others can have a significant effect on mental and physical well-being.

Their book draws not only on their own decades-long meditation practice but also their extensive experience as mental health professionals teaching MBCL. The 8-week MBCL course developed by the authors promises to be a significant contribution to the field of mindfulness-based approaches. It teaches in a step-by-step way how compassion training can support emotional resilience, heal the wounds of low self-esteem and reveal the strength of vulnerability. I heartily recommend this book, both for one's own personal use as well as for its rich possibilities for introducing others to compassion training.'

Linda Lehrhaupt, PhD, founder and executive director of the Institute for Mindfulness-Based Approaches, Zen teacher, co-author of *Mindfulness-Based Stress Reduction: An MBSR Course Handbook* and author of *Riding the Waves of Life* (in German).

'This book is thoughtfully and sensitively written from the depth of the Dharma. It is also easily accessible for people newer to meditation practice. May it touch many lives and offer a taste of freedom.'

Florence Meleo-Meyer, director of the Oasis Institute, Mindfulness-Based Professional Education and Training, Center for Mindfulness, University of Massachusetts Medical School.

'While the benefits of mindfulness in therapeutic settings are well known, new research suggests that self-compassion is also key to mental health. This book offers innovative techniques for helping both therapists and clients develop a more compassionate way of relating to themselves and others.'

Kristin Neff, PhD, associate professor in human development, University of Texas, and author of *Self-Compassion* (William Morrow, 2011).

'Compassion is at the heart of the mindfulness-based interventions in health care. It is encouraging to welcome the recent interest in compassion in both clinical practice and research. This book is a valuable contribution to this field, in particular with regard to offering compassion training to patients with psychiatric disorders such as depression and anxiety. Both authors have extensive experience with offering mindfulness and compassion training to this population. We are very happy to collaborate with them in examining the effectiveness of Mindfulness-Based Compassionate Living as a postgraduate training in a randomised controlled trial of patients with recurrent depression.'

Anne Speckens, PhD, professor of psychiatry of the Radboud
University Medical Centre in Nijmegen, the Netherlands.

Foreword

In this remarkable and accessible book, Erik van den Brink and Frits Koster have produced a masterpiece of integration of Western science with insights from the contemplative traditions that stretch back many centuries. In addition, they have developed a step-by-step 8-week programme that promises to have major benefits for people. Many of the ingredients of the programme are well researched and have established their efficacy.

What Western science has revealed, which was not available to the Buddha, is that humans evolved like all other species on this planet—under the influence of selective pressures. So we, like many other animals, have a brain that comes with a whole range of motives and emotions to enhance survival. Indeed, many of our motives are mammalian, focused on sexuality, status, attachment and group belonging. And like many other of our animal cousins we have a whole suite of 'built-in' emotions for dealing with threats, for seeking rewards and pleasures and for finding contentment, soothing, safeness and peace. These are the bedrock of the human mind.

But we are different from other animals in profound ways too, and this is both a gift and a curse. About 2 million years ago something quite remarkable happened to our human ancestors. Over a very short period of time we got smart. We became able to think, ruminate, anticipate and reason; to use symbols, have language and then science. We evolved the capacity for an objective sense of self and self-identity, being able to think about our own minds and futures, and the minds of others, in a way no other animal can. No chimpanzee sits under a banana tree worrying about its health or whether other chimpanzees like it or not, or even if it likes itself. We also became able to create images and fantasies that could stimulate systems in our body. In fact, we now know that all kinds of ruminations and imaginations can play on the physiology of our bodies like fingers on a keyboard. So anxious or angry ruminations will stimulate threat systems; 'wanting' achievements or pleasures can stimulate drive emotions. This is the fundamental reason why we need insight into how our minds are working, what they are focused on and what they are orientated to do. Without this the mind can be like a cork bouncing on the unpredictable seas of emotions and motivations. Without reflection we can end up doing very harmful things to ourselves and others. We do not need to look very far in the world to see the horrendous cruelties humans impose on others, the massive inequalities so many suffer and the very high rates of mental suffering of depression, anxiety and paranoia.

When Siddhartha set out on his quest into the nature and causes of suffering he came to recognise that the unenlightened and untrained mind was a source of suffering. The antidote was learning to pay attention to the contents of one's mind and be aware of 'the present moment'. But 'mindfulness', as it is now referred to, was embedded in a deep ethic linked to compassion and nonviolence. Indeed, mindfulness was a way of stabilising the mind and providing the basis for developing *bodhicitta*—where one dedicates the practice to the enlightenment and freeing from suffering of all beings. So the Buddha taught the importance of learning to pay attention to what is going on in one's mind and what part of one's mind is trying to take control of one's actions. But he also focused deeply on motivation because the way in which we cultivate motivation is central to the organisation of our minds. Erik van den Brink and Frits Koster have a deep appreciation of these roots of mindfulness and compassion in these ethical traditions.

In addition to deep insights from the contemplative traditions, Mindfulness-Based Compassionate Living (MBCL) builds on third-generation cognitive behaviour therapies that incorporate mindfulness and particularly on Compassion Focused Therapy (CFT) (Gilbert, 2000, 2009a, 2010; Gilbert & Choden, 2013). Although CFT draws on ancient wisdoms too, its basis for understanding the mind is deeply rooted in Western psychology and our increasing awareness of the evolution of the brain. Even a cursory look at how the brain evolved and now functions in the modern world suggests it can give us serious trouble. Science has now revealed how attention and physiology mutually and powerfully influence each other, that we are easily influenced and shaped by social circumstances for good or ill and that affiliative relationships strongly regulate both mind and body. So from the day we are born to the day we die, the care and compassion of others will play a huge role in the quality of our lives. Indeed, we now know that the human brain has evolved with a whole range of physiological systems to be sensitive to signals of care and selective in providing care. Be it at the level of the gene, the cardiovascular and immune system, the frontal cortex or other affect-regulating systems, science reveals that we function best when we feel loved and valued (in contrast with unloved and unvalued) and are loving and valuing (in contrast with hostile and contemptuous).

Many people with psychological problems find the essential and basic human processes of caring for others, being open to the care from others and being caring to oneself difficult. They may find it difficult to relate to other people, and they may live lives of loneliness and isolation; they may be mistrustful and live in an inner world of anger and disappointment; and very commonly they are disappointed in themselves, self-critical and at times even self-hating. So CFT began its journey by looking deeply into the nature of shame and blocks to caring experiences and how therapist and client could work to cultivate compassion in all three domains. The authors of this book have taken on the challenge of developing a mindfulness-based group programme that teaches participants to find their way in these domains while being their own mentors, coaches and therapists.

Compassion is very easily misunderstood as little more than kindness, tenderness or softness. Although these are qualities that would certainly enhance compassion, they are not the root of compassion. What is at the root of compassion is motivation, typically defined as 'sensitivity to suffering in self and others with a deep commitment to try to do something about it'. So, as in many motivational systems, there are two aspects to this: orientation and action.

Hence, compassion translates into the following:

1. Developing the willingness and courage to turn towards suffering both in oneself and others rather than turning away, and
2. Dedicating oneself to acquiring the wisdom and skills and engaging in the appropriate actions for the alleviation and prevention of suffering.

Western science and the wisdom of the older traditions have revealed deeper and deeper insights into why it is essential to cultivate compassion in the world today and pass it on to our children. We develop compassion because we see into the nature of our evolved realities that we are all vulnerable biological beings with bodies that are created as survival machines, quick to decay and fade away. It is not just that we experience impermanence, which the Buddha recognised as a source of suffering, but the process of impermanence is itself deeply painful—as we age we have to live more and more with physical pain, injury, illness, loss and disability. Compassion requires us to pay far more attention to the reality of people's lives and the ways they suffer. But we also see that humans are so caught up in self-interest and even greed that we are destroying our environment, imparting major problems to our children, not to mention the extraordinary disparities in wealth. Compassion reaches beyond the self. Although life involves pain and tragedy for us all in one form or another, suffering can be reduced or made tolerable in the landscape of compassion where each helps each.

So increasingly we are coming to understand what we are up against in terms of the reality of gene-built biological bodies and craving and fearful minds and what we can do to try to live a meaningful and happy life. This book seeks to provide readers with deep insights into these issues, and the MBCL programme offers a step-by-step approach to deepen the cultivation of mindfulness and compassion. Researchers are beginning to suggest that the combination of both mindful attention and compassionate motivation can be profoundly helpful for dealing with the way our minds work and for everyday living. And indeed it is everyday living with which this book is concerned. Building on the practice as taught in basic mindfulness training programmes, readers will find a whole array of deepening practices from many sources, such as soothing breathing rhythm, body awareness, guided meditations, using imagery, dealing with resistance and desire, recognising maladaptive patterns and cultivating compassion hand in hand with the other 'friends for life': kindness, sympathetic joy and equanimity. To pack this all into an 8-week training programme is quite remarkable.

In these pages you will find a very well researched and beautifully written account of how and why training ourselves in mindful compassion can lead to a meaningful, healthier and happier life with greater social harmony. This is a wonderful path for a mindfulness-based compassionate way to live. A book to be treasured.

Paul Gilbert, PhD, FBPsS, OBE, professor of clinical
psychology, University of Derby, author of *The
Compassionate Mind* (Constable & Robinson, 2009).

Preface to the First Dutch Edition

Nobody could have imagined that mindfulness would become so popular; not even Jon Kabat-Zinn, when he quietly started to experiment with his stress-reduction programme in a hospital basement. He succeeded in introducing the Dharma, that is, 2,500 years of Buddhist insight and know-how, into the conventional medical care system. When he wrote a book about it, he sent the manuscript to the Vietnamese Zen teacher Thich Nhat Hanh, asked him to write the preface and was surprised when he consented to do so. Thich Nhat Hanh wrote, 'This book can be described as a door opening both on the Dharma (from the side of the world) and on the world (from the side of the Dharma).' The book became extremely popular.

Success is a double-edged sword. Mindfulness has indeed opened doorways, but in being popularised it also threatens to be watered down. For some it has become no more than a cognitive psychological trick. In the hands of others it slides into cheap wellness, a 'woolly' feeling fine here now whilst not having both feet on the ground.

This is not so with Frits Koster and Erik van den Brink. They continue on the path first walked by Jon Kabat-Zinn and with the exploration of 'the door opening on the Dharma from the side of the world, and on the world from the side of the Dharma'.

The Dharma holds many treasures. One of them is that wisdom and compassion, the cognitive and the ethical, cannot be separated. The term 'mindfulness' emphasises the cognitive aspect. This has been well understood by cognitive therapists. But wisdom is not wisdom if it does not go hand in hand with compassion.

It has always been an open question for me whether Western psychology would be prepared to take this step as well and put compassion on the map. Frits Koster and Erik van den Brink offer an excellent example of how this can be done. From the understanding that mindfulness training is only truly mindfulness training when it is compassion training as well, they create a continuation of the original 8-week training programme where compassion becomes the explicit theme.

What has been addressed repeatedly in mental health care is the theme of aggression and abuse. How much mental suffering is directly or indirectly linked to violence and aggression? It involves physical, sexual and mental abuse, and often from earliest childhood. People tend to treat themselves as they have been treated. As if that weren't bad enough, the aggression of people towards themselves comes on top of the abuse they experienced. But what is aggression other than the absence of compassion? Particularly in cases like these, compassion is the only effective antidote.

The Dharma holds many treasures. I can only hope that more books like this will be published that further explore the immeasurable richness of the Dharma and make it accessible where it is most needed: wherever people are suffering.

Edel Maex, psychiatrist, author and pioneer
in mindfulness teaching in Europe

Introduction

For the bird of enlightenment to fly, it must have two wings: the wing of wisdom and the wing of compassion.

(Zen saying)

'Compassion' is the capacity to feel concern with pain and suffering, our own as well as others. It involves the wish to relieve this pain and suffering and also the willingness to take on responsibility in doing so. It is a universal human quality, inherently present in everyone, but often not fully cultivated. Fortunately compassion can be developed and deepened through practice, and this is the aim of compassion training. Whereas pity is primarily accompanied by fear and sentimentality, compassion requires courage and openheartedness. In the West the term 'compassion' is mainly used to indicate the concern for others' suffering, and we need to use the compound 'self-compassion' to specify being concerned with our own suffering. In a meeting between the Dalai Lama and Western scientists they came to the painful conclusion that the English language does not have a word for compassion for ourselves (Goleman, 2002) The Dalai Lama explained that in Tibetan one and the same word is used (*tsewa*) to refer to compassion for ourselves as well as others. In his view one cannot exist without the other, and it is a form of serious self-neglect to exclude ourselves from compassion. We take this view to heart in this book, and we see the practice of self-compassion not as self-centred but, on the contrary, as an important condition for a healthy relationship with ourselves as well as with others.

The compassion training or Mindfulness-Based Compassionate Living (MBCL) as we have developed it in mental health care is a follow-up course for people who have already completed a mindfulness training programme. The training springs from a science-based view of the importance of compassion and self-compassion and is based on the work of, amongst others, Paul Gilbert (2005, 2009a, 2010), Christopher Germer (2009), Kristin Neff (2011), Tara Brach (2004) and Rick Hanson (2009, 2013).

Many people with chronic or recurring mental, physical and behavioural problems, whatever form these may take, suffer from low self-esteem, self-reproach or shame. Their world can be gloomy, fearful, full of yearning, anger or suspicions, and they find it difficult to experience feelings of warmth for themselves and others. They may escape into isolation, busyness or relationships that do not bring real satisfaction. Talking therapies can provide certain insights, but they do not always reach the experiential level ('I understand what's going on but I can't feel it'). In such cases compassion training with exercises in how to *experience* more warmth, safeness, acceptance and connectedness with oneself and with others can be helpful.

The practice of mindfulness is usually described in the words of Jon Kabat-Zinn (1994) as 'paying attention in a particular way: on purpose, in the present moment, and nonjudgmentally' (p. 4). This practice can lead to more insight and wisdom in our lives and has been shown to have beneficial effects on physical and mental health. Therefore mindfulness trainings are increasingly offered in health care in the form of Mindfulness-Based Stress Reduction (MBSR) or Mindfulness-Based Cognitive Therapy (MBCT). From the very start of the course, mindfulness trainers stress that it is not only about developing mindfulness with an *open* attitude, but also with a *gentle* attitude. Edel Maex (2006) described mindfulness simply as 'a kind open awareness' (p. 49; translated from Dutch by the authors). Jon Kabat-Zinn said in *Coming to Our Senses* (2005, p. 69):

> More than anything else, I have come to see meditation as an act of love, an inward gesture of benevolence and kindness towards ourselves and towards others, a gesture of the heart that recognizes our perfection even in our obvious imperfection, with all our shortcomings, our wounds, our attachments, our vexations, and our persistent habits of unawareness.

Segal, Williams, and Teasdale (2002, 2013), the founders of MBCT, also referred to this kind and gentle attitude, albeit less explicitly. In the first edition (2002) of their handbook on MBCT, compassion practices are not mentioned. In the second edition (2013), a special chapter is devoted to the issue, but they expressed reservations about offering explicit practice as in patients vulnerable to depression it can easily reinforce the belief that they are not good enough when they fail to be kind with themselves. In their opinion a compassionate attitude is best conveyed implicitly by the practice of mindfulness itself and by the teacher's embodiment of loving-kindness. In the self-help book they published with Jon Kabat-Zinn, they stated that mindfulness could also be described as 'heartfulness' because it is really about a compassionate awareness (M. Williams, Teasdale, Segal, & Kabat-Zinn, 2007).

We do not want to imply by the subtitle of our book that mindfulness precedes heartfulness. Nor do we suggest that heartfulness is not included in MBSR and MBCT. However, with the words 'deepening mindfulness with heartfulness' we wish to indicate that our consciousness encompasses both an attentive mind and a compassionate heart. In Pali, a dialect spoken in the Buddha's time in Northern India, in which most of the original Buddhist scriptures were written, the word *citta* is used. In English this is usually translated as 'consciousness'; the word *citta*, however, includes the heart as well as the mind. The word 'mindfulness' was originally a translation of the Pali word *sati*, which refers to the pure quality of awareness, attentiveness, of being consciously present in the moment. The practice of *sati* paves the way to wisdom and insight into the workings of the mind and into the nature of reality. For many people mindfulness practice became synonymous with *vipassana* or insight meditation. In the West, mindfulness acquired an even broader meaning that also included cultivating the kind attitude with which we are mindful and developing loving-kindness and compassion. And so it became 'heartfulness'.

Nevertheless, there is a strong association in the West between mind and intellectual qualities, and between heart and emotional qualities. Not everyone immediately thinks that mindfulness also involves developing a compassionate heart and that heartfulness also includes developing mindfulness. We should really speak of 'heart-mind-fulness', which is an awkward and impractical construction. Therefore we choose to use both terms, referring to qualities that need to be cultivated side by side. It is useful to view them separately, but in viewing them separately we don't mean they can actually be separated.

In Asia the image of a bird is used. One wing represents 'wisdom', the other 'compassion' (R. D. Siegel & Germer, 2012). Both wings are needed for the bird to fly, keeping each other in balance. Trying to be caring and kind without insight can lead to foolish and unhealthy forms of compassion. Consider for example condoning and supporting addictive behaviour of a family member, or giving in to 'comfort eating'. Training in mindfulness without compassion can lead to cold insensitivity. An extreme example is when Japanese kamikaze pilots used their Zen training to drop their aeroplanes loaded with explosives ruthlessly on Allied ships during the Second World War.

For Whom This Book Is Intended

This book is meant for anyone who is interested in mindfulness and compassion practice in a health care setting. It is aimed at health care professionals, mindfulness teachers and interested nonprofessionals who wish to learn about the theoretical background, scientific foundation and content of MBCL. The heart of the book is meant for those who wish to familiarise themselves with the MBCL programme and is suitable both as an experiential guide and as a manual for professionals wishing to teach MBCL. It will also be a valuable source for therapists wishing to enrich their mindfulness-based approaches with compassion-focused work. In our view, familiarity with mindfulness practice is essential for a good understanding of compassion training as we present it, preferably by having followed an 8-week group training in MBSR, MBCT or Breathworks, the programme developed by Vidyamala Burch (2008) for clients with chronic pain and other physical problems. Having worked through a self-help book on mindfulness practice may also have laid down sufficient foundation (Stahl & Goldstein, 2010; Williams et al., 2007), or being familiar with mindfulness exercises from Acceptance and Commitment Therapy or Dialectical Behaviour Therapy (e.g., Bohlmeijer & Hulsbergen, 2013; Hayes & Smith, 2005; McKay, Wood, & Brantley, 2007). Of course it would also be sufficient to have an established practice in a more traditional form of meditation, such as *vipassana* or Zen.

Readers might get the impression that MBCL is mainly set up for clients accessing mental health services. This was indeed where we started. In the years that followed we have guided MBCL in various other settings. We saw that those with more stable backgrounds and fewer mental health issues, but nonetheless stressful lives, could benefit just as well from training in compassion. It is not easy to be a human being; we can all benefit from bringing more (self-) compassion into our lives.

The language and style we use is meant to be accessible to a wide audience. In exercises and parts where we invite the reader to do self-inquiry we have chosen to write in the more informal style that we use when we teach MBCL in our training sessions and workshops. At the same time we wish to be clear about the science basis of the curriculum. Whilst trying to avoid scientific jargon, we refer as much as possible to scientific and other sources in the text, with authors and publication dates in parentheses, so that the relevant literature can be found in the reference list.

The Structure of the Book

The book consists of three parts. Parts 1 and 3 are more theoretical and provide a framework for readers who are interested in acquiring more knowledge about the how and why of cultivating compassion in the health care setting. Part 2 is mainly practical and takes the reader session by session through the MBCL curriculum.

The first part, Approaches to Suffering, provides a theoretical background. In 1.1 we reflect on 'old truths' as regards human suffering and we compare *inner* and *outer science*. In 1.2 we mention a number of 'modern myths' that may be a pitfall when dealing with suffering. Then in 1.3 we suggest which 'timeless values' may support us in this. In 1.4 we show how Buddhist and Western psychologies of human suffering can complement each other as regards 'causes and remedies'. In 1.5 we describe how we as mindfulness trainers in the mental health care sector came to develop an advanced training module that we have called 'compassion training'. In 1.6 we give an overview of the results of scientific research that underpins its application in health care.

In the second part, Compassion Training in Practice, we present the structure of the training as it is now being offered. In this practical part we also include theoretical explanations that may be helpful when doing the exercises. First we mention a number of points for reflection before starting the training. In 2.1 to 2.8 we describe the compassion training in eight sessions. This part can be used as a guide for individual practice as well as for participating in or facilitating a group training. At the end of each chapter we give an overview of the content of the session. Transcripts of the exercises can be found in each session. Audio files of the exercises are listed in the Appendix: Guided MBCL Exercises That Can Be Downloaded on page 195 and can be downloaded free of charge from www.routledge.com/9781138022157

Part 3, The Compassionate Therapist, is specially aimed at health care professionals and mindfulness teachers who would like to work with compassion exercises. We offer three perspectives: the value of personal practice for the benefit of their own health and therapeutic efficacy (3.1); how the therapeutic work can be enriched with insights from Western and Buddhist psychology as regards compassion (3.2); and how therapists can explicitly teach their client compassion practices (3.3). Finally we reflect on which clients can be offered compassion practice, and by which teachers.

Personal Backgrounds

The heart has its reasons of which reason knows nothing.

(Blaise Pascal, 1669/1995)

Our motivation to write this book springs from our experience in teaching mindfulness in mental health care, where we work with clients with various mental vulnerabilities. Of course the motivation also grew from our own personal histories and our own vulnerabilities, so first we would like to introduce ourselves and show how this work is linked to our own lives.

Erik van den Brink

I started my medical studies highly motivated, but I frequently doubted whether I had made the right choice. This was mainly because of the many technical subjects involved; the approaches of the human body as a machine, a thing to be cut, prodded or worked on to make it function again. The person who lived in that body seemed of secondary importance. The primary concern seemed to be the exterior and not so much the interior, the inner experience of the sick person. In those days I had not yet heard about mindfulness. Sometimes I tried to meditate on my own, but I did not know where to find a good teacher. Words like 'compassion' were hardly used in the medical world. Looking back I realise that I had been looking for that.

I interrupted my studies on several occasions to gain valuable experience as a nursing assistant and to allow myself the time to become acquainted with the human side of working in health care. I also delved into psychology, philosophy and new thinkers in the Judaeo–Christian tradition. Although I had been raised lovingly by my parents in a rather traditional wing of the Dutch Reformed Church, from the last years of secondary school onward I felt attracted to broader ideas about spirituality and a just society. As an only child I had always been rather shy, and in my first years as a student I found it difficult to assert myself. I often tried to live up to the image I thought was needed to fit in, and I was excessively self-critical. Or I pretended to be independent and not needing anyone and then was highly critical of others. In both cases I was primarily concerned with looking for acknowledgment and appreciation, and I was more preoccupied with self-esteem than with self-compassion.

Because I interrupted my studies to work as a nursing assistant and to travel, my self-confidence increased and I conquered my reservations about sharing my inner quest with others. During the last phase of my studies I met my wife Anja, and we journeyed through India and Nepal. We worked as interns in the Himalayas of Northern India, travelled to South India and back up again, and on the way visited several health projects, ashrams and Mother Teresa's House for the Dying. We met inspiring people and got to know other forms of spirituality. I am still deeply grateful for all the experiences on this journey. Looking back I realise how much was touched in me then that was cultivated only much later. It was enriching to learn more about the Eastern wisdom traditions, even though I never felt the need to formally become a follower of any of these traditions. I did however increasingly realise how important a respectful meeting of the *inner science* of spiritual traditions and the *outer science* of the exact sciences is.

After working for a year as a medical practitioner in the accident and emergency department of a British hospital, I decided to train to become a psychiatrist. Psychiatry seemed to be the speciality that devoted the most time to the inner experience of the patient, which interested me most. In the U.K. we could do the training part time from the time our children were born. In this way, Anja and I could grow in our working lives as well as raising our two sons. There was also time for inner science. We attended silent Quaker meetings—the Quakers being one of the few lay movements that grew out of Christianity that focus on formal contemplation in silent meetings. Here we encountered a warm circle of people. For the first time I fully experienced the power of meeting each other in silence, which I later encountered in retreats. I was impressed by the nonjudging attitude of the Quakers, their radical nondogmatic approach in the quest for peaceful and sustainable solutions for problems and their method of only reacting to conflicts from the silence and after careful attunement with themselves and the other party.

Back in the Netherlands I started to work as a psychiatrist in the mental health services in Groningen, at first in ambulatory crisis work, later in an out-patient team for patients with mood disorders and then, from its inception, at the Center for Integrative Psychiatry. I continued to be in touch with like-minded people who were interested in spirituality, and I began to devote myself more to formal meditation practice, first *vipassana* and later Zen. Initially I preferred to keep my personal journey and my professional life separate. This felt safer, even though I suffered from the gap between them.

Immediately after we experienced a number of bereavements at close hand, there was more upheaval in our lives when Anja developed breast cancer and had to undergo drastic treatments. We experienced the advantages of high-tech medicine but also the scant attention to care and self-care in the treatment, which we had to find mainly outside the conventional medical world. During that stage we noticed how one develops resilience in the face of setbacks. Being confronted with the vulnerability and finiteness of life, there was a growing sense that every day is the first day of the rest of our lives. We began to take the question 'What do you want the rest of your life to stand for?' increasingly seriously. I familiarised myself further with methodologies that increase the potential for self-healing with as few harmful side effects as possible (Van den Brink 2006a, 2006b) and started to go to retreats guided by the Dutch Zen master Ton Lathouwers. The first time I heard him speak, I was deeply touched by the story of Kwan Yin, the female bodhisattva of compassion—she who listens to all cries for help and does not accept liberation for herself until *all* living beings have become liberated. I was also moved by the similar old Russian legend, mentioned in *The Brothers Karamazov* by Dostoyevsky, about the mother of God who descends to the depths of Hell to save those whom God has forgotten (Lathouwers, 2013). These feminine images of boundless compassion made a deep impression on me because I grew up with predominantly male religious role models.

When *Mindfulness-Based Cognitive Therapy for Depression* by Segal et al. (2002) was published, I was overjoyed because I saw the possibility of bringing my personal journey and my professional life closer together. I soon started to teach mindfulness courses to groups of patients as well as to colleagues in the mental health profession. I participated in inspiring training weeks with pioneering mindfulness teachers, and my life moved into a wholesome flow. Now I work harder than ever but with more inner peace. Even though fruitful collaboration is not possible with everyone, it has become easier to accept all human beings as they are, which for a therapist is not a bad thing, of course. It is also satisfying that my self-acceptance has grown. Introducing *metta* (loving-kindness) and compassion has deepened my meditation practice, although at first I felt a rather allergic reaction—as though I was artificially covering myself in a pink cloud. Now I understand how much courage is needed to encounter the pain and imperfection of life and face it with kindness and love rather than with resistance. I have also come to understand how my old patterns and my looking for approval were related to a lack of self-compassion and that my attitude to others often was unnecessarily harsh. I realise now that self-compassion and compassion for others are inherently connected.

I am grateful to have found a friend and colleague in Frits to expand the mindfulness work in mental health care. I first met him in his role as meditation teacher in the Vipassana Meditation Centre in Groningen. When he wanted to know what my job was, I felt rather embarrassed. At that time I still preferred to do meditation incognito and to keep it separate from my work. I had to admit that I was a psychiatrist in front of the whole group. When years later we started to co-teach the first groups, I looked up to Frits as the experienced meditation teacher and retreat facilitator. I was surprised to hear during an intervision meeting that he encountered feelings of inferiority where I was concerned. Apparently both of us were experiencing feelings of inferiority whilst sitting side by side. By now we are much less in the grip of the tendency to compete in feeling inferior, and many people have told us we complement each other well.

Frits Koster

After a relatively carefree childhood, I experienced an identity crisis during puberty. I did well at school and finished my secondary education with good marks, but I did not know what I wanted to study at university and often felt like a rudderless ship. After a failed attempt to study, I decided to travel through Europe and explore the world. I picked grapes in France, olives in Greece, worked in a home for the disabled and later served in a bar in the U.K. For friends in the Netherlands all of this seemed rather 'cool', but I felt an unpleasant emptiness and did not really know how to relate to myself and to the world around me.

At the age of 22 I met the Venerable Mettavihari, a Thai Buddhist monk who taught me the basic principles of *vipassana* meditation, where developing mindfulness is at the heart of the practice. Although I did not find meditating easy, for the first time in my life I had discovered something I really wanted to devote my time and energy to. From the very start it gave me the impression that I would be able to understand life better.

Like so many young men in those days I had to do my military service, but I decided to be a conscientious objector and started the alternative national service. In my spare time I meditated and prepared myself to travel to Asia; I planned to study psychology on my return to the Netherlands. I had a recommendation letter from my meditation teacher, and in Thailand I went on retreat under the guidance of Achahn Asabha Mahathera, a Burmese monk who had been invited to come and teach in Thailand.

After this long retreat in Thailand, I was offered the opportunity to become a monk. When I heard that in Southeast Asia 85% of all monks are only temporarily ordained, I decided to ordain. Initially I thought in terms of 1 year, and to start my studies after that. However, after a year I was so content that eventually I lived as a Buddhist monk for more than 5 years in Thailand, Burma and Sri Lanka. I experienced this as a precious time in my life. I could meditate and study Buddhist psychology with very experienced teachers, and I am extremely grateful for what they have given me and others.

After 5 years my first meditation teacher asked me to return to the Netherlands to help him support the Thai community there. He also asked me to help establish a meditation centre in the city of Groningen. It appealed to me that I would see my parents and old friends again, and I would be able to see if I could integrate the knowledge and wisdom I had developed into Western society. This was not at all easy at first. In Asia I had become accustomed to the peaceful atmosphere in the monasteries, I could go on daily alms rounds and need not worry about anything. Just as people can become 'hospitalised' in a hospital, I noticed that I had become 'monasterised'. I am glad I stayed in the Netherlands though, and gradually I began to feel at home again. However, it was difficult to live as a monk. I was given the freedom to interpret monkhood in a more Western way, but I began to feel less and less comfortable in Eastern robes. Eventually I disrobed because I began to feel unhappy as a monk; besides, I fell in love.

Subsequently I started to work in psychiatric health care, while in my spare time I guided meditation activities. I have been aware of a curious change in psychiatry. When early on in my work I mentioned meditation, most psychiatrists tended to avoid me. After mindfulness became well known this changed completely; I was fully accepted. About 6 years ago, after finishing training as a mindfulness trainer, I have shifted my field of work to primarily giving MBSR/ MBCT courses, and now also compassion training courses, to clients and professionals in the mental health care sector.

I now live in a small village in the Dutch province of Groningen and am happily married to Jetty. Apart from offering training courses in two mental health care organisations, Jetty and I organise and teach various meditation activities under the auspices of the Training Bureau of Kindness & Mindfulness that we have established and officially registered. I am also connected to several training institutes for mindfulness teachers in the Netherlands, Belgium, Germany, Ireland and other European countries. A Dutch publishing house called Asoka has published a number of my writings. The Thai publisher Silkworm Books has brought out English translations of *Liberating Insight, Buddhist Meditation in Stress Management* and *The Web of Buddhist Meditation* (e-book).

Looking back I can say that particularly in the first years I was meditating, I was extremely driven, and at the same time very harsh, if not ruthless, towards myself. I was mindful, but a large part of the practice was coloured by self-criticism. Thoughts were not allowed, emotions were suppressed. Sometimes Thai and Burmese meditation teachers advised me to practise loving-kindness meditation, but I thought this was only for 'softies'. Very slowly, over many years, I began to realise how ridiculously harsh I was on myself, and I began to practise meditations on kindness and compassion and am still discovering the richness of these practices.

In those days there were not many meditation teachers who recognised the very pervasive Western 'disease' of lack of self-compassion. Whereas I had to go through a process lasting more than 15 years, I am pleased to be able to illustrate to others who might have similar negative attitudes towards themselves that a lighter and kinder attitude is possible and offer them something so that they don't need to go through the same struggle as I did.

Erik and I met around 15 years ago in the Vipassana Meditation Centre in the city of Groningen. He was a participant in an open meditation evening. I remember how touched I was to meet a psychiatrist during a meditation activity for the first time. Nowadays this is quite normal. About 10 years later Erik asked me whether I would like to start working in the Center for Integrative Psychiatry in Groningen as mindfulness trainer. This was the beginning of an extremely fruitful and smooth collaboration. It was a pleasure to write this book together with Erik.

Acknowledgments

Many people have been involved in the writing of this book in one way or another. First of all we express our gratitude to our parents for the love they gave us and for the seeds of compassion they consciously or unconsciously planted in our hearts. Then we thank all teachers, guides and fellow travellers on the path who have nourished us in our personal growth in the area of meditation and study as well as in our development as mental health care professionals. In particular we are grateful for and appreciate the work of Paul Gilbert, Kristin Neff, Christopher Germer, Tara Brach, Daniel Siegel and Rick Hanson; they were our inspiration when we developed the compassion training.

We thank Paul Gilbert for his heart-warming Foreword and Edel Maex for the encouraging Preface. We are very grateful to Tara Brach, Vidyamala Burch, Rebecca Crane, Barbara Fredrickson, Christopher Germer, Willem Kuyken, Sister Stan, Linda Lehrhaupt, Florence Meleo-Meyer, Kristin Neff and Anne Speckens for their supportive endorsements.

We owe much gratitude to our beloved partners, Jetty Heynekamp and Anja Sanders, who have been very patient with our writing passion over the past year and who offered valuable suggestions for improving the manuscript. We are also grateful to all our colleagues at the Center for Integrative Psychiatry in the Dutch city of Groningen, who have supported us from the very start and who enabled us to embark on this adventure. For the English translation we are very grateful to Marjo Oosterhoff and for support and suggestions for revision to Joanne Forshaw, Susannah Frearson, Kirsten Buchanan and others at Routledge. The result is a thoroughly revised text with updated scientific references, thanks to the researchers taking an interest in compassion and the exponential increase of publications in recent years. We particularly wish to express our deep gratitude to Victoria Norton. Without Victoria's enthusiasm, encouragement and perseverance we would not have been able to publish this English edition. Besides, she generously recorded all the audio exercises.

Last but not least, thanks and appreciation for the courage, patience, openness and trust of all participants, clients and professionals who were prepared to follow the Mindfulness-Based Compassionate Living programme and share their precious insights and experiences with us. Without them this project could never have grown into what it is now.

Sources and Permissions

Naomi Shihab Nye

Excerpt from "Kindness" from *Words Under the Words: Selected Poems* by Naomi Shihab Nye, © 1995. Reprinted by permission of Far Corner Books, Portland, Oregon.

Leonard Cohen

Two lines from the song "Anthem" from the album *The Future* © 1992 Leonard Cohen. Reprinted by permission.

Sister Stan

Excerpt from the entry for January 4th from *Day by Day* © Sister Stanislaus Kennedy 2013. Reprinted by permission of Sister Stan and Transworld Ireland.

Sri Nisagardatta

Two excerpts from *I Am That: Talks With Sri Nisargadatta Maharaj*, pp. 8 and 236. Translated by Maurice Frydman, edited by Sudhakar S. Dikshit (2nd rev. ed., Durham, NC (USA) SBN: 978-089386-0462) © 2012 Acorn Press. Reprinted by permission of Acorn Press.

Tommy Wieringa

Excerpt from *Joe Speedboat*, p. 186. © for the English Translation Sam Garrett 2009. Reprinted by permission of Portobello books (U.K. and worldwide except U.S.) and Grove Atlantic Inc. (U.S. and Canada).

Vidyamala Burch

Excerpt from *Living Well With Pain and Illness*, p. 72. © 2010 Vidyamala Burch. Reprinted by permission of the author.

Disclaimer

Part 1

Approaches to Suffering

A man who fears suffering,
is already suffering from what he fears.
(Michel de Montaigne)

When I (Erik) was working as an intern in a psychiatric hospital in the U.K., I saw the letters 'TLC' under the heading 'treatment plan' in the file of an elderly, seriously ill patient. Nothing else was mentioned to indicate what was meant. When I asked the nurses what the letters stood for, they smiled at the Dutch doctor's ignorance. They told me that the meaning of the abbreviation, used widely in English-speaking countries, was 'tender loving care'. When 'TLC' was written in a file it was obvious that nothing more could be done for the patient medically and that the nurses could only offer loving care. This was one of the few occasions that a compassionate approach was explicitly mentioned in a medical file. Fortunately many nurses also lovingly cared for their patients without such instructions—even when they were still being treated—but doctors only seemed to write down this particular order after all treatment possibilities had been exhausted.

As a quality to be developed, compassion plays only a marginal role in our modern Western culture. Perhaps we should expect some room for it in health care because patients by definition suffer a lot, but even here it is seldom mentioned. This has not always been so. Hippocrates, generally seen as the father of Western medicine, stated that some patients get better simply because of their physician's kindness. In the Middle Ages, the monastic traditions evolved where caring for the sick was inspired by the 'love thy neighbour' ideal of the gospels. But also empirical practitioners like Ambroise Paré, a well-known French surgeon from the Renaissance period, believed it was the physician's duty 'to cure occasionally, relieve often, console always' (Czerniak & Davidson, 2012, p. 771). And he was not exactly suffering from the 'soft touch' as he performed heroic surgery on the battlefield. Since the age of Enlightenment and the rise of scientific materialism in medicine, the care arising from Christian neighbourly love has been gradually replaced by a rational approach stressing the correct technical implementation of treatments. Increasingly, the nonspecific factors in treatments were regarded as less important 'placebo' effects. Hospitals and other health organisations have nowadays become large modern enterprises, where as many patients as possible have to be treated according to protocol in the shortest possible time. Efficiency and producing measurable results have become more important than loving care.

It seems that compassion only comes into the picture when doctors and therapists have come to a dead end. This is not only because of them but because of modern culture in general. Modern society expects its doctors and therapists to continue with 'proper' treatments as long as possible. *Cure* is more important than *care*.

Compassion requires a different attitude to suffering than the prevailing one. In the first part of this book we reflect on various approaches to suffering and make comparisons between 'inner science' and 'outer science'. We explore a number of old truths and modern myths that are significant in dealing with suffering and wonder what guiding values can be of service to us. Subsequently we draw parallels between Buddhist and Western psychology as regards the causes of suffering and the remedies for alleviating suffering. Then we discuss the development from mindfulness training to compassion training and conclude with an overview of the results of scientific research that underpin its application in health care.

1.1 Old Truths

In this chapter we compare two important empirical approaches to human suffering. One is more typical of Eastern culture, the other is more typical of Western culture.

We can view the Buddha's attitude as an example of an approach to suffering that grew out of empirical research. 'Empirical' means tried and tested by careful observation of the experience. The 'Four Noble Truths' are the basic principles of a practical manual for understanding and alleviating human suffering, which can be viewed not as dogmas but more as four working hypotheses for life that can be repeatedly tested by means of our own experience. It is striking how the Buddha's method reflects that of a physician. Just like a physician, he made a diagnosis, analysed the cause (aetiology), offered a prognosis and proposed a therapy. He worked as a scientist of the inner world. He called for careful investigation of the processes in our own mind and body, advising people not just to believe him but to investigate everything for themselves. Subsequently various Buddhist schools arose in Asia—dependent on historical and cultural conditions—advocating specific adjustments and religious practices in which the original principles are not always so recognisable. A growing number of representatives from these different schools have come to the West, resulting in a meeting and exchange of ideas. Many of the modern teachers in the West have been schooled in several traditions and are more open than ever to what it is that connects the different schools and to their common source. Joseph Goldstein (2002) wrote about the emergence of a Western Buddhism, and before him Stephen Batchelor (1998) described a non-religious Western form of Buddhism. In this context it is useful to realise that the historical person Siddhartha Gautama, who later became the Buddha, was not a Buddhist himself and probably did not intend to establish a new religion. What particularly appeals to us as health care professionals is the method of self-inquiry he used to alleviate human suffering and the fact that anyone can test its efficacy by their own experience, irrespective of whether they are a Buddhist or not. In this book we refer to this empirical method of self-inquiry, from the perspective of the first person, as 'inner science'. Only the person involved can carry out this intimate investigation of his or her own inner world. This does not mean however, that it cannot result in useful knowledge that can be shared and compared with others who apply the same method of self-investigation.

Buddhist psychology is the fruit of this methodical self-inquiry, which was practised for centuries in monastic and lay communities and the results of which were passed on from master to student and discussed with fellow practitioners. It is not true to say that Western scientists never considered this form of scientific practice. They have talked about 'mental empiricism' or 'contemplative psychology', which can be viewed—like clinical and experimental psychology—as a form of scientific practice (De Wit, 1991, 1999; Wallace & Hodel, 2008). Even though contemplative psychology uses a different method, namely meditation and self-inquiry, its results are equally verifiable by everyone who applies the same research method. Buddhism is not unique in this, and we can find comparable methods in other spiritual schools as well as in the contemplative traditions of the West (Goleman, 1988). However, Buddhism was the first of these traditions to come up with an elaborate analysis and psychology of the human mind, the *Abhidhamma* (Koster, 2014).

In modern Western health care, many manuals have been developed as a response to human suffering, in medicine as well as in clinical psychology. And these are also based on an empirical method—but more from the perspective of the third person—which we call 'outer science' in this book. This science does not make use of the 'inner eye' that is focussed on our inner world but of the external senses to study the outer world. Where necessary, these senses are supplemented by measuring devices and precision instruments so that everything can be recorded as precisely as possible in size and number. In the West this outer science is often regarded as the only 'true' science. Only this form of scientific practice is believed to lead to knowledge that can be taken seriously, and inner science is regarded as 'unscientific'. In Eastern culture inner science played a much more important role, and thus it is not surprising that both cultures developed divergent approaches to human suffering.

Whereas in Buddhism 'Four Noble Truths' are the point of departure, in the modern Western world 'Four Noble Aspirations' appear to determine the attitude to suffering. We can distinguish two basic attitudes that differ significantly from each other:

Table 1

East—Inner science FOUR NOBLE TRUTHS	West—Outer science FOUR NOBLE ASPIRATIONS
1. There is suffering ('dis-ease', illness, aging, death).	1. Suffering is avoidable (health is 'makeable').
2. There is an inner cause: greed, aversion, delusion (here-now).	2. Causal factors can be analysed and manipulated (past-future).
3. Inner liberation is possible.	3. Control is possible.
4. There is a path towards inner liberation.	4. There is a path towards more control.
'Existential' suffering	**'Pathological' suffering**

We will compare the different approaches as regards the diagnosis, cause, prognosis and treatment of suffering.

1.1.1   The Diagnosis

The First Noble Truth is the simple acknowledgment ('diagnosis') that suffering is an inevitable part of existence: 'There is suffering.' Just consider the universal phenomena of illness, aging and death. And apart from these there are, of course, many forms of inevitable suffering, like not being able to get what we want, being confronted with unwanted situations or being separated from what is dear to us, experiencing unpleasant emotions and thoughts. The Pali word in Buddhist scriptures is *dukkha* and was used to refer to an axle off-centre or a bone out of joint (Mikulas, 2007). It is not easy to be a human being. Our lives often do not run smoothly. There may be many moments of happiness, but we cannot hold on to them. Inherent to human life is a fundamental state of dissatisfaction or 'dis-ease'. The First Noble Truth acknowledges this fundamental empirical fact. The story of Siddhartha Gautama relates how he grew up as a prince in the luxurious palace of his father, who wanted to protect him from all the evil influences of the outside world. Yet Siddhartha could not resist the temptation to secretly go outside the palace walls, where for the first time he came across illness, old age and death. He was so moved by these encounters with human suffering that he gave up his luxurious life to find a way to alleviate suffering. He started his quest from an attitude of compassion and a caring concern for human life in all its uncontrollability and unpredictability. But just as we, from very basic stress reactions, initially tend to try to fight pain and suffering, the young prince at first fought suffering in various ways as a wandering ascetic for 7 years. Then he realised that he did not need to struggle *against* suffering but could find a way to freedom *with* human suffering. He discovered an inner attitude where he did not need to repress pain and suffering but at the same time did not need to drown in it. By acknowledging what is there with a nonjudging awareness, Siddhartha discovered a way to inner freedom.

The modern Western aspiration, which seems to be the counterpart, states that 'suffering is avoidable'. Or formulated in a positive way: 'Health is makeable'. In our culture a militant attitude toward suffering is more prevalent than an accepting one. The diagnosis should be made as specifically as possible so that the cure (solution) for our suffering can be found. Western health practice seems to be so preoccupied with searching for the best cure that there is less and less space for care (loving attention), even when a cure turns out to be incomplete or impossible.

Thus it seems justified to approach existential suffering with a more accepting attitude and pathological suffering more militantly. Care is appropriate for existential suffering, whereas we should continue to look for a cure for pathological suffering. Both approaches are valid, particularly when existential and pathological suffering can be clearly distinguished. It becomes problematic, however, when existential suffering is considered abnormal and is fought in the same way as pathological suffering. Much emotional pain is normal, for example anxiety in situations you previously experienced as threatening, anger because your colleague gets more appreciation for the same job than you or sadness about the loss of a loved one. And if we avoid or fight emotional pain, the suffering only grows and may eventually grow to such an extent that it becomes pathological suffering. This suffering, however, could have been prevented by a more accepting attitude of normal emotional pain.

Researchers often simply choose a cut-off point on the questionnaires they use. Disorder is on one side of this cut-off point, and normality is on the other side. In every new edition of the *Diagnostic and Statistical Classification of Mental Disorders* (American Psychiatric Association, 2000, 2013), more disorders are being added, particularly in the mild spectrum (Frances, 2009). Many of us could easily meet the criteria for an anxiety disorder, a depressive disorder, an eating disorder, an attention-deficit disorder, a stress-related disorder or an addictive disorder. It is also quite easy to fulfil the criteria for a personality disorder. Normal suffering increasingly seems to be viewed as pathological. Several authors have drawn attention to 'the depression epidemic', as a modern phenomenon, where normal sadness is transformed in pathological depression for which antidepressant drugs are prescribed abundantly (Dehue, 2008; Healy, 1997; Horwitz & Wakefield, 2007). In modern Western health care, it seems difficult to accept that existential suffering is a normal part of human life.

1.1.2   The Cause

The Second Noble Truth—there is a cause of suffering—unveils that cause. It involves three phenomena that are called the 'three poisons' in Buddhism. They are greed, aversion and delusion. Delusion is sometimes also referred to as confusion, illusion or ignorance. Whenever we are overpowered by desire for experiences that are impermanent by nature, this causes suffering. When we are overpowered by aversion to pain or unpleasant experiences that are inevitable, this only adds more suffering. When it is not possible to see reality clearly because we are blinded by prejudices, judgments and fixed opinions, this can lead to much suffering. It involves phenomena that can be investigated here and now in our consciousness by meticulous self-inquiry, as formally practised in meditation. If these causes remain unconscious, they constantly condition our actions and keep us imprisoned in our suffering. If we practise self-inquiry regularly, we learn from our own experience which processes reinforce suffering and which alleviate it. The advantage of this method of inner science is that we ourselves are the experts, because nobody is in a better position to carry out this investigation than ourselves. The disadvantage is that we cannot discover causes that are hidden from view, even when we can see extremely clearly with our inner eye.

The Western aspiration, which seems the counterpart of this Second Noble Truth, is to strive to discover the causal factors of suffering that cannot be seen by the suffering persons themselves by analysing the cause-and-effect sequences of an illness process or psychological disorder. Usually these sequences are viewed as linear from past to future. Through investigating the past, looking for causal connections and testing hypotheses that make predictions about the future, we steadily gain insight into the processes of suffering. These analyses do not take place in our inner world, as with inner science, but on the outside, accessible to the objective observation of others (outer science). These analyses are supported by sophisticated research tools, like laboratory research, imaging techniques and standardised questionnaires, which help to translate the inner processes—which cannot be seen with the physical eye—into an 'outside' by providing measurable data that everyone can see. These analyses are preferably carried out by independent researchers with predetermined research methods that can be repeated by other researchers, who should find the same results under the same conditions. However, behind identified causes lie numerous other causes that are in turn part of other cause-and-effect sequences, so that the theories become ever more complex, and an increasing number of hypotheses are added that also need validating. What makes it even more complicated is that in contrast to the laboratory situation, human situations rarely if ever remain the same. Individuals differ from each other, and individuals themselves change over time with new experiences and circumstances.

It is obvious that all outer science work could never be done by inner science, and self-inquiry could never be replaced by outer science. Both forms of research have their value and supplement each other. An important advantage of outer science may be that it takes on the responsibility for tracing causes and effective solutions that are outside the perspective of the suffering person. The disadvantage of this approach, however, is that as the cause-and-effect sequences become more complex and further removed from our subjective experience and understanding, we become increasingly dependent on expert knowledge. Because professionals are better at interpreting all the data they manage to obtain from the outside than the suffering persons themselves, there is a danger that the person involved no longer feels responsible for his or her own well-being.

1.1.3   The Prognosis

The Third Noble Truth offers a 'prognosis', namely that liberation or inner freedom from suffering is possible. Through awareness of and insight into suffering as a result of greed, aversion and ignorance, we can wake up or 'awaken' to a state of more inner freedom. When we 'see' our conditioning, space arises for other possibilities. Acknowledging and accepting the processes as they naturally occur without fighting them favourably affect the prognosis. We are not dependent on others but can create the conditions for a good prognosis ourselves. The word 'Buddha' means 'awakened'. We all have 'Buddha-nature' and the potential to awaken.

This Noble Truth is the counterpart of the Western aspiration to link a good outcome to successful management and manipulation of the causal factors of suffering. The aspiration is to manipulate the cause-and-effect sequence—even without us being aware of it—with the help of medication, surgery or other remedies in such a way that suffering can be alleviated or even cured. Fighting, not acceptance, promises a favourable prognosis, which usually means we have to surrender to the expert opinion of doctors and therapists who know more about these matters than we do. Of course this is completely acceptable when it involves acutely dangerous or ultimately life-threatening illnesses, but we can also go too far. We only need to recall the World Health Organization (WHO) definition of 'health' as a state of complete social, physical and mental well-being (WHO, 1978) and the extremely ambitious striving for *Health for All by 2000* (WHO, 1979). Even though that target has obviously not been reached, the pursuit for more control over suffering and the 'makeability' of health knows no limits. Natural processes are influenced by all kinds of unnatural methods, not only at the time of birth and impending death but also in everyday inconveniences, imagined blemishes or normal aging processes.

1.1.4   The Treatment

The Fourth Noble Truth prescribes the Eightfold Path (the 'treatment') as a way to liberation from suffering. This is a path of practice and self-inquiry that everyone can follow. The Eightfold Path involves cultivating insight (right view, right intention), ethics (right speech, right action and right livelihood) and meditation (right effort, right mindfulness and right concentration). 'Right' should not be understood here in the moral sense, as something that can be laid down in norms and behavioural codes, but as 'wholesome', 'alleviating suffering'. We need to discover for ourselves what is wholesome, skilful or beneficial by testing it against our own experience. Here we are our own healer and not dependent on a professional therapist. We can seek advice from a more experienced teacher and support from fellow practitioners, but nobody can take over the actual work. The various stages of this Eightfold Path of practice are not independent from each other. Practising one aspect reinforces the other aspects; neglecting one part will have a detrimental effect on the others. What is striking is the caring concern that is inherent in these guidelines for living our life as a whole. The 'treatment' is not aimed at specific causes but encompasses all dimensions of life.

Tara Brach (2004) clarified two different ways in which we can look for inner wisdom and happiness. In the first—'vertical'—approach we look for something higher than this mundane existence, something perfect, and try to connect with that. This approach can be found in many cultures and religions, but it does have a downside. The more we focus on that perfection as an ideal image, the more we might have a negative view of the limitations and shortcomings of life because we are imperfect human beings, and so is the world around us. In the second approach we look for inner wisdom and happiness on a 'horizontal' level. In this more pragmatic approach, we do not look for something higher, transcendent, but we connect more with the limitations and imperfections in life. In this view we make friends, as it were, with ourselves and with life as we experience it. We look for healing instead of cure. This can result in more self-worth, and paradoxically this approach seems to be at least as liberating and enlightening as the first, more idealistic, approach. The Buddhist way is more compatible with the horizontal perspective.

The modern Western aspiration seems more focussed on specific aspects of our lives and strives for better control over suffering, preferably by means of evidence-based treatment methods. An important characteristic of an evidence-based approach is that the applied treatment methods proved effective in independent scientific research, in line with the highest level of evidence (Sackett, Straus, Richardson, Rosenberg, & Haynes, 2000). A hierarchy has been established in the different levels of evidence. Highest in this hierarchy are the methods that have been validated more than once in controlled research, where the group of patients that gets the treatment in question is compared with a control group. This control group receives either a conventional treatment, a placebo or is on a waiting list to be treated. Ideally the assignment to the groups is random. The choice and preferences of the patient and the practitioner are eliminated as much as possible because they affect the results. Subjective self-inquiry is considered to be the lowest level of evidence, and case studies from clinical practice are not much higher on the list. It is clear that in this approach, the alleviation of suffering can easily take place outside our consciousness and our responsibility and that outer science is superior to inner science. The treatment is preferably aimed at specific causes within certain aspects of our existence and is less concerned with our life as a whole. Because pathological processes are so complex that lay people cannot really understand them, we are expected to let experts make the choice for the correct treatment.

We could say that the Four Noble Truths encourage an attitude of care, whereas the Four Noble Aspirations offer more chance of finding a cure. But what happens if cure is not possible? Then we have nothing to lose with care. And if there does turn out to be a cure, an attitude of care will still be beneficial and only support the cure.

1.2 Modern Myths

Most Westerners would find it extremely dangerous if we were to prefer inner science to outer science when dealing with human suffering, and we are definitely not advocating this approach. One-sided emphasis on inner science can too easily make us accept and passively resign to conditions that could have been treated by outer science. Many diseases are still prevalent in non-Western cultures that could be cured if the knowledge and means of Western medicine were more available. A one-sided emphasis on outer science on the other hand is also not without its dangers and can give rise to modern forms of superstition. Some advocates of outer science reject in advance everything that has not been investigated, but the absence of evidence of efficacy is not the same as the evidence of absence of efficacy.

It might be true that the practice of inner science in a pure form would have much to offer in the field of spiritual growth, but should it play such an important part in health care? Moreover, the principles might be 'noble' but they are definitely not free from being clouded by less noble interests of its practitioners—personal, ideological or economic. We know enough examples of how elevation of an individual's truth, or that of a master or guru, over other truths can have unwholesome effects and have resulted in the abuse of credulous followers. Many people fear that too much emphasis on inner science would only result in a return to magical thinking, outdated superstitions and 'woolly' practices that leave treatable conditions untreated. All this while we had hoped to have left these old methods behind once and for all with the help of modern science. A well-known example in the Netherlands is the Dutch actress Sylvia Millecam, who died from breast cancer in 2001 while she was relying on alternative therapists who did not take her diagnosis seriously. Partly because of this case, the Center for Integrative Psychiatry where we work has adopted the Dutch Complementary and Alternative Medicine protocol to ensure the safe and evidence-based use of unconventional treatment methods (Hoenders, 2014; Hoenders, Appelo, Van den Brink, Hartogs, & De Jong, 2011).

In this chapter we will discuss a number of modern myths, namely the myth of controllability, the myth of specific remedies, the myth of dependence on experts and the myth of freedom from values.

1.2.1   The Myth of Controllability

The approach to suffering according to the method of outer science seems at first glance to be superior to that of inner science, for it has achieved impressive results and contributed to many effective treatments for serious forms of suffering. Diseases that previously killed many, such as smallpox and measles, have now been brought under control. Operations that seemed impossible in the last century are carried out every day. Painkillers render the pain in our bodies manageable, and psychotherapeutic methods manage the pain in our minds and souls.

Even though a lot has been achieved through medical science and modern psychology, it remains to be seen if suffering in general has become more controllable. Often we gain control in one area only to lose it elsewhere. Perhaps vaccination programmes eliminate certain diseases, but we do not know if this makes us more susceptible to other illnesses. The younger premature babies can be kept alive, the more complications may be in store for them. The more we can prolong life, the more difficult the last stage of life can be. Effective medication can have side effects that cause new problems. For example, the elderly patient who becomes lightheaded as a side effect of her medication consequently falls and breaks her hip.

Costs keep rising in the health care sector and seem just as uncontrollable. Although more people are working in health care than ever, the waiting lists get longer. The wealthier we become, the less tolerant we seem to be of discomfort and the more demands we make as regards our health. The less acceptance there is in our culture of normal, existential suffering, the more forms of suffering are considered pathological and become incorporated as diseases and disorders that need to be treated.

The mental health care sector has an elaborate range of psychopharmaceuticals at its disposal to eliminate unpleasant, but not such unusual, states such as depression, anxiety, restlessness, insomnia and concentration problems. Many people in Western countries take antidepressants. In the Netherlands, for instance, where the overall population is around 16 million, an estimated 1 million people are prescribed these drugs (CVZ, 2011; CVZ is a collective of health insurers in the Netherlands), undoubtedly partly for conditions and complaints that were previously accepted as 'normal' and being part of life.

The number of psychotherapeutic methods is growing steadily as well. The more psychotherapeutic help is accepted for various forms of intrapersonal and interpersonal distress, the more psychotherapeutic models and protocols are added. It has been estimated that well over 10,000 handbooks on psychotherapy have been published since the 1960s and that more than 400 psychotherapeutic methods have been documented, of which there are 145 manualised treatment protocols for about 50 diagnostic groups (Beutler et al., 2005; Wampold, 2001). Many of these treatments, just like psychopharmaceuticals, are directed at conditions for which people did not seek specific professional help half a century ago.

Outer science is no doubt helpful in many forms of suffering, but to try to control what is uncontrollable creates a lot of unnecessary suffering. Practising inner science can help us to accept uncontrollability and be compassionate towards the suffering that is part of life. We recall the Serenity Prayer. Though the source is controversial (Shapiro, 2008), its message is very fitting here:

> *God, grant me the serenity to accept the things I cannot change;*
> *The courage to change the things I can;*
> *And the wisdom to know the difference.*

1.2.2   The Myth of Specific Remedies

The wish to find medication for every ailment and a specific remedy for every discomfort seems closely connected to the high demands we make on our quality of life and the associated expectations we have of modern science. We imagine that the ongoing search will eventually result in finding the specific causes and solutions for our problems. But the more we know, the more complex the search becomes and the more cause-and-effect sequences are involved in the process. The specific cause is as elusive as the proverbial needle in the haystack. The assumption that mental disorders are caused by too much or too little of certain substances in the brain, a specific imbalance that could be rectified with a specific drug, was evidently far too simple (Healy, 1997, 2002). It was thought that depression, for example, was caused by a shortage of the neurotransmitter serotonin. Drugs that inhibit the reuptake of serotonin proved effective in depression but subsequently also turned out to help with anxiety and obsessive–compulsive disorders, eating disorders and even premature ejaculation. So apparently the serotonin reuptake inhibitors were not that specific after all. Even if there could be specific intervention in certain chains of chemical reactions, the required specific effect is often accompanied by unintended nonspecific side effects because the drug also has effects on many other reaction chains. These effects are usually unwanted, but not in all cases. And then suddenly a drug can acquire a different field of application (like premature ejaculation). So one drug can often be applied to various disorders, and more than one drug can be effective for one disorder or various combinations can be used. A depressed patient whose mood improves after she takes an antidepressant usually does more to improve her frame of mind. She talks to her psychologist, goes out for walks more, drinks less alcohol, starts taking a multivitamin supplement with her meals and cancels a number of stressful appointments. Has she improved because of the antidepressant, the talks with the psychotherapist or through better self-care?

Although the number of evidence-based psychotherapy protocols is steadily increasing, at the same time there is growing evidence that the psychotherapeutic model that is used only makes a small specific contribution to the successful outcome of the treatment. Nonspecific factors like offering hope, unconditional positive regard and empathy are important contributors to the success of psychotherapy. The quality of the therapeutic relationship—as experienced by the patient!—seems the most important predictor for success; in any case, the relationship is far more important than the method that is used, whether it is evidence based or not (Beutler et al., 2005; Wampold, 2001). One study even showed that doctors who have a better relationship with their depressed patients have more success with a placebo than their colleagues who do not have such a good relationship using a genuine antidepressant (McKay, Imel, & Wampold, 2006).

So our remedies are not as specific as they seem, and the causes of many forms of suffering are probably not either. An increasing number of health problems are caused by our lifestyle. It has been known for some time that many physical problems, like obesity, heart and coronary disease, some forms of cancer, diabetes and conditions of the musculoskeletal system are the result of unhealthy habits. Up until now it has also been greatly underestimated how much our lifestyle affects psychological disorders (Walsh, 2011). It may also be the case that for many mental health problems, changes in lifestyle may be more effective than specific treatments. This would involve qualitative modifications on many levels, such as nutrition and diet, physical activity and relaxation, relationships with others and with nature, spirituality, meaning and social engagement. This approach is nonspecific and focuses on more than one dimension of life, and it can be compared to the Buddha's guidelines of the Eightfold Path for it similarly concerns a combination of self-inquiry, insight and living a virtuous life.

The practice of inner science can prevent us from being blinded by the belief in specific causes and specific cures. It is not about disqualifying insights from outer science but about having respect for the endless complexity of our existence.

1.2.3   The Myth of Dependence on Professionals

The more ambitious we become in striving for control over more and more forms of suffering, the more dependent we become on health care professionals and their growing supply of treatments. Powerful companies and the economy have a lot to gain from this. And perhaps we ourselves do too, because as long as scientists and experts deal with these forms of suffering, we do not need to take responsibility ourselves.

When our suffering is caused by our lifestyle, however, it can be tempting to push away our own responsibility because we are so busy and lifestyle changes need a lot of effort. Particularly if enough professionals are ready to fulfil the role of expert and advocate specific treatments, we often choose the line of least resistance. Yet the outcome of patiently learning healthier habits will ultimately be more beneficial and sustainable than these short-term external solutions and will make us less dependent on experts. In health care we are beginning to see a gradual shift from therapies to training courses that emphasise the individual's responsibility and the value of regular practice and training in healthy behaviour. Here the trainer is more a teacher than a therapist, teaching the participants a method so that they can become their own therapist. The mindfulness training and the compassion training that is described in this book are examples of this. Martin Appelo (2011) has stressed how important reflection and discipline are when making lifestyle changes. Everyone who has tried to break a persistent habit knows how difficult it is. Discipline easily collapses, even more so when the motivation is predominantly external ('I am doing this because my partner wants me to' or 'because the doctor tells me to'). Internal motivation can be hard to find if the reflection remains superficial. In our view, the practice of mindfulness can deepen this reflection and help us to become aware of our intrinsic motivation. And the practice of self-compassion can contribute to self-discipline, not from an imposing or commanding attitude but out of kindness towards ourselves.

Of course, more objective research in this area is important and this needs outer science. But unfortunately economic forces are not conducive. The tragedy of modern Western society is that on the one hand there are powerful commercial forces at work that tempt us to make unhealthy lifestyle choices (smoking, drinking, lack of physical activity and stressful working conditions), whereas on the other hand there is a powerful industry promoting drugs and professional treatments that claim to make us healthy again in easy ways, without having to go through the trouble of learning how to have a healthier lifestyle. Self-inquiry helps us to become aware of our own responsibility and prevents us from becoming needlessly dependent on professionals.

Economic forces also determine to a large extent the research areas of scientists, the preference for certain research methods and, at worst, the results that get published. This brings us to the fourth myth.

1.2.4   The Myth of Freedom From Values

The belief that scientific research is independent and value free, as well as the associated superior status of Western science, is increasingly up for discussion, and therefore the reliability of evidence-based treatments is too. The choices that are made as regards *what* is studied, *how* it is studied and the interpretations of the results are anything but value free. This would not be so bad if the choices were made based on 'noble values', but there seems to be contamination at many levels. Scientists and others point out that there is a worrying entanglement of economic, academic, ideological and personal interests (Dehue, 2008; Healy & Thase, 2003; Moncrieff, 2003; Vandereycken & Van Deth, 2006). One could speak of a credibility crisis in science.

There is a preference for publication of positive results, for instance. Negative results are published less often because the editors of scientific journals do not find them 'interesting' or because they simply do not get submitted as too much is at stake. Meta-analyses showed that the efficacy of antidepressants versus a placebo was seriously undermined when unpublished research was also taken into account (Kirsch et al., 2008; Turner, Matthews, Linardatos, Tell, & Rosenthal, 2008). Pharmaceutical industries have far more control than is generally suspected. They influence which research results get published, and partly determine the choice of research areas of academic centres because these are financially dependent on them. Professional organisations and patient lobby groups are also dependent on the industry's financial support, and pharmaceutical companies put their stamp on the content of educational and professional training programmes for doctors and on the information that is put out via the media and the Internet.

As evidence-based practice in health care becomes more complex, there are calls for giving more emphasis to 'values-based practice' (Fulford, 2008). Because we are influenced by values in any case, whether we want to be or not, it is important to acknowledge that and to make conscious and explicit what values determine our direction. Whether we are scientific researchers, clinicians or 'hands-on' experts, our approach to suffering does not *end* with ethics but *starts* with ethics. How do we want to approach suffering, and which are the values that guide us?

Instead of pitting the various approaches to suffering of East and West *against* each other, we would do better to reap the fruits of both. We can safely assume that nonnormative or value-free scientific practice does not exist. The claim of being value free only results in dangerous dogmatism and intolerance. There are many examples in the history of religions as well as science where people with new ideas were seen as heretics who much later received public recognition. Science is always practised within a cultural and historical context and is based on assumptions and preferences as regards views of humanity and the world. Norms and values always play a role, and they can be more, or less, 'noble' or virtuous. Without the self-reflection of inner science there cannot be an awareness of the values that guide us, for outer science overlooks this. What is of real value is not seen by the external eye but is experienced inwardly.

When the results of inner and outer science are viewed as irreconcilable opposites, this usually leads to fruitless discussions about who is right. A well-known example is the discussion about 'mind' and 'brain'. Advocates of scientific materialism propose that only the brain is real and that an independent mind is an illusion. The mind, in their view, is only a product of the chemical and physiological processes of the brain. Idealists in the humanities say that the mind is the only thing that is real and that it exists independently from the brain. This discussion will never end as long as both camps do not acknowledge that it is a discussion about values and not about facts. We could also choose a middle way and take as our premise that neither the mind nor the brain exists absolutely independently from each other but that they are interconnected and mutually dependent.

Both inner and outer science can contribute to a better understanding of how they are interdependent. Because one method leads to knowledge that is inaccessible to the other, they can supplement and enhance each other. Inner science studies the mind as an immediate experience to which outer science has no access; outer science studies the processes in the brain upon which inner science cannot comment. When this is acknowledged, a meeting between inner and outer science can take place. Such a fruitful meeting can be found in the work of a growing number of Western scientists who are familiar with both inner and outer science. Examples are B. Alan Wallace, who is a physicist and expert in religious studies (Wallace & Hodel, 2008), neuropsychologist Rick Hanson (2009) and psychiatrist Daniel Siegel (2010b), who have also written for the general public.

We hope to have clarified that the approach to suffering, from a scientific perspective also, is a 'valuable' matter (a matter of values). It is now time to pause at a number of 'timeless values' that may give us guidance and that may bring compassion back from the side-lines to the heart of health care.

1.3 Timeless Values

The choice to recognise inner and outer science as equally valuable ways to knowledge and insight that complement each other is, of course, based on values. We hope to make clear that we are talking about 'noble' values, values that call on us again and again to reexamine our attitude to suffering and to strive for an approach that involves as many wholesome and as few harmful effects as possible. Characteristic of noble values is that they are 'timeless', or at least enduring. They last throughout the centuries, survive wars and disasters and help us time and again to transcend temporary limitations and short-term interests. Such timeless values can be found in all great wisdom traditions.

We would like to mention three values that we consider guidelines in our search for the relief of suffering and that can contribute to more wisdom and compassion in medicine and psychology. You could call them golden rules for practitioners of both inner and outer science. The first is concerned with *what*—the content of what we do to alleviate suffering and the methods that are applied. The second and third are concerned with *how*—the way in which we deal with each other and with ourselves.

1.3.1 'Put Everything to the Test and Keep What Is Good'

This biblical instruction (I Thessalonians 5:21) is perhaps taken out of context but concisely describes the open attitude that is called for in our search for what works to alleviate suffering. The integrative approach in medicine and psychiatry (Hoenders, 2014; Hoenders et al., 2011) does not want to preclude anything but wants to give all treatment methods an honest chance and investigate them with an open mind.

'Put everything to the test' does not only apply to manualised treatments of groups of patients with the same characteristics but also to the exploration of what works to alleviate the unique suffering of this unique person in this unique situation. Thus research into what works never comes to an end. Naturally a treatment that has been proven to be effective should be applied first where possible, and there would have to be good reasons to depart from this. Yet 'keep what is good' refers not only to what is shown to be most effective in large controlled studies, for these always concern other people than the patient in question, but also to what proves to work best for this particular individual.

Because all research takes place in a cultural–historical context, it will never be able to yield absolute guidelines, or protocols that should be followed blindly, but will continually require a critical openness to new possibilities. 'Keep what is good' is, in our view, not a call for conservatism but a pragmatic call for doing more of what works. What is important is not whether a method suits a certain view of humanity or the world, or a certain culture, but whether *the method alleviates suffering and promotes health in the least harmful and the safest possible way.* It is of less concern whether the current medical models can explain it. What matters more is whether there is an openness to adapt theories and explanation models to the findings. Science would never have progressed if there had not always been people who had thought outside the box of the prevailing scientific model. But for these people we might still think that the Earth is flat, that the sun rotates around the Earth or that atoms are the smallest particles in the universe.

1.3.2   'Treat Others as You Want to Be Treated Yourself'

This adage is the positive version of the so-called Golden Rule: 'Do unto others as you would have them do unto you.' The British religious historian Karen Armstrong (2011) shows how the Golden Rule is endorsed by almost all religious, ethical and spiritual traditions. It can be found in monotheistic religions like Judaism, Christianity and Islam as well as in the Chinese, Hindu, Buddhist and other great wisdom traditions. The founders of these traditions did not envisage a world that suffered from religious wars and that is still afflicted by hatred, intolerance, extremism and violence. Hostility arises from old innate survival instincts and the associated need to emphasise differences and to elevate one's own personal identity and own group over others. The Golden Rule, on the other hand, points to the similarities between all people and acknowledges the needs and wants of friend and foe. It is aimed at the survival and well-being of all, not only that of one's own personal identity or group.

Armstrong, together with others, drew up a Charter for Compassion. It invites us to let ourselves be inspired by the ancient ethical principle of the Golden Rule and to let our moral actions be guided by our unlimited potential for compassion and altruism. They recommended reinstating the Golden Rule in health care as well, which has inspired Dutch medical students to draw up a charter Compassion for Care (www.compassionforcare.com). Imagine if caregivers would treat their patients as they would want to be treated themselves, researchers would study their subjects as they would want to be studied themselves and adherents of different scientific explanation models would respect each other as they would want to be respected themselves. The Golden Rule invites a friendly connection not only between those of similar views but particularly between those who have different opinions. The essence of compassion is that boundaries between mine and yours are transcended and that we acknowledge that none of us wants to suffer and that everyone wants to be happy.

You may think 'The Golden Rule doesn't seem so sound to me at all. I treat myself so badly and would never wish that on anyone!' This gives us all the more justification to practise self-compassion first and to wonder how we would really want to be treated. It is also a reason to reflect on the third value we want to mention.

1.3.3   'There Is More Right Than Wrong With Us'

From the very first session of mindfulness training Jon Kabat-Zinn (1991) emphasised that there is more right than wrong with us and that there is good reason for this. Human beings quickly and instinctively zoom in on negative signals (Hanson, 2009). This is an old survival mechanism that helps us whenever we encounter acute danger. But when we are in psychological pain we are also inclined to focus on what goes wrong, has gone wrong or could go wrong. Without noticing it we become bitter or gloomy and lose the objective view and often enjoyment of life as well.

Many people in our Western culture seem inclined towards a high degree of harshness or ruthlessness, particularly towards themselves. This ruthlessness is often linked to a low sense of self-worth and to self-hatred. Tara Brach (2004) called this 'the trance of unworthiness'. When the Dalai Lama heard about this for the first time during a meeting with Western scientists and meditation teachers at the third Mind & Life Conference in 1991, he initially did not understand what was meant; he was painfully moved when Western meditation teachers told him about this, and he found it hard to believe that many Westerners do not love themselves (Goleman, 2003). It was remarkable that he then asked whether these people were looking for happiness. When this was answered in the affirmative, the Dalai Lama said that this was a sign that compassion is indeed one of the most fundamental emotions and driving forces in our lives.

We do not need to take the saying 'there is more right than wrong with us' to imply that we have to approve of every type of behaviour. Even if our behaviour is reprehensible and needs improvement, there is the potential for self-healing deep down in us. We do not want it to be a superficial statement against better judgment but really see it as a value, a guiding compass under all circumstances. On the surface many things might be wrong with us, but every human being has a potential for insight and growth. Just as we carry the old innate survival mechanisms—which are not 'sinful' but natural—we also have the natural ability to cultivate awareness and compassion, whatever our starting position might be. Mystics and respected teachers from all traditions have pointed out time and again that the essence of wisdom and compassion—Buddha-nature, the Tao, Christ-consciousness, the True Self, or whatever it is called—is always present in us, although we usually do not live from that awakened state of mind. It seems healthy to remind ourselves from time to time of this valuable insight.

For a long time, the focus in medicine and psychology has been on what is wrong, on our ailments, disorders and failings. In the second half of the 20th century, however, in the humanistic and client-focussed schools we can also see a shift in attention to inner strength and self-healing potential; and in the past several decades these have been increasingly underpinned by outer science, for example in solution-focussed approaches (De Jong & Berg, 1998; De Shazer & Dolan, 2007), in positive psychology (Carr, 2011; Seligman, 2002), in the interest in resilience (Appelo & Bos, 2008) and in the shift in focus from symptoms to strengths (Bos & Appelo, 2009). However, there are pitfalls in being biased towards what is right as well as in being biased towards what is wrong. It is an *art* both to accept inevitable suffering and to pay attention to what is positive in life. A new school of psychology is called the 'psychology of the art of living', which unites both sides of life (Westerhof & Bohlmeijer, 2011).

The 'rightness' this third value refers to is of a considerably deeper level than the more superficial joys and sorrows that characterise our existence. Outer science will never be able to explore it directly, and inner science can only refer to it with inadequate words. We conclude by listing the guiding values with which we align ourselves and that we apply to meet human suffering compassionately:

- 'Put everything to the test and keep what is good' gives guidance on how we deal with the world in the broadest sense in our search for effective remedies.
- 'Treat others as you want to be treated yourself' gives guidance on how we deal with each other (and other living beings), acknowledging that we all want to be happy and free from suffering.
- 'There is more right than wrong with us' gives guidance on how we deal with ourselves, giving space to the possibilities of awakening and healing qualities that are present in us.

As far as we are concerned these values are durable and they give direction and guidance, even if they might never be fully achieved. We might not always act in accordance with them, but that does not make them less valuable. Regular reflection and mindfulness make it possible to return to them again and again, just as the beams of a lighthouse remind us of the desired direction at all times.

In the next chapter we no longer contrast East and West. Both offer vital and complementary approaches to suffering. We explore how a meeting between inner and outer science might look and focus on the meeting of Buddhist and Western psychology.

1.4 Causes and Remedies

The libraries of medicine and psychology contain many manuals about specific forms of suffering. However in this book we choose a transdiagnostic approach to suffering. It is not a substitute for all those manuals but an addition. We do not focus on specific complaints or disorders, nor do we deal with specific causes or remedies. We do focus, however, on the fundamental causes of suffering that—whatever the specific form—may play a role, and the possibility of freeing ourselves from them. The second part of the book, although a practical guide, also contains relevant theoretical background. Because we do not wish to dwell too much on theories in advance, we will suffice here with a broad outline of the parallels between Buddhist and Western psychology and how they can complement each other. (For an integrative review, see Mikulas, 2007.)

1.4.1 Causes of Suffering: A Meeting Between East and West

When we look at old Buddhist representations of the wheel of life (*samsara*), we see images of various realms in which the mind can dwell, and they all symbolise different forms of suffering (Epstein, 1995). This Eastern imagery may seem strange to us, but we want to point out how the wheel of *samsara* is propelled at the centre by three fundamental causes of suffering. We have already met these causes before as the 'three poisons' in the discussion of the Second Noble Truth (1.1.2). These are symbolised by three animal figures that bite each other's tails: the cock represents greed and attachment, the snake hatred and aversion and the pig ignorance, confusion and delusion (see Figure 1).

The three causes of suffering as pointed out in Buddhism (1. in Figure 1) can also be found in important schools in Western psychology. In classical *psychoanalysis* (2. in Figure 1) instinctual drives, which we experience as pleasure and displeasure, are seen as the driving forces behind our neurotic suffering, particularly when they are unconscious. Just as in the Buddha's teachings, here too the investigation of the inner world is essential, although it was assumed that the therapist often 'saw' more of the inner world of the patient than the patient him or herself, and in any case understood more of it than the patient. Psychoanalysts did not consider the inner science as it was practised by the Buddha very reliable and were of the opinion that a capable therapist was needed to point out the causes of

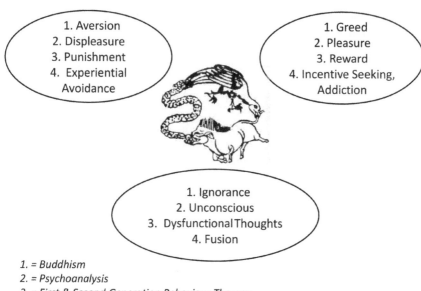

1. = *Buddhism*
2. = *Psychoanalysis*
3. = *First & Second Generation Behaviour Therapy*
4. = *Third Generation Behaviour Therapy*

Figure 1 Causes of suffering East/West.

suffering. For them it was important to trace repressed experiences and to analyse unresolved processes in earlier relationships that imprisoned the patient in their suffering and that they unconsciously transferred to the relationship with the therapist. When the therapist thought the patient was ready, the therapist offered his or her insights in the form of interpretations. The patient's reactions were an indication whether the therapist was on the right track. The therapists themselves tested their hypotheses about the causes of suffering and this had its drawbacks. If the relationship with the patient deepened, then this was a positive confirmation of the hypothesis. If the patient showed resistance, however, then the hypothesis could still be correct but the patient was not yet ready for that insight.

Psychoanalysts were not so inclined to let their hypotheses be tested by independent researchers. The first behavioural scientists therefore considered psychoanalysis unscientific. They abhorred the exploration of the inner world, which they viewed as a 'black box'; in a scientific sense nothing could be said about it. Like other scientists they arrived at their knowledge by means of outer science and developed objectively verifiable methods to study and influence behaviour from the outside. As this was rather complex with human behaviour, initially they often used animal models. In doing so, they seemed to be further removed from the Buddha's inner science than ever. Yet even in the learning theory of behavioural scientists there are echoes of Buddhist psychology because it describes in a very recognisable way the outside (behaviour) of the processes that inner science explores from within. In *first generation* behaviour therapy (3. in Figure 1) the emphasis was mainly on reinforcing and aversive stimuli (reward and punishment), which condition our behaviour in a desirable or undesirable direction. In *second generation* behaviour therapy—cognitive behaviour therapy—dysfunctional thoughts, interpretations and beliefs, comparable with 'delusion' in Buddhism, were seen as playing a significant role in unhealthy behaviour. This brought our inner world back into the picture, and it became the cognitive therapist's task to trace these unhealthy interpretations and beliefs.

In the *third generation* behaviour therapy (4. in Figure 1) we see that a meta-cognitive aspect has been added (Hayes, Follette, & Linehan, 2004). It is no longer so much the content of our thoughts that matters as the relationship to our thoughts, for that determines the amount of suffering. Acceptance and Commitment Therapy (ACT), which is an example of a third generation therapy model, argues that universal human suffering should no longer be pathologised (Hayes, Strohsal, & Wilson, 1999). Much of our suffering could be normalised again as existential suffering, which is as much part of mental health care as pathological suffering, because the distinction between the two is arbitrary by nature and creates more problems than it solves. Third generation therapists position themselves less as experts who apply therapeutic interventions to the patient and more as teachers or trainers who pass on a method for self-inquiry that they practise themselves because they also share in the existential suffering of humankind. Therapists apply the model of ACT to themselves as much as to their clients. This is even more evident in mindfulness teaching, in which trainers are expected to integrate the exercises they ask participants to do into their own lives. Self-inquiry has returned as a valuable inner science and has again become the responsibility of the person involved. The therapist/trainer can be a companion but can never do the work of self-inquiry for another person. Only the individual concerned is able to look directly into their inner world, and only from that perspective can 'insight' arise into how reactions to inevitable primary suffering cause secondary suffering. Attachment to pleasant experiences (dependence, addictions), aversion to unpleasant experiences (experiential avoidance) and 'fusion' (overidentification, merging) with thoughts about ourselves, the world, past and future, are recognised again as important causes of suffering. Here the language of modern Western psychology gets very close to the original Buddhist psychology and paves the way for a genuine meeting between East and West. It remains to be seen if they have enough in common to 'marry' each other.

1.4.2   Liberation From Suffering: A Marriage Between East and West

What if the meeting between East and West became a joint venture to alleviate suffering? If we compare the remedies for liberation from suffering that have been developed in Eastern and Western psychology, we see that in *Buddhist psychology* (1. in Figure 2) three antidotes are distinguished that are effective against the poisons of greed, aversion and ignorance. All three of these can be cultivated by the practice of the Eightfold Path: *generosity*, or not being attached to what

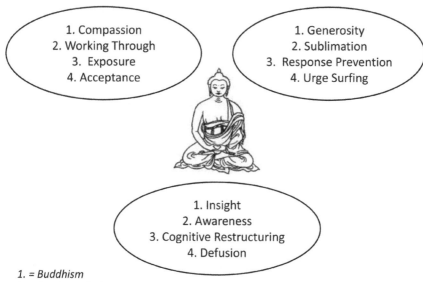

1. = *Buddhism*
2. = *Psychoanalysis*
3. = *First & Second Generation Behaviour Therapy*
4. = *Third Generation Behaviour Therapy*

Figure 2 Liberation from suffering East/West.

is impermanent; *compassion*, or facing pain with care and concern; and *insight* into the fact that all phenomena are ultimately impermanent, unsatisfactory and uncontrollable. Insight into our 'selfless' nature is part of this too because our 'ego' or 'self' and everything we identify with is just as temporary and impermanent as all other phenomena. Getting attached to what is fleeting is what creates 'dis-ease' and suffering.

The *psychoanalysts* (2. in Figure 2) described similar processes that could be initiated with the help of a therapist to alleviate neurotic suffering. Making *conscious* what was hidden in the unconscious and what kept the patient imprisoned in their neurosis was particularly important. Furthermore, *working through* repressed pain and delayed grieving was of significance, as well as *sublimation*, that is, the expression of unacceptable primitive urges at an acceptable level— for example by channelling aggressive impulses through engaging in sports, and sexual desires through creating works of art. It was thought that working within the therapeutic relationship where transference processes could be interpreted would be a powerful means for liberation. Later there were doubts about whether psychoanalytical interpretations were helpful, and in accordance with attachment theory the emphasis was shifted to the safe environment the patient could experience with the therapist. Individuals who had grown up with insecure relationships to parents or caregivers could at last begin to feel accepted in their needs and wants in the *holding* of the therapeutic environment (Epstein, 1998). In this way their self-confidence could grow, and the mental and interpersonal suffering that had arisen from insecure attachment could be alleviated. The client-centred approach of Carl Rogers (1995), which inspired many subsequent psychotherapeutic schools, underlined the importance of a trusting relationship with the therapist. Later this was indeed confirmed by research into the efficacy of psychotherapy, as we already pointed out when discussing the myth of specific remedies (1.2.2). Qualities like authenticity, unconditional positive regard, acceptance and empathy proved to be far more important than the theoretical model that the therapist favoured. It is also interesting to note that Buddhist students praise these qualities in their teachers. Apparently meeting the other in an atmosphere of trust, from heart to heart, is a significant support for liberation from suffering. We also see a shift in focus in the client-centred approach from 'what is wrong' to 'what is right' about the client. Good qualities are naturally present and can begin to blossom as soon as they are welcomed with kind attention in the appropriate therapeutic context.

The liberating processes of Eastern psychology show similarities with the technique of first generation behaviour therapy (3. in Figure 2), although they were developed in a completely different way. *Exposure-based* methods are commonly used, that is, being exposed to and learning to tolerate unpleasant situations. For example, the object the phobic patient is afraid of is gradually brought nearer for as long as is needed for the fear to subside. Another technique is *response prevention*: abstaining from unhealthy behaviour and resisting giving in to urges and desires in the short term because they sustain the suffering in the long term. For example, a patient with an obsessive fear of contagion and compulsory hand washing (which causes skin irritation that maintains the fear) forgoes the urge to wash his hands. The cognitive therapy of the second generation chose to work in the area of correcting dysfunctional thoughts and beliefs—*cognitive restructuring*—by inviting patients to view themselves and the world from healthier cognitions and to act accordingly.

In third generation behaviour therapy (4. in Figure 2) we see that the work of *exposure* is also extended to exposure to painful emotions and thoughts. Thus experiential avoidance can be replaced by *experiential acceptance*, and *mindfulness* practices can support this (Hayes et al., 2004). Mindfully observing painful experiences, without running away from them, is a form of radical inner exposure. Not giving in to a tendency but mindfully observing an impulse or burning desire for as long as necessary to experience that the desire can also diminish and disappear is called 'urge-surfing' (Bowen, Chawla, & Marlatt, 2011). This mindfulness exercise is particularly suitable for people with addiction problems who are in the abstinence stage. In the ACT model, mindfulness-based exercises are taught to *defuse or dis-identify* from views about ourselves, the world, the past and the future with which we are fused or overidentified. Defusion of our self-image opens up our awareness and shifts the perspective from self-as-content to self-as-context, the 'empty space' that the stream of experiences flows through and is somewhat similar to the Buddhist teaching on selflessness. Thus, our consciousness becomes a constantly available holding environment with unconditional space and acceptance for all our experiences, pleasant or unpleasant.

Fusion and experiential avoidance are processes that prolong our suffering and prevent us from aligning our lives with our *values*, with what really matters. Defusion and acceptance pave the way for a life where we are committed to our values. Self-inquiry into our inner world, where we can find the causes for our suffering as well as the keys to free ourselves from it, seems to have become as essential to Western psychology as it always was in Buddhist psychology. Mindfulness trainers are not so much engaged in 'therapy' but practise a mindful dialogue with the participants (McCown, Reibel, & Micozzi, 2010). This so-called 'inquiry' has no other aim than to bring participants back again and again to the experience of the present moment, so that they themselves learn to make the distinction between wholesome or unwholesome reactions to their suffering and learn to trust the secure holding of being tenderly and mindfully present with whatever is happening. Mindfulness becomes *heartfulness*. In doing so we develop a relationship with the suffering part of ourselves comparable to that of a good therapist with his patient or a teacher with his pupil: authentic, respectful, nonjudgmental and empathic.

Practising inner science and the introduction of mindfulness training courses in mental health care is not a marginal phenomenon or a fad but a powerful development in line with the important theories concerning mental suffering in Eastern and Western psychology. The approaches to suffering from East and West are far more similar than might be suspected at first glance. If the role of inner science were more powerful, we would be less blinded by the modern myths we discussed in the previous chapter.

Reinstatement of the practice of inner science does not mean that Western psychology should turn away from the methods of outer science. On the contrary, the processes that are only visible to the 'inner eye' are accompanied by processes that can be examined by the outwardly focussed eye. For the first time we see that these inner processes, which for centuries were shared subjective experiences in cultures where meditation was practised, are now supported by objective neuroscientific and clinical psychological research. Scientific literature concerning the effects of meditation and applications of mindfulness is growing exponentially (Didonna, 2009a; J. M. G. Williams & Kabat-Zinn, 2011). East and West, inner science and outer science seem to have a fruitful marriage. The effects of the practice of compassion and loving-kindness are increasingly being studied. Before giving an overview of this, we describe the development from mindfulness training to compassion training in the mental health care sector in the next chapter.

1.5 From Mindfulness Training to Compassion Training

In this chapter we reflect on the place mindfulness training has acquired in the health care setting and how we came to develop Mindfulness-Based Compassionate Living (MBCL) training as a deepening course in the mental health services where we work.

1.5.1 Mindfulness Training in Health Care

The green light for mindfulness courses in mental health care was given in 2002 when Zindel Segal (from Canada) and Mark Williams and John Teasdale (from the U.K.) introduced Mindfulness-Based Cognitive Therapy (MBCT) as an evidence-based method to prevent relapse in patients with recurring depression (Segal, Williams, & Teasdale, 2002). MBCT was an adaptation of Mindfulness-Based Stress Reduction (MBSR) that had been developed from 1979 onward by Jon Kabat-Zinn (U.S.) in the Stress Reduction Clinic (now Center for Mindfulness) of the University of Massachusetts Medical School (Kabat-Zinn, 1991). MBSR was developed in general health care and was offered initially mainly to patients with chronic pain and persistent physical diseases where conventional treatment had unsatisfactory results.

MBCT and MBSR have much more in common than differences. In both cases they involve eight weekly group meetings of, on average, 2 and a half hours, supplemented in MBSR with usually a day or part of a day of silent practice. The number of participants in MBSR can be larger (30–40) than in MBCT (10–16). For the duration of the course, participants practise mindfulness exercises at home for an hour every day, with the support of audio CDs and a course manual or handouts for every session. The formal practices (body scan, movement exercises while standing or lying down, sitting meditation) are the same in MBCT and MBSR. In MBSR there is somewhat more emphasis on the body scan and mindful movement or yoga, and in MBCT sitting meditation is practised a bit more. The themes of communication and nutrition are elaborated on in MBSR, whereas in MBCT psychoeducational and cognitive–behavioural therapeutic material has been added, focussed on the specific vulnerability to depression. The theme 'dealing with thoughts' gets more attention in MBCT, as do the '3-minute breathing spaces'—short mini-meditations that form a bridge between the formal practices and the informal practice in daily life.

Besides MBCT for recurring depression, other similar mindfulness-based pro-grammes and interventions (see Baer, 2006; Didonna, 2009a for an overview) have been developed or are still being developed for people with anxiety disorders (Orsillo & Roemer, 2005), obsessive–compulsive disorders (Didonna, 2009b), per-sonality disorders (Rizvi, Welch, & Dimidjian, 2009), eating disorders (Wolever & Best, 2009), addiction problems (Bowen, Chawla, & Marlatt, 2011), attention-deficit/hyperactivity disorder (Zylowska, Smalley, & Schwartz, 2009), autism spectrum disorders (Spek, Van Ham, & Nyklicek, 2013), susceptibility to psychosis (Chad-wick, Newman Taylor, & Abba, 2005), chronic pain (Burch, 2008; Gardner-Nix, 2009), cancer (Bartley, 2012; Carlson, Labelle, Garland, Hutchins, & Birnie, 2009), chronic medical illness (Bohlmeijer, Prenger, Taal, & Cuijpers, 2010) and medi-cally unexplained symptoms (Van Ravesteijn, Lucassen, Bor, Van Weel, & Speck-ens, 2013) and for certain age groups like children (Goodman & Kaiser Greenland, 2009), adolescents (Biegel, Brown, Shapiro, & Schubert, 2009) and the elderly (Smith, 2004; Zellner Keller, Singh, & Winton, 2013). These programmes are often based either on the MBSR or the MBCT module.

Much of the qualitatively better research has so far been done with homoge-neous groups, where all participants suffer from the same disorder or vulnerabil-ity, like MBCT for patients with recurring depression. Because the training is primarily aimed at the nonspecific causes of suffering, it seems advantageous to offer them to heterogeneous groups, made up of participants with different disor-ders and vulnerabilities. In practice this is happening already because logistically this has many advantages. Studies have now been published indicating that the results of MBSR and MBCT for mixed groups are on a par with those of homoge-neous groups (Bos, Merea, Van den Brink, Sanderman, & Bartels-Velthuis, 2014; Green & Bieling, 2012). As far as we are aware, to what extent the specific com-ponents of MBCT are essential additions or whether clients with recurring depres-sion would not benefit equally from the MBSR module have not been studied. Because most clients in mental health care suffer from stress, often from chronic stress, or because in acute stress situations they get stuck because of unhealthy coping strategies, we, along with many mindfulness trainers, are of the opinion that it is more efficient and practical to present both modules as one course so that as many clients as possible can benefit. We have chosen to integrate MBSR and an MBCT into one programme and have adjusted the training material to suit mixed groups of psychiatric outpatients with various diagnoses and to add an additional silent practice session.

It is our experience that there are not only logistical but also therapeutic advan-tages to including participants with a variety of problems in the same group. This makes it less easy for them to shift attention to the content of their problems, enabling them to focus on investigating the experience of and the relationship to the symptoms or complaints, whatever the underlying disorder or illness. Mind-fulness practice does not so much bring relief from the primary stress, the suf-fering that is inevitable, but the secondary stress, the suffering that arises from unhealthy reactions to primary stress. Therefore mindfulness training is a comple-mentary methodology *par excellence* that does not replace conventional forms of treatment but adds the healing power of mindfulness and self-inquiry. Mindfulness practice promotes a more conscious and a healthier lifestyle that can benefit our physical, emotional and social well-being.

1.5.2   Compassion Training in Health Care

The compassion training we have developed, referred to as MBCL, can also be offered to mixed groups, as a transdiagnostic learning programme that builds on the mindfulness training. In MBCL, as in MBSR/MBCT, a caring, compassionate attitude is cultivated that can be beneficial in many forms of suffering.

Why did we think it necessary to develop a compassion training as a follow-up to the mindfulness course? An important reason is that we noticed that the 8-week foundation course is too short for many people, particularly for participants with persistent unhealthy or dysfunctional patterns. After the course many people have said that they benefited from the exercises. They were more aware of what was happening in their lives and more open to the richness of their sensory experiences. They had begun to feel more 'at home' in their bodies and started learning to observe feelings and thoughts as passing events without identifying with them. They felt more freedom as regards their options in stressful situations. And often they have reported that they have become kinder towards themselves and others. Yet there are quite a number of participants who find it difficult to really take the gentler, kinder attitude to heart, particularly those who have always been harsh, severe and critical towards themselves (and/or others) and those who are tormented by feelings of shame, guilt, unworthiness or a sense of being wronged. The persistent nature of their complaints, symptoms and unhealthy habits—whether it is anxiety, depression, irritability, physical pain, tiredness, obsessive–compulsive or addictive behaviour, loneliness, social problems or the more general or varying complaints associated with stress—can easily change the gentle attitude back into its opposite. They often find it difficult to continue the exercises after the course without the guidance of a trainer and without the support of the group meetings. It is as though the inner critic or bully quickly raises its head with harsh judgments and reproaches them that they are not doing enough practice, or not doing it well enough, or that everything is meaningless anyway. Old patterns do not disappear overnight, and they easily creep back in again. In people with chronic or recurring health problems, the inner bully, in one form or another, often plays an important part in the continuation or worsening of these problems. Although the basic course introduces the attitude of kindness, it is often insufficient to soften these persistent patterns. These participants in particular may experience the advanced course as valuable. It can also help all others who are interested in finding ways to deepen their mindfulness practice and be more compassionate in life.

The attitude of loving-kindness and self-compassion is already part of the original MBSR and MBCT programme, although mostly implicitly. In the MBCL programme, we explicitly address loving-kindness and self-compassion as a practice. There are many parallels between the compassion training and MBSR and MBCT as regards the number of participants, the structure of the course (eight sessions and an additional silent practice session), the duration (2 and a half hours) and structure of the sessions, practising at home with formal and informal exercises and the guidance by means of a course book and audio CDs. This model is familiar to participants, and this supports the process of deepening the practice. Participants do exercises in cultivating compassion and loving-kindness for themselves and others, and these exercises can also further hone their mindfulness skills. There is a broader range of exercises than in the basic course, with more options to invite participants to choose the exercises that meet their individual needs and are appropriate for their phase of self-inquiry. The psychoeducational material is more elaborate; there is more information about evolutionary psychology, the workings of the brain, emotion regulation and dealing with stress. The exercises use the imagination to further cultivate the kind and compassionate attitude. You might say that where mindfulness training helps to open our eyes so that what appears to us from moment to moment can be seen more clearly, compassion training can help to open the heart to what is being seen, particularly when it is painful and unpleasant. We welcome the secret revealed in *The Little Prince* by Antoine de Saint-Exupéry (1943/1971): 'It is only with the heart that one can see rightly; what is essential is invisible to the eye' (p. 86). The heart has access to deeper levels of 'seeing', and at these deeper levels compassion can be a healing force, even if all else fails.

So far the feedback on compassion training has been very positive, and most participants have reported that they experience the training and the power of compassion and self-compassion as extremely beneficial. The training as it is described here is relatively new, and a controlled trial is currently being carried out at Radboud University in the Netherlands. The training has a solid scientific foundation, and most elements of the course have proven to be effective in scientific studies. There is more on this in the next chapter.

1.6 Research

In this chapter we focus on research concerning the relationship between mindfulness, compassion and health and studies of compassion-focused interventions in healthy subjects and in therapeutic settings. Many other references to scientific work underpinning theory and practice of the Mindfulness-Based Compassionate Living (MBCL) training programme are given in the description of the sessions in Part 2 of this book.

1.6.1 Correlation Studies: Mindfulness, Self-Compassion and Health

It falls outside the scope of this book to discuss the extensive research into the effects of mindfulness, so we refer the reader to reviews and meta-analyses by Baer (2003); Grossman, Niemann, Schmidt, and Walach (2004); Hofmann, Sawyer, Witt, and Oh (2010); Chiesa and Serretti (2011) and Piet and Hougaard (2011). Meanwhile it is crystal clear that mindfulness has positive effects on both physical and mental health. Less is known about *how* it works, and this requires more research. Shapiro and Carlson (2009) have argued that the time is right to shift the focus in mindfulness studies from reducing complaints and symptoms to cultivating wholesome mental qualities such as wisdom, compassion and virtue. The concept of mindfulness has gradually broadened and cannot be clearly distinguished from (self-) compassion. The first self-report questionnaires assessing mindfulness mainly measured bare attentiveness. More recently used questionnaires also have addressed other components, including the accepting and non-judgmental attitude with which one pays attention. It is easy to see an overlap here with a compassionate attitude when pain and suffering emerge in the field of awareness. Often it is assumed that alongside mindfulness practice the capacity for self-compassion develops 'by itself'. It has been shown, for example, that mindfulness training can promote self-compassion in health care professionals and therapists in training who had participated in a Mindfulness-Based Stress Reduction (MBSR) course (Shapiro, Astin, Bishop, & Cordova, 2005; Shaprio, Brown, & Biegel, 2007). This was also found in a sample of patients with recurring depression who were trained in Mindfulness-Based Cognitive Therapy (MBCT; Kuyken et al., 2010). Interestingly, self-compassion appeared to be a mediator for stress reduction in MBSR and for preventing recurrence of depression in MBCT. One could therefore argue that self-compassion could well be a central mechanism in the effectiveness of mindfulness (Baer, 2010). Also, in a sample of healthy individuals who did not have a regular meditation practice, self-compassion appeared to be a crucial attitudinal factor in the relationship between mindfulness and happiness (Hollis-Walker & Colosimo, 2011).

The instrument that is generally used to measure self-compassion is the scale developed by Kristin Neff (2003a). She pioneered the research into self-compassion amongst relatively healthy populations, mainly students. Here also the different contributions of mindfulness and self-compassion cannot be separated because *mindfulness* itself, as the ability to mindfully acknowledge our pain and suffering, is a component of the self-compassion scale. The other two components of the scale are *common humanity*, the ability to see our suffering as part of our shared human condition, and *self-kindness*, the ability to offer kindness to ourselves when we suffer. All three components turn out to be significant in self-compassion and are interdependent. The practice of mindfulness and self-compassion probably reinforce each other, but more empirical research is needed to determine how they relate. It is plausible that both contribute to health in their own way. A growing body of evidence, suggests that the cultivation of self-compassion deserves more explicit attention (for reviews, see Barnard & Curry, 2011; Hofmann, Grossman, & Hinton, 2011; Neff, 2012). A recent study of more than 500 respondents from the general population who enrolled in a self-help method for anxiety showed that self-compassion as measured on Neff's scale as a whole was much more strongly associated with mental well-being (less anxiety, fewer depressive symptoms and better quality of life) than mindfulness measured according to a specific scale (Van Dam, Sheppard, Forsyth, & Earleywine, 2011).

In samples of the general population, self-compassion had a positive correlation with psychological strengths like happiness, optimism, wisdom, curiosity, personal initiative, emotional intelligence and social connectedness and a negative correlation with self-criticism, depression, anxiety, ruminating, thought suppression and perfectionism (Heffernan, Griffin, McNulty, & Fitzpatrick, 2010; Hollis-Walker & Colosimo, 2011; Neff, Rude, & Kirkpatrick, 2007). In a meta-analysis of 20 samples using Neff's scale a large effect size was found for the association between self-compassion and mental health (MacBeth & Gumley, 2012).

There are more and more indications that the kind of 'self' we identify with is affecting our well-being and our social relationships. Students followed during their first semester at university who pursued compassionate goals had significantly better outcomes than those pursuing self-centred goals (Crocker & Canevello, 2008). For a long time, cultivating self-esteem was thought to be crucial, but more recent data suggest that self-compassion is actually a better predictor of well-being whereas a strong sense of self-esteem is associated with narcissism (Neff, 2008; Neff & Vonk, 2009). Gilbert and colleagues have demonstrated, using social rank theory, that competitive behaviour can be motivated by striving for dominance but also by striving to avoid inferiority (Gilbert et al., 2007). The latter especially appears to be associated with social evaluative fears, submissiveness, stress, anxiety and depression and is predictive of psychopathology. Although modern society may make us believe the contrary, a caring mentality proves to be more beneficial for our health than a competitive mentality; 'getting along' is more important than 'getting ahead' (Gilbert, 2005; Liotti & Gilbert, 2011). Even in relation to competitive activities like sport, two studies amongst young women showed that high self-compassion scores were associated with more intrinsic motivation, fewer concerns with ego-related goals, less anxiety about failure and social judgment of their physique and less obligatory exercise behaviour (Magnus, Kowalski, & McHugh, 2010; Mosewich, Kowalski, Sabiston, Sedgwick, & Tracy, 2011). Another study amongst female undergraduates showed that higher levels of appearance-related self-compassion were associated with lower levels of disordered eating, even when controlled for self-esteem (Breines, Toole, Tu, & Chen, 2014).

In adversity, self-compassion also seems more protective than self-esteem. Many correlation studies showed that self-compassion is associated with healthier coping with difficult circumstances, such as academic failure (Neely, Schallert, Mohammed, Roberts, & Chen, 2009; Neff, Hsieh, & Dejitterat, 2005), personal weakness (Neff, Kirkpatrick, & Rude, 2007), traumatic events (Thompson & Waltz, 2008), homesickness (Terry, Leary, & Mehta, 2013), the consequences of maltreatment in childhood (Vetesse, Dyer, Li, & Wekerle, 2011), divorce (Sbarra, Smith, & Mehl, 2012) and chronic pain (Costa & Pinto-Gouveia, 2011; Wren et al., 2012). Individuals who were more compassionate towards themselves appeared to function better in relationships (Baker & McNulty, 2011; Neff & Beretvas, 2012) and reported more empathy, altruism, perspective taking and forgiveness (Neff & Pommier, 2012).

It is not just a caring attitude towards ourselves but also compassion for others that is associated with beneficial effects on well-being and stress regulation. The students in the study by Crocker and Canevello (2008) who showed greater compassion for others also perceived others to have greater compassion for them and appeared to create better social supportive environments. In a community sample of healthy females, higher scores on compassion for others were associated with decreased physiological reactivity (measured by blood pressure, cortisol and heart rate variability) and increased ability to receive social support whilst performing a stressful task (Cosley, McCoy, Saslow, & Epel, 2010).

In clinical samples, self-compassion appears to be protective of distress and levels of disability. In patients with cancer, self-compassion was found to significantly predict lower levels of depressive and stress symptoms and increased quality of life (Pinto-Gouveia, Duarte, Matos, & Fráguas, 2013). In women who were studied after completion of active treatment for breast cancer, self-compassion was correlated with fewer disturbances of body image and less psychological distress (Przezdziecki et al., 2013). An interpretative phenomenological analysis of patients with diagnoses of anxiety and depression using semistructured interviews on the experience and meaning of self-compassion revealed that they could meaningfully connect with the concept. They thought being self-compassionate would help them cope with their anxiety and depression, whilst at the same time they thought it would be difficult to put into practice (Pauley & McPherson, 2010). Compared with healthy controls, patients with generalised and social anxiety disorder scored lower on self-compassion. Within the patient groups, self-compassion was correlated with lower levels of anxiety, worry and sensitivity to anxiety and less fear of social evaluation (Hoge et al., 2013; Werner et al., 2012). In patients with schizophrenia and schizoaffective disorders, higher self-compassion scores were correlated with less psychopathology, including fewer psychotic symptoms, less excitement and less emotional discomfort (Eicher, Davis, & Lysaker, 2013).

In general, self-compassion seems to be associated with beneficial exposure to painful emotions and thoughts; having self-compassion makes it easier to be exposed to the inevitable forms of pain and suffering in our lives. Self-compassion seems a natural remedy against experiential avoidance, a basic mechanism that lies at the root of many forms of mental suffering (Hayes, Strohsal, & Wilson, 1999; Kashdan, Barrios, Forsyth, & Steger, 2006). It is therefore of utmost importance to develop effective interventions that help this capacity to grow, in preventive as well as therapeutic settings.

1.6.2 Intervention Studies in Nonclinical Samples

A number of controlled studies have been done with nonclinical, healthy respondents about the effect of practising loving-kindness meditation (traditionally called *metta*, and comparable to what we call 'kindness meditation' in the MBCL programme). In comparison with a neutral exercise, a short loving-kindness practice increased feelings of social connectedness and involvement with strangers (Hutcherson, Seppala, & Gross, 2008). Another study investigated the practice of loving-kindness meditation amongst employees of a software company (seven weekly sessions of an hour with additional exercises that focussed on the participants themselves and others, as home practice with CDs). Compared with the control group, there was a positive effect on the scores for positive emotions, mindfulness, experiencing meaning, future and social support, and there was a decrease in depressive symptoms and physical complaints (Fredrickson, Cohn, Coffey, Pek, & Finkel, 2008).

In a controlled study with female undergraduates, a brief self-compassion training (listening to *metta* recordings for 10 minutes during 5 days) attenuated biological and psychological stress responses to social evaluative threat (Arch et al., 2014). Controlled research also showed that brief interventions promoting self-compassion helped in avoiding unhealthy foods in women who placed strong dietary limitations on themselves (Adams & Leary, 2007), in smoking less in participants who tried to stop smoking (Kelly, Zuroff, Foa, & Gilbert, 2010) and in managing self-criticism, rumination and concern over mistakes in women athletes (Mosewich et al., 2011). In a number of studies, writing compassionate letters to themselves helped people to cope with adverse life events (Leary, Tate, Adams, Allen, & Hancock, 2007), diminished depressive symptoms (Shapira & Mograin, 2010) and facilitated creative originality, particularly among individuals who were prone to critical self-judgment (Zabelina & Robinson, 2010). In another experiment, students were asked to address a personal weakness in a brief writing exercise. Those who were instructed in a compassionate approach viewed their weakness as more changeable than those instructed in a self-esteem-enhancing approach or those in a no-intervention control group (Breines & Chen, 2012). The findings of this study paradoxically suggested that taking an accepting approach to personal failure makes people more motivated to improve themselves. In a recent study on the effect of a brief training and application of a compassionate image, healthy students were randomly assigned to the intervention group or the control condition (training and application of a neutral image). Following exposure in imagination to a distressing situation, participants applying the compassionate image showed significantly lower levels of negative emotion, higher self-esteem and fewer paranoid thoughts compared with those in the control group (Lincoln, Hohenhaus, & Hartmann, 2013).

Several more elaborate compassion training programs have been developed and evaluated in controlled studies. These have probably more in common than they differ from each other and they also overlap considerably with the MBCL course. Whereas MBCL has been developed in the mental health care setting as an advanced training program for those already familiar with mindfulness practice, these programs are mostly offered in community or primary care settings for people who are not required to have previous experience with mindfulness. One of these, The Mindful Self-Compassion (MSC) programme developed by Neff and Germer (2012) combines exercises in self-compassion and mindfulness in eight weekly sessions of 2 hours, to which a 4-hour silent session and 40 minutes of home practice daily are added. The MSC programme was evaluated with a pilot study and a first randomised controlled trial with a waiting list control group. The results showed significant improvements on measures for mindfulness, compassion for oneself and others, social connectedness, well-being and happiness and a decrease in measures for depression, anxiety, stress and avoidance of unpleasant thoughts and feelings.

Compassion Cultivation Training (CCT) is another programme. It was developed at the Center for Compassion and Altruism Research and Education at Stanford University and is based on Tibetan Buddhism. It is shaped in a secularised 9-week format and offers systematic practice on compassion in three domains: compassion for others, being the recipient of compassion from others and self-compassion. A first randomised controlled trial in a community sample of healthy adults, comparing CCT with a waiting list control group, showed significant improvement in all three domains of compassion (Jazaieri et al., 2013). Among the effects were also increased mindfulness and happiness as well as decreased worry and emotional suppression (Jazaieri et al., 2014). Results correlated with the time spent on practice.

Cognitive-Based Compassion Training (CBCT) is a secularised programme, based on the Tibetan *lojong* tradition, which was developed by Lobsang Tenzin Negi. It has been researched in a number of controlled studies with healthy subjects. In two studies, a 6-week version of the programme was compared with an active control group who followed an interactive health programme with similar time investment. Both groups were compared in a standardised laboratory stress test on neuroendocrine response (blood cortisol levels), immune function (blood interleukin-6 levels) and behavioural distress (Pace et al., 2009, 2010). Although there were no differences between intervention and control groups, the results suggest that engagement in compassion meditation may reduce stress-induced immune and behavioural responses because participants in the meditation group who had practised more than average showed better results than those who had practised less than average. It already had been shown previously that inducing a state of compassion had a positive effect on another indicator of immune function (S-IgA), whereas inducing and trying to regulate anger had a negative effect (Rein, Atkinson, & McCraty, 1995). An 8-week version of the CBCT programme was also studied in a design with an active control group, this time focussing on the effects on empathy and changes in the brain on functional magnetic resonance imaging (fMRI) scans (Mascaro, Rilling, Tenzin Negi, & Raison, 2013). The CBCT group showed significantly more empathic accuracy as measured by the Reading the Mind in the Eyes Test, which correlated with neurobiological changes on fMRI.

A Swedish randomised controlled pilot study of an 8-week Buddhist meditation program, built around the practice of the Four Immeasurables and *tonglen* (which are also included in the MBCL course) showed significant increases in mindfulness and self-compassion and a significant decrease in perceived stress in the intervention group (Wallmark, Safarzadeh, Daukantaitė, & Maddux, 2013). There was also a trend towards an increase in altruistic orientation (empathic concern for others in need) that significantly correlated with practice time.

Whilst the evidence is steadily growing that compassion training makes us feel better, the question arises as to whether it also makes us behave better. Does compassion training lead to actual prosocial behaviour? Positive effects on empathic accuracy and altruistic orientation point towards this, and the question was specifically addressed in a Swiss–German study by Leiberg, Klimecki, and Singer (2011). Subjects who received short-term compassion training showed more prosocial behaviour towards strangers in a training-unrelated task, unlike the control group who received short-term memory training. An American study confirmed this: Brief compassion training increased altruistic redistribution of funds to a victim encountered outside of the training context (Weng et al., 2013). In both studies, the increase in prosocial behaviour correlated with fMRI changes in the brain.

1.6.3 Intervention Studies in Clinical Samples

A number of small-scale uncontrolled studies have been done amongst patients in mental health care, especially around Compassion Focused Therapy (CFT) and Compassionate Mind Training (CMT), which is based on CFT (Gilbert, 2009a, 2010) and of which many ingredients are integrated in the MBCL course. The description of theory and practice of the compassion focused approach applied to various clinical problems, such as shame and self-attack (Gilbert & Irons, 2005), depression (Gilbert, 2009b), shyness and social anxiety (Henderson, 2010), posttraumatic stress and other anxiety disorders (Lee & James, 2012; Tirch, 2012;

Welford, 2010), bipolar disorders (Lowens, 2010), recovery after psychosis (Gumley, Braehler, Laithwaite, MacBeth, & Gilbert, 2010), deliberate self-harm (Van Vliet & Kalnins, 2011) and eating disorders (Goss, 2011; Goss & Allan, 2010), are a prelude to various clinical studies that will no doubt lead to more publications in the near future. The clinical use of exercises that involve visualisations and compassionate imagery is scientifically supported by Gilbert & Irons (2004, 2005); Lee (2005); Rockliff, Gilbert, McEwan, Lightman, and Glover (2008); Brewin et al. (2009) and Longe et al. (2010).

Significant reductions were found in depression, anxiety, shame and self-criticism in heterogeneous samples of clients with severe and enduring mental health difficulties who received group CFT in a community health setting (Judge, Cleghorn, McEwan, & Gilbert, 2012) or CMT added to a day-centre therapy programme (Gilbert & Proctor, 2006). Similarly, CFT delivered to a group of outpatients with personality disorders who had histories of previous mental health care of at least 2 years revealed a beneficial impact on a range of outcome measures (Lucre & Corton, 2013). Interestingly, all variables showed a trend towards further improvement at 1-year follow-up. CMT also proved beneficial for people with persistent psychotic symptoms, like hearing voices with negative content (Mayhew & Gilbert, 2008). CFT showed a positive effect on mood, feelings of self-worth and sense of social appreciation, while there was a decrease in mental health symptoms in patients in a high-security psychiatric ward (Laithwaite et al., 2009). Another study showed significant positive results of adding CFT to a standard treatment programme for patients with eating disorders, more so for those with bulimia than those with anorexia (Gale, Gilbert, Read, & Goss, 2014).

A comparative study examined patients referred for cognitive behaviour therapy (CBT) following a trauma-related incident (Beaumont, Galpin, & Jenkins, 2012). Participants were randomly assigned to CBT alone and to combined CBT and CMT. Although there was only a nonsignificant trend in better treatment outcome in the group who received the combined therapy, participants in this group scored significantly higher on self-compassion, which is linked to a decrease in anxiety and depression and trauma-related symptoms. A qualitative analysis of patients with posttraumatic stress disorder (PTSD) receiving CFT showed that the road from self-criticism to self-compassion can be tough but worthwhile (Lawrence & Lee, 2014). For those with high self-criticism self-compassion was an entirely new experience and at first evoked an adverse emotional response. This shifted towards a positive emotional response later in therapy.

A first randomised controlled trial of CFT was carried out on patients with schizophrenia who received an outpatient group program of CFT. They proved to be functioning better clinically than the control group and an increase in compassion correlated with a decrease in depressive symptoms and experience of social exclusion (Braehler et al., 2013). These findings are in line with an earlier pilot study examining the effects of a 6-week programme of loving-kindness practice for outpatients with schizophrenia, which showed significant decrease of negative symptoms and an increase in positive emotions (Johnson et al., 2011). Another pilot study of loving-kindness meditation was carried out with veterans suffering from PTSD. The course (12 weekly sessions of 90 minutes; 30 minutes of daily home practice) was well attended and appeared safe and acceptable. Results showed significantly reduced symptoms of PTSD and depression, mediated by enhanced self-compassion (Kearney et al., 2013). In a controlled study, a 6-week CBCT was offered to at-risk adolescents in foster care, most of whom had one or more psychiatric diagnoses (Reddy et al., 2013). Here the qualitative reports of improved functioning, better emotion and stress regulation and more capacity to respond compassionately towards others were much more promising than standardised self-report measures, suggesting the need for measures more sensitive to the positive changes noted or longer training periods to demonstrate effects.

An 8-week loving-kindness meditation programme for patients with chronic low back pain, compared with standard care, reduced pain as well as general psychological distress, anxiety and hostility after the intervention and 3 months later (Carson et al., 2005). Distressed acne sufferers were randomly assigned to either one of two self-help interventions (self-soothing or resisting self-attacks) or a control condition (Kelly, Zuroff, & Shapira, 2009). The interventions consisted of instructions by a computer program, including a short writing exercise from the perspective of either a soothing image or a resilient image who stood up for them against their inner critic, and daily imagery-based self-talk exercises. In 2 weeks, the self-soothing intervention lowered shame and skin complaints. The attack-resisting intervention lowered depression, shame and skin complaints and was especially effective at lowering depression in those with high trait self-criticism.

1.6.4   The Neurobiology of Compassion

It is outside the scope of this book to cover the vast and rapidly growing research on neurobiological processes thought to be involved with compassion and related concepts like love, happiness, empathy and altruism. For scientific reviews readers are referred to Wang (2005), Esch and Stefano (2011), Decety (2011) and Engen and Singer (2012). Recent books written by scientists for a wider audience make the rather complex scientific literature in this field more accessible for educative purposes (see for instance Fredrickson, 2013; Hanson, 2009, 2013; Keltner, 2009; D. J. Siegel, 2010b). We highlight a number of findings in three areas.

'The Plastic Brain'

The term 'neuroplasticity' refers to the brain's capacity to change in response to experience. We can change our brains with mental practice, and when the brain changes certain experiences become more likely than others. So we can use our minds to change our brains, which will change our minds (Hanson, 2013). Richard Davidson (2012) and his team have been studying the influence of the practice of meditation and compassion on the brain. A study amongst long-term meditators (Tibetan monks) showed that there are significant differences between long-term compassion meditation practitioners, compared with beginners, in the brain function on the electroencephalogram, particularly in gamma activity and neural synchronicity (Lutz, Greischar, Rawlings, Ricard, & David-son, 2004). Independent of the circumstances, those who had undergone a more intensive training could evoke loving feelings more easily. A subsequent study with fMRI, which gives more detailed information on the activity of different brain regions, revealed that the practice of compassion towards others produced changes in brain areas that are associated with empathy and emotion regulation (insula, cingulate cortex; Lutz, Brefczynski-Lewis, Johnstone, & Davidson, 2008). Experienced meditators showed a stronger response to sounds of others in distress than beginners. But a study of inexperienced individuals showed that even a brief intervention can have a remarkable result. An Internet programme of instructions in compassion meditation (30 minutes daily for 2 weeks) led to more activity in the circuit associated with feeling positive emotions compared with the control group who received a cognitive training of similar time investment (Weng et al., 2013).

A German–Swiss research group led by Tania Singer studied fMRI changes in healthy females who followed a short-term compassion training based on loving-kindness practice with an active control group who did a memory training with similar time investment (Klimecki, Leiberg, Lamm, & Singer, 2013). Neural functional and subjective responses were measured before and after the training during a standardised video task witnessing others in distress. The results showed that compassion training elicited activity in a neural network of brain regions associated with positive affect, affiliation and reward, suggesting that the deliberate cultivation of compassion offers a new coping strategy that fosters positive affect even when confronted with the distress of others. An interesting variation on this study was done in another all-female sample with a similar memory training control group (Klimecki, Leiberg, Ricard, & Singer, 2013). In this sample the intervention group first received training in empathic resonance and subsequently compassion training. Watching others in distress following the training in empathy increased negative affect and activated brain regions associated with empathy for pain. These effects were neutralised following the compassion training. The increase in negative affect was reversed and a nonoverlapping brain circuit was activated similar to that in the previous study. The findings suggest that empathy and compassion indeed rely on antagonistic affective systems and that even short-term training of compassion can counteract empathic distress. This gives neuroscientific backing to the impression that compassion training can protect overempathic caregivers against burnout and to Matthieu Ricard's pledge to replace the misnomer 'compassion fatigue' by the more appropriate concept 'empathy fatigue' (Ricard, 2010).

Research with fMRI has become increasingly sophisticated, and recent data show that the practice of mindful or focused attention affects other brain regions than the practice of compassion or loving-kindness, which particularly affects areas relating to the experience of positive emotions and emotional processing when faced with distress. Results suggest that effects of meditation grow with the level of practice and are also transferred to nonmeditative states (Desbordes et al., 2012; Lee et al., 2012).

The story goes that Tibetan monks who were the subjects in studies on the effects of meditation and compassion practice had a lot of fun when they were hooked up to the machines. They thought it was hilarious that scientists who wanted to explore the mind placed the electrodes on their heads and not on their hearts! Is this our typical Western tendency to focus on the brain, even when we study experiences of the heart? Meanwhile, there is strong scientific support that there are intimate neuroendocrine connections between the brain and the heart.

'The Wandering Nerve'

The polyvagal theory as described by Stephen Porges states how the role of an important cranial nerve, the vagus (or 'wandering') nerve, evolved and changed when mammalian species became increasingly dependent on attachment and care for each other (Porges, 2003). The vagus nerve and its branches represent a major part of the parasympathetic autonomic nervous system and connect the brain with the inner organs and particularly the heart. In the course of evolution, emotional and motivational systems developed to support the care-seeking and care-giving behaviour that mammals needed to survive. Species with low numbers of vulnerable offspring require long-term protection from birth until adulthood and need to form close bonds between parents and offspring and within social groups. The newer branches of the vagus developed in a way that could support soothing and attachment behaviour (Porges, 2007). An increase in parasympathetic activity or 'vagal tone' can be measured as an increase in the physiological arrhythmia of the heart rate as it correlates with the breathing rhythm. In a calm state with optimal balance between sympathetic and parasympathetic activity, every in-breath is accompanied by an acceleration of the heart rate and every out-breath by a deceleration. An increase in heart rate variability (HRV) correlates with the natural state of feeling contented and connected. When one feels stressed, the sympathetic tone overrules, which is accompanied by a decrease in HRV.

Compassion is a capacity that is grounded in the ability to soothe and care for others and for oneself and is dependent on these physiological systems. The intensity of the vagal tone is a durable characteristic and shaped by the quality of attachment with caregivers and subsequent social relationships. A powerful vagal tone means autonomic flexibility and correlates with the capacity of the parasympathetic nervous system to calm the body after it has become aroused in stressful circumstances because of threat or excitement. It does this by regulating respiration, heart rate and blood pressure and enhancing digestion and immune function. This state of 'rest and digest' neutralises the fight or flight reactions. The vagus nerve is anatomically linked not only to visceral organs but also to nerves involved in coordinating eye gaze, generating facial expressions and tuning the ear to the frequency of the human voice, all functions that are important for forming social connections (Porges, 2007). An increase in vagal tone correlated with psychological flexibility, emotional well-being and social engagement (Geisler, Kubiak, Siewert, & Weber, 2013; Kok & Fredrickson, 2010). High HRV was associated with less inclination to blame others and reduction in anger (Léon, Hernández, Rodríguez, & Vila, 2009).

Although the vagal tone is a durable trait, research suggests that it can be trained in relatively short time by mental practice that enhances positive emotions. Barbara Fredrickson's team measured the vagal tone as an index of physical health in a controlled study among university employees before and after a course of loving-kindness meditation (six weekly sessions of 1 hour and facultative home practice; Kok et al., 2013). During a 2-month period, emotional experiences and perceived social connections were assessed daily. They found that the intervention produced more positive emotions, an effect moderated by the baseline vagal tone. Increased positive emotions, in turn, produced increased vagal tone, an effect mediated by an increase in perceived social connections. The results support the hypothesis that positive emotions, supportive social connections and physical health influence one another in an upward-spiral dynamic.

'The Love Hormone'

Another player in this positivity game is oxytocin. Like the vagus nerve, it plays a key role in social bonding and attachment. Although oxytocin is often called 'the love hormone', it is actually a neuropeptide that is produced in the brain and released in the bloodstream to have effects in the body (Olff, 2012). Oxytocin was originally discovered to play a role during giving birth and breastfeeding. Later it became clear that the release of oxytocin facilitates social bonding in general in both men and women. It is released during intense and subtle kinds of pleasurable social contact, such as making love, cuddling, massaging, having a kind conversation, playing with a child or petting a dog. It increases vagal tone and HRV (Kemp et al., 2012) and attenuates biological stress reactions. It is the motor behind the so-called 'tend and befriend' reaction as opposed to fight or flight (Taylor, 2006). It shifts attention from self-protection to protection of others, which is crucial for the survival of vulnerable beings that are dependent on caring others.

Oxytocin plays an important role in interpreting social cues and enhances the capacity for social engagement and prosocial behaviour. Oxytocin can be administered as a drug by nasal spray, and even a single dose has proved to increase trust in others (Kosfeld, Heinrichs, Zak, Fischbacher, & Fehr, 2005). Its effects depend on the social and individual context, however. Not every individual will respond in the same way. Those with insecure attachment, childhood maltreatment and borderline personality disorder may respond with decreased trust. When the environment is interpreted as 'safe' oxytocin may promote trust; when it is interpreted as 'unsafe' mistrust may increase (Olff et al., 2013). This is in line with the findings of researchers who studied the effects of intranasal oxytocin on compassion-focused imagery and compared this with intranasal placebo (Rockliff et al., 2011). Results showed that overall oxytocin increased the ease of imagining compassionate qualities, but there were important individual differences in how these were experienced. Participants with high scores on self-criticism and low scores on self-reassurance, social safeness and attachment security had fewer positive experiences with compassion-focused imagery under oxytocin than placebo.

High and Low Roads to Compassion

There seems to be a condition of the neurobiological soil on which the flowers of compassion grow best. The qualities of compassion grow on the innate abilities to seek and give care, to nurture the young and vulnerable, to tend and befriend and to empathise with each other. Previous positive experiences of secure attachment and social bonding leave traces in our brain circuitry and neurobiological systems that promote approach rather than avoidance tendencies in social encounters (Vrticka & Vuilleumier, 2012). When we are in need or feeling stressed we are more likely to seek the presence and reassurance of caring others and respond with increased vagal tone and oxytocin release. Our brains and bodies are already prepared for compassion by old mechanisms that evolved when mammals adapted their survival strategies. Daniel Goleman (2006) spoke of 'the low road to compassion'. When the neurobiological systems of this low road are well trained, a compassionate response is more likely. That is why we often start compassion exercises with a soothing breathing rhythm (increase in vagal tone and HRV), or we touch our heart with one or both hands (release of oxytocin).

But there is also a 'high road to compassion'. When caring others are absent we can still be caring towards ourselves and make use of soothing compassionate images. When we use our much younger capacity to be mindfully present with the pleasant and the unpleasant and work with the power of our minds using kind wishes and compassionate imagery, we can strengthen the neurobiological circuits of the low road (see also the section 'The Plastic Brain' earlier in this chapter). Researchers found that a few minutes of compassion-focused imagery (as opposed to neutral imagery as a control) could increase HRV and decrease the stress hormone cortisol, although this was not straightforward (Rockliff et al., 2008). Individuals with high self-criticism and an insecure attachment style could respond to compassionate imagery with a decrease in HRV. Those with a history of insecure attachment may actually feel threatened by compassionate images and first need to learn that compassion is safe. We cannot force our biology in the desired direction by imposing a compassionate image, but in the right context compassionate images are likely to increase vagal tone and oxytocin levels. Likewise, we cannot make people experience compassion by simply telling them to slow down their breathing or spraying oxytocin into their noses, but in the right context naturally raised HRV and oxytocin levels do make a compassionate response more likely. It makes sense that we respect individual differences and make use of both the high and low road to compassion in a safe, gentle and balanced way. Then both roads could well reinforce each other in an upward spiral.

In her latest book, Barbara Fredrickson (2013) offered a scientific update on 'love', which she called 'our supreme emotion' and defined as 'positivity resonance'. In her innovative view love is defined not as an ongoing state but as micromoments of positivity resonance that come and go. She distinguished love from the durable bonds that can grow between people over time. Durable bonds are certainly positively influenced by these short-lived experiences—and vice versa may increase their frequency—but they are not the same. Moments of love can happen any time when the circumstances are favourable, between friends as well as strangers. These moments of love resonate in our emotions, our social behaviour and our bodies. They resonate in regions of our brain, in vagal tone, HRV and oxytocin levels. They cannot be forced but are more likely to happen when our neurobiological systems are trained to resonate with the experience of love. In this way love can create more love by causing ripples that flow through our bodies as well as into our relationships with others and into their bodies.

Likewise one can describe compassion as the experience of love when we face suffering. Compassion is thus viewed as an emotional experience of positivity resonance when we meet pain and suffering. It is, just like love, more likely to occur when the neurobiological soil is fertilised by practice. Compassion *practice* is more about cultivating good will than good feelings, however (Germer, 2009). Good feelings cannot be forced, but the practice may indeed generate positive emotions and feeling connected with oneself and others. It may feel unpleasant however, particularly when old pain surfaces or when we do not get what we expect. This does not mean failure, but by patiently resetting our intention to relieve suffering and promote happiness in an unforced way, we increase the likelihood of positivity resonance, not just between ourselves and others but also between the compassionate and the suffering parts within ourselves.

We end this chapter on research with the conclusion that insights from inner science that have been generated over 2,500 years are in fact being increasingly supported by outer science. Research into the practice of compassion is still in its infancy but rapidly growing. The results support that we can *train our brains* and neurobiological systems. Just as our physical condition and muscle power can grow by exercise, so our mental condition and neurobiological capacity to respond compassionately can grow with practice. And this can contribute to healing and well-being—physically, emotionally and socially.

In Part 2 of this book we invite the reader on a practical journey to discover how our capacity for compassion can grow. We therefore change to the more informal style that we use when we take participants through the MBCL programme.

Part 2

Compassion Training in Practice

Part 2 takes you through the full Mindfulness-Based Compassionate Living (MBCL) programme and the practices. The course consists of eight sessions with an extra silent practice session between Sessions 6 and 7. If you are going to use this book on your own, we would advise you to reflect first on the questions we usually ask participants before they start the training.

Do You Need a Different Form of Professional Support First?

If you have serious health issues, we advise you to familiarise yourself with first-choice treatment methods that have proven to be effective for your condition. Perhaps you never considered asking for professional help, or had support but were disappointed with the outcome. If you are seeing a health care professional or are in therapy already, it is advisable to discuss the compassion training with them. We consider this training, as we present it here, as a form of complementary health care for all phases: prevention, treatment or when problems recur or cannot be treated.

Compassion training is mainly aimed at care (dealing with the problem with kindness and support) and less at cure (solving the problem). It is not a substitute for treatments that can cure. However, it can offer additional care that supports methods aimed at curing. And when cure is not or only partially possible, the care of compassion training may make the suffering more bearable. Striving for cure where no cure is possible can in itself become a source of suffering. Pain, and especially emotional pain, is inevitable in life. Gentle acceptance and care will be more beneficial than judging, fighting or avoiding the inevitable pain because this will only lead to more suffering. Paradoxically, when there is a lot of emotional pain, it is often care that can lead to cure. However, if you are suffering from severe trauma, are vulnerable to psychoses or manic–depressive mood swings, have neurological problems or are addicted to alcohol or drugs, we urge you to find professional advice before starting the MBCL training.

Are You Sufficiently Experienced in Mindfulness Practice?

It is advisable to complete a mindfulness training, preferably Mindfulness-Based Stress Reduction (MBSR) or MBCT, before the compassion training because MBCL is based on these. Obviously, this book will also be of benefit if you have become familiar with meditation practice in a different context or have followed a similar training course, for example Breathworks (Burch 2008; Burch & Penman, 2013).

Is This the Right Time to Do Compassion Training?

It is important that you have sufficient time and space to continue and deepen the process of self-inquiry that you already started with mindfulness practice. Do you have the opportunity to practise regularly, preferably about an hour every day? This will not be easy if all your time and energy is taken up by stressful situations as a result of, for example, a new job, a financial setback, going through a divorce or moving house. You might ask yourself if it would be better to put your energy towards a more direct and practical approach in dealing with the source of stress first. Creating time and favourable circumstances is important, but the next question is even more essential.

Are You Sufficiently Motivated?

This method is not a magical formula. You will not learn special techniques to make your problems disappear, but you will learn to deal with them differently. Persistent unhealthy habits are not so easy to change. They usually only disappear gradually when new, more helpful habits are put in place, which can only be developed by regular reinforcement. If this does not happen, old habits easily resurface, particularly when life presents us with a new challenge. So it comes down to practising, and you need motivation to do so. This does not mean strong discipline or self-torture. We are inviting you to be compassionate with yourself when practising, not from an attitude of forcing anything but in a relaxed, caring and playful way. As is common in mindfulness training, you are likely to meet unpleasant experiences and obstacles in compassion training; indeed, meeting obstacles is an essential part of the training process. So the training requires a willingness to investigate these unpleasant experiences with gentleness and respect for your boundaries. Knowing why you are undergoing the training will strengthen your motivation. Therefore do not skip the last question.

What Benefits Do You Wish to Gain From Compassion Training?

When participants apply for the training course, we send them a questionnaire to fill out before they start. We invite you to reflect on the questions, too, and to write down the answers if you like.

What changes do you wish the training to bring about, regarding the way you

- treat yourself?
- treat others (family, friends, colleagues etc.)?

- deal with present difficulties in your life?
- deal with other areas of your life that are important to you, for example daily activities, relationships, work, social involvement, meaning and spirituality?
- work towards your goals in life (short term and long term)?
- deal with future challenges?

Look at the answers to the above questions and ask yourself whether they are realistic. Do your answers leave scope for inner change? Or do you imagine that change will only happen as a result of external events? If you have unrealistic expectations, for instance, 'I want to get rid of all my problems' or 'other people or circumstances need to change before I can change', or the method of mindfulness and self-inquiry does not appeal to you at all, or you do not have much time and space, or you are not very motivated, then it might be better to put this book aside for the time being.

If you anticipate many changes, perhaps your expectations are too high. It is good to realise that these practices are more about coming to an acceptance of how life is than at bringing about drastic changes. Interestingly, Carl Rogers (1995) said that

> the curious paradox is that when I accept myself as I am, then I change. . . . We cannot change, we cannot move away from what we are, until we thoroughly *accept* what we are. Then change seems to come about almost unnoticed. (p. 17)

Perhaps you already recognise how you are inclined to strive, which in itself can involve a lot of suffering. Wanting and striving is, of course, part of life, and it is possible to accept this without being swept away by it. To emphasise this, we ask participants to hand in their desired outcome list at the first session. We symbolically put this in a drawer to leave it there until the end of the training. Often quite a few desired outcomes have been achieved, but not always. Sometimes beneficial change occurs in unexpected areas, such as being less change focussed.

Maybe you are anxious about what you might encounter during the training and you may already feel resistance, fear or tension. It is normal to feel resistance when feeling threatened by unfamiliarity, and a first step towards acceptance can be to acknowledge this without getting pulled into the tendency to avoid or to postpone. Compassion practice certainly demands courage in order to face what frightens us. Have you gathered enough courage for further exploration of your resistance during this training course?

Have you become curious, are you motivated to continue to explore the path of mindfulness with compassion and do you sense that your life could become richer if you opened your heart to the suffering that is inevitable? If so, then let us start.

The Self-Compassion Test

If you want to get an idea to what extent you are self-compassionate right now, there is an online self-compassion test. It was developed by Kristin Neff (2003a), one of the pioneers in the field of scientific research on self-compassion. See www.selfcompassion.net for Neff's test. You could repeat the test later on in the training or after you have finished.

2.1 Session 1

Three Emotion Regulation Systems

2.1.1 Why Do We Need Compassion?

In Session 1 we usually give the participants a somewhat paradoxical reflection exercise to ponder over individually or to share in small groups over a cup of tea or coffee. The question is, 'What reasons can you come up with for *not* participating in compassion training?' Participants are often a bit surprised at this question, but we can usually draw up a list of understandable reasons such as the following:

- It does not appeal to me at all to meet my old pain and disappointments in life.
- I feel ashamed to have compassion for myself while so many people have a lot more serious problems. I don't deserve it.
- I might become self-centred.
- When I tell my friends that I am doing compassion training, they will think I am a 'wimp'.
- I may become lazy and too easy going.
- I don't want to have any compassion for people who have hurt me.
- People who have infringed human rights in terrible ways do not deserve compassion.

Sometimes these reactions point to inner fears or defences, or to misunderstandings about compassion. There is no harm in acknowledging your fears and reservations. They are common. It may be reassuring to know that so far nobody wanted to quit as a result of this reflection and that you will not be forced to be compassionate towards yourself or someone else if you are not ready to do so. We teach that compassion starts with learning to look kindly at your experience. Like mindfulness practice, compassion training always starts where you are *in this moment*, and it is quite possible that right now, you observe mixed feelings about compassion training.

Now, why would we want to practise compassion? The first and most primary reason is that it helps us survive. Pain and suffering are inherent to human life. We all get our share, whether we want it or not. It might differ in amount, and the distribution might appear random and unfair, but despite the differences, we have in common that we all suffer at some stage in our lives. One of the people who inspired us to develop this training, Paul Gilbert (2009a), stated that we are all in the same boat:

- we all ended up in this life
- with a brain, body, emotions and a socially developed self
- that were not our choice but with which we have to manage
- in a life full of tragedies (threats, losses, illness, ageing, death), unpredictable circumstances and dilemmas.

This may not cheer us up, but we cannot escape it by ignoring or fighting it. The family, the circumstances and the culture in which we grow up and unpleasant events that happen to us are *not* our choice. We did not design our brain and our body, and much of what we experience is not our fault either. Because pain and suffering are unavoidable, we need compassion. Compassion involves mindfully acknowledging our experience, with kindness, but also with the courage to face our pain and take responsibility for what we *can* choose, namely how we deal with it.

A long evolutionary history is the foundation of this survival strategy to express warmth and care when confronted with suffering and vulnerability. This ability is not unique to humans; we share it with many other mammals. So, compassion is not a luxury to which we only need pay attention after all other basic needs have been met. The Dalai Lama has called compassion itself a basic prerequisite for our survival, and also for our happiness (T. Gyatso, 2003). Although compassion deals with suffering, it is a gateway to happiness. And that is the second good reason to practice compassion. Most ancient wisdom and spiritual traditions regard compassion as the core value for the human race (Armstrong, 2011). And finally, compassion practice benefits our health in many ways, physically, mentally and socially. The growing amount of evidence for this we have reviewed in the chapter on research (1.6).

The MBCL programme offers a mix of theory and practical exercises. The theory is like a swimming pool: It provides a framework and foundation for the training. The practical part, where various exercises and practices are offered, is the water in the pool. The real practice starts when we begin to swim and benefit from the pool and the water.

Why not start with a dip in the pool and do a short exercise? The following builds on the basic Three Minute Breathing Space as used in MBCT (Segal, Williams, & Teasdale, 2013). In exercises like this one and in other basic mindfulness practice we are usually invited to simply observe the breath in whatever way it behaves. However, in many ancient and modern practices a *slow* breathing rhythm has been recognised to have a calming influence on our body and mind (Brown & Gerbarg, 2012; see also 1.6.4). In the following exercise and in many to come, we will therefore invite you not just to 'be' with the breath but also to gently 'work' with the breath and allow it to slow down into a comfortable rhythm. In Compassion Focused Therapy (CFT) this is called the 'soothing breathing rhythm' and is considered to be a basic skill in the process of cultivating compassion (Gilbert, 2009a, 2010).

2.1.2　Exercise: 'The Breathing Space With Kindness'

Being Present With Open Awareness

Put yourself in a comfortable position. You will probably be sitting down right now, but you can also do this exercise while standing or lying down. Be open and focus your attention on what you are experiencing right now. Be aware of what thoughts, feelings or physical sensations are there. Recognise and note what is presenting itself, without seeing anything as a disturbance or hindrance. Feel and accept whatever is there in this moment.

Allowing a Soothing Breathing Rhythm

Bring your attention back to the breath and follow every in-and-out-breath with a relaxed attention, with a kind and caring attitude. Allow a soothing breathing rhythm. You can

- *gently and intentionally slow down and deepen the breath if it is quick and superficial, without forcing;*
- *adjust your posture so that it supports a calm breathing rhythm: allow your muscles to soften, allow a soft smile;*
- *follow the breath in your belly and let the belly become soft;*
- *intentionally breathe through the heart area and allow feelings of space, lightness and warmth—you can place one or both hands on your heart to help with this;*
- *allow an image to form that supports a calm breathing rhythm, for example, a safe place, a soothing colour, relaxing music or somebody whose presence calms you.*

Expanding the Awareness With Kindness

You can now become aware of the body as a whole, the breathing body that is sitting, standing or lying down. See if you can hold a kind, gentle or supporting wish for yourself. For example, 'May I be . . . safe . . . healthy . . . happy . . . at ease . . .' See what is appropriate for you. Use your own words and let them come from your heart. You can let them flow through the body on the rhythm of the breath. With each inhalation you could hold the first half of the wish, and with each exhalation you could hold the second half of the wish, for example, 'May I . . .' (on the in-breath) '. . . be at peace' (on the out-breath). Or 'May I . . .' (in-breath) '. . . have courage' (out-breath). And however you feel when you are doing this, it's okay.

Let a kind wish for yourself flow through you in a soft, natural way, on the rhythm of the breath or independently of the breath if that feels better. Then you could perhaps take this caring attention and good intentions with you, or remind yourself of them later in the day.

Feedback from a participant:

> 'It is great to realise that you feel better when you don't put yourself down, but look at yourself with compassion.'

2.1.3   The Evolution of Our Brain and Our Capacity to Be Compassionate

It may not be obvious why we should delve deeply into the history of evolution when we talk about compassion. Yet it can result in a better understanding of the how and why of our compassion practice and strengthen our motivation. We take to heart what the Dutch biologist Frans de Waal (2009) said in *The Age of Empathy*: 'Instead of fixating on the peaks of civilisation, we need to pay attention to the foothills' (p. 16).

The human brain evolved over millions of years (see Figure 3), and from an evolutionary perspective it has developed into an extremely sensitive survival organ. It contains a huge range of potential reactions for adapting to difficult situations, but it is not perfect. It enables us to develop healthy patterns but also unhealthy ones. It is clear that the brain is an extremely complex organ with intricate mechanisms that are anchored in the different layers of the brain, corresponding to different phases in evolutionary history. Older and newer parts of the brain can easily come into conflict and unsettle each other. Therefore Gilbert (2014) has called our brain a 'tricky brain' that can easily get us into trouble. The model of the *triune brain* (MacLean, 1990) can help our understanding, as several authors have shown (for example Appelo, 2011; Hanson, 2009; D. J. Siegel, 2010a). Three layers are distinguished:

- the *reptilian brain*, or 'brain stem', is the oldest part and serves to defend territory, hunt prey (survival of the individual) and reproduce (survival of the species);
- the *old mammalian brain*, or 'limbic system' or 'emotional brain', serves living in groups, enabling social bonding, caring and rank formation;
- and the *new mammalian brain*, or 'neocortex', the youngest part, offers great learning and adaptation potential in new situations, enabling more complex forms of society.

The reptilian and old mammalian brain together are simply called 'old brain' and the neocortex 'new brain'. The *reptilian brain* is of vital importance for basic processes such as feeding, fighting, fleeing and mating. These are mainly inborn, instinctive and automatic. It controls all the automatic and unconscious bodily functions such as heartbeat, blood circulation, respiration and digestion. New reactions can be learned without conscious interventions, and then they also happen automatically. Recall the famous experiment by Pavlov, where his dogs began

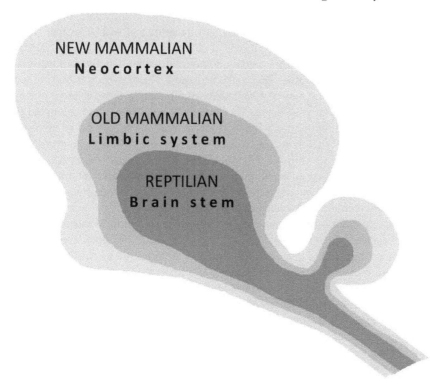

NEW MAMMALIAN
Neocortex

OLD MAMMALIAN
Limbic system

REPTILIAN
Brain stem

Figure 3 The evolved brain.

Adapted from MacLean, 1990.

to salivate when they heard a bell after he had first sounded the bell a few times while simultaneously offering food. We call this 'classical conditioning'.

The *old mammalian brain* is important for the experience of emotions. When you are angry, afraid, sad or happy, your limbic system is active. These are often instinctive reactions; however, there is more scope for learning new reaction patterns than in the reptilian brain. In the limbic system this happens through reward and punishment, also called 'operant conditioning'. If something is pleasant we continue; if it is unpleasant we stop. These processes are also mostly automatic; we don't need to think about them, there is mainly 'feeling'.

The *new mammalian brain* enables us to think and reason about what we experience and how we act. Reactions can be automatic, but there is a lot more scope for learning new patterns because we can postpone the fulfilment of needs. We can refrain from satisfying desires and continue to do something that is unpleasant. We can consciously remember previous experiences and imagine various future scenarios. We can have conversations with others and with ourselves about them.

In humans the new mammalian brain has developed expansively because of the acquisition of many new skills such as the use of language, imagination and symbols. Furthermore we have the ability to remember and anticipate, analyse and deduct, fantasise and ruminate, organise and integrate and have concepts about our 'self' and what happens in the minds of others. Because we apparently can do so much with this new brain we usually do not realise that it evolved to increase our chances of survival rather than make us happy. The drawback is that we are also able to create many new problems that actually decrease our chances of survival and certainly our well-being. An example is how we can get entangled in constant worry and rumination without any benefit at all. We can get so involved that we forget to care for ourselves and our loved ones. When our new-brain functions are driven by old-brain impulses the effects can be disastrous. Consider wars, overproduction, depletion of natural resources and the awful cruelties people can engage in. Even though we may think that our brain is controlling our impulses and emotions, the opposite is usually the case.

Reptiles generally have numerous offspring with a low survival rate and do not have the capacity for social bonding or for concern about each other's vulnerability. Their young quickly disperse after birth, on the principle of 'each for itself', and this increases their chances of survival. Mammals on the other hand have few offspring, which are vulnerable and need protection for a relatively long period of time. Therefore the ability to bond and care for each other is crucial for survival. In lower mammals this ability serves their own survival and that of their immediate offspring, the social group and the species. More evolved mammals like apes, dogs and dolphins can also direct this capacity to members of other species. The more protection and care the young need (the human child being especially vulnerable), the less 'instinctive' the brain is and the larger the capacity for learning. This shows itself in heightened sensitivity to giving and receiving care, an elaborate repertoire of social behaviour and a strongly developed capacity for empathy and compassion.

Empathy and compassion are not exclusive to the human species (De Waal, 2009). What makes human beings special is that their capacity for compassion, and likewise their potential for cruelty, is unlimited; both can extend to all living beings. Frequently our compassion is quite limited, however—limited to those we feel most strongly connected with. Many people find it difficult enough to have compassion for themselves. If compassion is such an important quality for our survival and well-being, why then do we have such difficulty with it? Apparently it is because it gets tangled up in the emotions of other survival mechanisms.

2.1.4   The Threat, Drive and Soothing System

Emotions can be viewed from an evolutionary perspective as messengers that indicate whether we are moving in the right direction of survival. These messengers inform us about threat or safety, failure or success, social isolation or connectedness. Although they can be experienced as pleasant or unpleasant and judged as positive or negative, they are morally neither right nor wrong. They are all useful for survival. So let us not act like the king who ordered the messenger from a hostile country to be killed because he did not like the message. (He soon lost his kingdom to the enemy.)

Feedback from a participant:

'When I see emotions as messengers, I become much more tolerant towards my emotions.'

It is helpful to distinguish three basic types of emotion regulation systems, when we want to make sense of our complex emotional life (Gilbert, 2009a). The diagram in Figure 4 we adapted from the model used in CFT.

The Threat System. This system is activated by threat and danger; it is aimed at self-protection. Attention is narrowed and focussed on what is threatening. Emotions are unpleasant: anger, anxiety and/or disgust, accompanied by physical sensations such as increased heartbeat, shallow rapid breathing, dry mouth and tensed muscles. Affiliated behaviour is active, namely *fight* or *flight*, or inhibited, namely *freeze*, when fighting or fleeing is too risky. It is the most fundamental system for immediate survival. We cannot afford to miss a threat; it could cost us our lives.

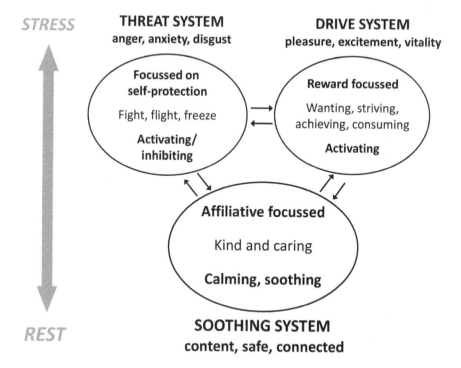

Figure 4 The three emotion regulation systems in balance.

Reproduced and adapted with kind permission from *The Compassionate Mind* by Paul Gilbert, 2009, London: Robinson.

The Drive System. This system is triggered by desire such as hunger for food, sex, possessions, success, status and power. It is incentive and resource seeking and is aimed at satisfaction. Attention is narrowed and focussed on reward. Emotions are predominantly pleasant but short lived: desire, excitement, vitality, joy. Physical sensations depend on the focus of the desire, for example, salivation, hunger pangs, sexual arousal, quickened heartbeat and breath, increased muscular tension and the urge to move. Affiliated behaviour is active and centres around striving, achieving, consuming. This system is also very basic to survival. After all, we cannot do without food for very long.

The Soothing System. The soothing system can come up when 'nothing needs to be done' (the danger has passed and the hunger is stilled). It is aimed at social connectedness, care and 'safeness' (to be distinguished from 'safety', which is what the threat system seeks). The attention is open, evenly divided between the internal and external world, between self and other. Emotions are pleasant, like emotions in the drive system can be, but with a different quality and longer lasting: warmth, calmness, contentment, well-being. Affiliated behaviour is caring and kind, peaceful, relaxed and playful. This system is less important for immediate survival but very important for longer term survival in mammalian species. Mammals can only survive when they are able to seek care, receive and give care and form social bonds.

These three emotion regulation systems are all anchored in the old brain. They colour the feeling state we are in from moment to moment, the threat system giving rise to unpleasant emotions (LeDoux, 1998) and the drive and soothing systems to pleasant emotions of different qualities (Depue & Morrone-Strupinsky, 2005). Several neural networks, neurotransmitters, hormones and physical reactions are involved. Serotonin is a neurotransmitter believed to play an important role in the threat system and dopamine in the drive system; in the soothing system it is oxytocin, also called the 'love hormone' (Olff, 2012; see 1.6.4). The release of endorphins, opium-like substances that are naturally present in the brain, is also linked to the soothing system (Hsu et al., 2013).

The sympathetic nervous system is especially active in the threat and drive systems, and the stress levels are high; the parasympathetic nervous system is involved in the soothing system, and stress levels are low. 'Stress' we define broadly here as disturbed homeostasis, a state of strain or tension caused by a stimulus, which can be experienced as negative or positive; metaphorically speaking, as a 'stick' or as a 'carrot'. A stressful stimulus evokes a range of psycho–neuro–endocrine reactions. It is not so much the sticks or carrots themselves that give us stress but how we react to them. Hans Selye (1976), a pioneering researcher on stress, later in his career made a distinction between healthy 'eustress' and unhealthy 'distress'. For a healthy functioning organism a certain amount of stress is mandatory. Excessive activity from both the threat and the drive system can cause unhealthy levels of stress, however, especially when insufficiently balanced by a restful state. Sympathetic and parasympathetic systems are very old from an evolutionary point of view and are rooted in the reptilian brain. Together they form the autonomic nervous system, which can function autonomously, without conscious prompting. They are the body's neural accelerator-and-brake system. The sympathetic nervous system alerts us: Our breathing becomes more rapid and more superficial, our heart rate goes up, our blood pressure rises, the blood circulation increases in the muscles and decreases in the digestive organs. Digestion is less important for immediate survival, and the same goes for the immune system, which is weakened by stress. When the sympathetic nervous system is overactive we get exhausted and will not be able to recover adequately. Energy-consuming, threat-avoiding or incentive-seeking actions and an overactive sympathetic nervous system lead to exhaustion. In order to recuperate we need the calming influence of the parasympathetic nervous system to 'rest and digest' (Porges, 2007). Then the breathing becomes slower and deeper, the heart rate slows down, the blood pressure falls, the muscles relax, the blood circulation in the digestive organs increases and the immune system becomes stronger. In mammals newer parasympathetic branches of the vagal nerve evolved, wandering from brain to inner organs, particularly the heart (see 1.6.4), and a soothing quality of contentment was added to the resting state to support social bonding.

Unlike the CFT diagram, which places the threat system at the bottom because it is evolutionarily the oldest (Gilbert, 2009a), we decided to put the soothing system at the bottom because it is the system we settle into when we feel at ease and 'at home' (Hanson, 2013). It is our 'being mode', whereas the other two stir us up into the 'doing mode' to get away from the unwanted or get hold of the wanted. Ideally the situation is as presented in Figure 4 with a healthy balance between stress and rest, between the sympathetic threat or drive activity and the parasympathetic soothing system.

The emotion regulation systems alternate in their dominance, depending on the situation, and this can happen extremely quickly. Mammals have a greater chance of survival when all three systems are functioning well and when one system can take over from the other as soon as it is necessary. If there is a real danger, a well-functioning threat system can be life saving. In a safe situation the threat system becomes inactive and another system can take over. The drive system gets activated when there is a desire for food or for mating. Once these needs have been satisfied (full stomach = own survival; sexual partner for offspring = survival of the species), then the drive system can calm down again. If in the meantime there is still no threat of danger, the soothing system can take over: being contentedly together, relaxed, safe and connected, just 'being' rather than 'doing'. In this relaxation phase there is time for recovery and growth, for social bonding and care (for example apes start to groom each other), but also for play, creativity and new discoveries. If danger arises unexpectedly, the threat system is alert again; when there are hunger pangs the drive system takes over.

The Cat

Observe the three regulation systems in a cat. When a cat gets hungry you see it creep around the garden looking for prey; the drive system has been activated. When its belly is filled, it lies down to rest, relishing the sun. The soothing system prevails and it purrs when you stroke it. If a dog suddenly comes near, its threat system is alerted. In a very short space of time it jumps up and faces the enemy, spitting, with an arched back and fluffed-up tail. After the danger has gone, it returns to just lying in the sun. Now, it is hard to imagine a cat being in the threat or drive system 24 hours a day. The cat naturally returns to the soothing system any time it can so it spends no more energy than necessary. In contrast, human beings often keep their threat and drive system going even when their minds and bodies need rest.

These three systems enable humans and animals to survive, but in humans the situation is more complicated. We very easily lose the balance displayed in Figure 4. Information from the external or internal environment can enter through the sense organs and sensory neural pathways and quickly alert our emotional brain via the *short route*, informing us about the feeling tone (pleasant, neutral, unpleasant) of an experience (LeDoux, 1998). There are also neural pathways from the old to the new brain so that we can be consciously aware of sensory input and our emotions, postpone the tendency to react on autopilot and respond with intentional behaviour. This is the *long route* in our brain. The new brain is affected by the old brain, but in turn also affects the old brain. Thoughts and images can activate our threat system, drive system or soothing system. Thus there is two-way traffic between the old and the new brain. Unfortunately, our new brain can keep us much longer in the threat system or the drive system than necessary. In our imaginative mind we can see danger and shortcomings everywhere, even when all our basic needs are met. It is much harder for humans to naturally gravitate to their soothing system than it is for most mammals, which is why we are more prone to suffer from all kinds of stress-related problems. An influential work about this difference by biologist Robert Sapolsky (1994) was given the title *Why Zebras Don't Get Ulcers*.

To gain better insight into the three emotion regulation systems, we invite you to do the following exercise.

Feedback from a participant:

'Insight into the three regulation systems makes me understand how I operate as a human being and helps me to deal with my fear much better.'

2.1.5   Exercise: 'The Three Circles'

Which emotion regulation system has been 'practised' more and which has been 'practised' less in your life? Draw the three circles of the threat, drive and soothing systems on a sheet of paper. You can draw a bigger circle for a system that has been developed more strongly and a smaller circle for a system that is less developed. Reflect carefully on the following questions and make or write down key words in the circles. Take your time to pause at each system and see what arises. Observe it with a gentle and open attentiveness, even though it may be painful. Don't force anything; respect your limits.

1. *What experiences, events, persons have possibly played a key role in how your threat, drive and soothing systems function?*
2. *What was your biggest fear or threat in these situations? Your most desired outcome? Your deepest need or yearning?*
3. *What are the most prevalent strategies you developed to protect yourself and to survive psychologically? Which are external—for example, social avoidance, dependency on others? Which are internal—for example, avoiding certain emotions, cherishing certain views and opinions about yourself, making high demands on yourself?*
4. *What are the unintended and undesirable effects of these strategies?*
5. *What do you actually need most and what would you genuinely wish for yourself?*

You can end the exercise with loving-kindness towards yourself and wish for yourself what came up at the last question, for example, 'May I . . .' (on an in-breath) '. . . be safe, strong, calm, happy, contented . . . ?' (on an out-breath).

2.1.6 A Matter of Balance

The emotion regulation systems react to information from our body and surroundings through the senses and transfer information to the new brain. In turn they also react to information from our new brain. Through images and language we can both soothe ourselves and cause ourselves to panic. Feeling actual pain from harmful external influences can trigger our threat system, but so can an imaginary threat. Just the memory of a traumatic event or the thought of a recurrence can trigger a fear reaction that shoots through our body. The thought that we lack something or see some potential 'prey' can activate the drive system, even though we have more than enough to fulfil our basic needs. Fortunately, through visualising a safe place or a person we love and care about, or through positive wishes, warm feelings can be evoked as well and activate our soothing system. The new brain can work for us as well as against us. It can stimulate our soothing system and strengthen our capacity for compassion and loving-kindness or obstruct them. If the threat and drive systems are activated too frequently and too easily and take turns being dominant, the soothing system will be insufficiently developed.

Now, we are not saying that any of the emotion regulation systems is redundant. All three are essential for our survival; we need them to function well in the right circumstances. It is important for our health and well-being, however, that they are in balance. If you feel your soothing system can do with some more practice, the next exercise might be worthwhile.

2.1.7   Exercise: 'The Safe Place'

General Introduction

It is important that the exercises that are described in this book be done in a comfortable posture. You are invited to find a posture in which you can sit upright and relaxed, on a cushion, a kneeling bench or a chair. If you have physical limitations you can also lie down. Whichever way you feel, you can always begin with mindfully acknowledging your experience in this moment, just as it is. There may be thoughts, physical sensations, emotions, sounds . . . Allowing in your awareness whatever is predominant, moment by moment, the pleasant and the unpleasant, in a nonjudgmental way, is already a first step in any practice of kindness and compassion.

Then, a second step is to observe the breath wherever it is felt most clearly, in the belly or the chest and, without forcing, allowing a soothing breathing rhythm to emerge by gently slowing down and deepening the breath movements, inviting the breath to flow freely through the body. When you experience the breath movements as soothing, you let the breath flow by itself, without needing to influence it any further.

During any exercise in this training, at any stage, you can always pause and come back to the simplicity of mindfulness and acknowledge whatever is experienced; for example when you get stuck, tired or overwhelmed by a strong emotion. This pausing in the moment is like an internal resetting. Again you can allow a soothing breathing rhythm. And then reconnect with the instructions of the exercise when you feel space to do so.

Instructions: 'The Safe Place'

In this exercise, we imagine a safe place that evokes feelings of calmness, contentment and safeness. When you are stressed or depressed it may be difficult to feel this way. That doesn't matter. What is being asked is only to imagine this place and to practise it. Feelings can come later. The place can be indoors or outdoors. No one else needs to be present so that you can feel completely at ease just as you are, unthreatened and unobserved (exercises where others are also included in the practice will follow later on). We will give you some examples and invite you to find out which ones appeal to you. Feel free to go your own way in imagery exercises like this.

Your safe place could be, for example, a beautiful spot in the woods where the leaves move gently in the wind and rays of sunlight nourish the earth with light and warmth . . . Imagine how a gentle breeze caresses your face and patterns of light dance before your eyes. Hear the leaves rustle and smell the scent of the trees and the forest soil . . .

Or your safe place could be a beautiful golden sandy beach in the sun, with a blue sea stretched out to the horizon and a sky with friendly fluffy clouds. You watch the sparkling water. You hear the waves break on the shore, the murmuring of water against the sand, the sounds of seagulls flying in the sky. You smell the salty air; you feel the rays of the sun warming your skin and the sea breeze ruffling your hair. You feel your feet slowly sinking into the warm sand, the grains of sand passing through your toes . . .

Or your safe place could be near a roaring fire . . . or sitting in a cosy corner of your garden . . . or under your favourite tree in the park . . . lying in a hammock . . . drifting in a boat . . . or wherever. Alternately focus on all your senses: what do you see . . . what do you hear . . . what do you smell . . . what do you feel . . . at the surface of your skin . . . inside your body . . . Allow your body to relax in your safe place . . . your face to assume a peaceful expression . . . a smile to form on your lips . . . your eyes to emanate joy . . . your heart to open, like a flower opens towards the light.

The safe place is your creation and therefore has a unique relationship with you. Imagine how the place itself rejoices that you are here. Allow yourself to feel that joy. Allow yourself to feel gratitude for this place of safeness, for the possibility of returning to it whenever you like, knowing that you are always welcome. A place to come home to, time after time, even though it may present itself in different forms.

As if you reach a place.
Look about you and know
that you're home.

. . .

As if you knew this
before it had been seen.
Had been there
before you would arrive.
So at home.
>   (From 'Home', Kees
>   Spiering, 1996)

2.1.8   Out of Balance: More Stress Than Rest

If we have a personal history with a lot of threat or trauma, our threat system may become easily activated because it has been trained to do so (see Figure 5). It was not a conscious choice, but we have acquired an overdeveloped threat system that has become extremely sensitive to all kinds of real or imagined threats. Even neutral events can activate it, through associations and links that are made with the aid of language and imagination. When the coast seems clear and our threat system calms down, we quickly want to satisfy a few needs before the next threat arises, and so our drive system is triggered immediately. In this way there is little opportunity for the soothing system to develop, and we experience more stress than rest. A safe place may first of all be associated with a place of safety that protects us from immediate danger rather than a place of safeness where we can truly feel at ease and welcomed as we are.

If we have been raised with a lot of competition and were frustrated in our need for recognition and success, every feeling or image of lacking something

Figure 5 Background with a lot of threat.

Reproduced and adapted with kind permission from *The Compassionate Mind* by Paul Gilbert, London: Robinson, 2009.

or having less than others can easily activate the drive system (Figure 6). Once we have achieved a moment of satisfaction (drive system switched off), soon the fear arises that we cannot hold on to this (threat system switched on) and we cannot enjoy it. Before we realise it we already feel frustrated, and we chase after the next moment of satisfaction. Again, we experience more stress than rest. In modern society, consumption, competition and achievement are actively encouraged; indeed the economy depends on these. We easily get caught on the so-called 'hedonic treadmill', vainly trying to achieve happiness by getting satisfaction from the next desirable thing (Brickman & Campbell, 1971). Thus our drive system is kept going, but also our threat system, because not having enough is often experienced as not being good enough. We are ashamed and fear disapproval when our mobile phone, laptop or TV are too old, our clothes outdated, our partner too boring or our achievements not up to par. It is not surprising that we have little time left for our soothing system and that we suffer from burnout, depression, anxiety or addictions. Even in our 'leisure' time we are often more busy keeping our threat and drive systems in good shape than cultivating our soothing system.

The soothing system is also insufficiently developed when someone has been emotionally neglected in his or her younger years. Those who have received little warmth and love usually find it difficult to give loving care to themselves or to others. An extreme example is the Rumanian orphans who were severely neglected during the Ceauşescu dictatorship and were later barely able to have

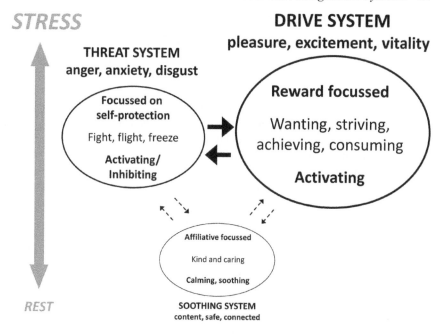

Figure 6 Background with a lot of competition.

Reproduced and adapted with kind permission from *The Compassionate Mind* by Paul Gilbert, London: Robinson, 2009.

social interactions (Rutter et al., 1999). People may also have learned to distrust a safe situation because of frequent unpredictable behaviour or abandonment by their parents or carers. Then warm feelings and attachment bonds with others can even be experienced as threatening. The soothing system can become a trigger for the threat system (see also 2.2.12). Attachment theory emphasises that secure attachment bonds between the baby and its mother are essential for a healthy development. Research has indicated that the attachment style of 1-year-olds is a good predictor of the measure of happiness, well-being and stability in relation-ships in adulthood (Ainsworth & Bowlby, 1991). Secure attachment goes hand in hand with a well-developed soothing system on which compassion is more likely to thrive (Gillath, Shaver, & Mikulincer, 2005). If there is insecure attachment this system is less well developed, but fortunately research suggests that it can be remedied by training in later life (Canterberry & Gillath, 2013).

Feedback from a participant:

'Awareness that my threat system has become so much stronger chal-lenges me to be more attentive to developing the drive and soothing systems.'

2.1.9 Restoring the Balance

It is important to restore the balance when the threat or drive systems have been overactivated and the soothing system has been underactivated. Only then will we be able to face the inevitable pain and corresponding suffering in ourselves and others with a kind and open awareness.

As early as the middle of the previous century it was argued that 'neurons that fire together, wire together' (Hebb, 1949). A system becomes stronger and more easily activated only through practice, but the opposite is also true, 'If you don't use it, you lose it.' Neurons connect with each other through synapses and form stronger circuits in our brain the more frequently they are stimulated. Neuroscientists confirm that parts of our brain are sensitive to giving and receiving care and kindness only when they are adequately stimulated during the course of our life. Specific areas of the brain are active when compassion is practised, and the extent of the activity is related to the amount of practice (Lutz, Brefczynski-Lewis, Johnstone, & Davidson, 2008; see 1.6.4). There is also a connection between our emotional brain and our heart. Our heart rate variability increases when we breathe calmly and imagine situations that evoke warm feelings and gratitude (Servan-Schreiber, 2005). There is a link between objectively measurable physiological phenomena and subjective experience. Compassion is aptly called a 'quality of the heart' because the emotional quality is most noticeable in our heart area.

Fortunately our brains can change, and it is never too late to start practising. Regular mindfulness training has already provided us with a solid foundation, and this very moment we can start to feed our soothing system. Like the old, wise tortoise says in the animation film *Kung Fu Panda*, 'Yesterday is history. Tomorrow is a mystery. Today is a gift. That's why it is called the present.'

Throughout the compassion training we will practise various forms of kindness meditation, the first of which is given below.

2.1.10 Exercise: 'Kindness Meditation—Yourself'

Everyone accepts me as I am.
Now it's my turn.

(Loesje)

Just as we can train our physical fitness through exercise, we can also cultivate mental qualities like mindfulness and kindness. In order to make a start with the last one we would like to invite you to repeat softly and gently a kind or compassionate wish towards the person you most often deal with in your life—namely yourself. Life is easier when we are on good terms with ourselves, for we take ourselves with us wherever we go. Wishing something kind for yourself doesn't mean that you are selfish. Just like all people and animals want to be happy and live in peace, you probably have the same wish, and that is totally justified. And when we can look with kindness on ourselves and treat ourselves in kind ways, this will most likely have a deep effect on those around us.

1. *The exercise may start as described in the introduction in 2.1.7.*
2. *We would like to invite you to repeat softly a kind wish for yourself and in doing so starting the practice of kindness or friendliness meditation. You can use one of four traditional phrases:*

   • *'May I feel safe';*
   • *'May I be as healthy as can be';*
   • *'May I be happy'; or*
   • *'May I be at peace' or 'May I live with ease.'*

   You can let these wishes, in the above order or in a different order, softly flow through you or keep repeating one that is particularly appropriate right now. But you can also use a wish tailored to your needs in this moment. You can wish kindness for yourself, or inner harmony, gentleness, courage or rest . . . Choose a wish that opens your heart and can be appreciated.
3. *It may be helpful to find a certain rhythm, which makes it easier to keep the attention on the phrases. You can do this by letting the wish coincide with the breath, letting the first half of the wish flow with the in-breath . . . and the second half with the out-breath. For example, 'May I . . .' (on the in-breath) '. . . be at peace' (on the out-breath), or 'May I . . .' (in-breath) '. . . be kind' (out-breath). There is no need to force the breath, just allow a soothing breathing rhythm on which you let the wish flow . . . Another option is to let the wish be carried by every exhalation . . . If both options are too complicated you can just repeat the wish softly without connecting it to the breath.*
4. *This practice is not about striving for the wish to be fulfilled. The intention with which you wish something kind for yourself already has a healing power, irrespective of whether the wish is realistic or not. You are not selfish in wishing something good and wholesome for yourself. On the contrary, the less kind we are to ourselves in life, the more this bitterness influences those around us. So do not hesitate to repeat gently a kind wish for yourself and let it flow through you, on the rhythm of the breath, or independently from the breath.*
5. *At times you might be carried away by thoughts or be distracted by a sound, a physical sensation or an emotion and forget to repeat the wish. When you notice your attention has wandered, you can also deal with this in a kind way and mindfully note that there is hearing, thinking or feeling. And when there is space again you can return to softly repeating the wish and let it flow gently through you.*
6. *To simplify the practice it is suggested that you don't think of a new wish all the time, because doing so can be quite tiring. However, if during the practice another wish spontaneously arises that seems more appropriate, you can of course continue with the new wish. And when you get tired of repeating the whole phrases you can also make the phrases shorter. In this way you could abbreviate a wish like 'May I be kind to myself' to 'be kind', or you can abbreviate 'May I be at ease with my body' to 'be at ease'. You don't need to keep repeating the phrase or the words either. When, for example, you notice that*

you are in a peaceful, gentle state of mind, you can also let go of the wish completely for a while and only observe and enjoy the peaceful atmosphere—and resume the phrases when you notice that your mind begins to wander again.

7. *However you feel is fine. Sometimes during the practice you can feel quite peaceful, or at the beginning you might feel moved, angry, sad or doubtful. When such an emotion is clearly there you can label it as 'feeling moved', 'anger', 'sadness' or 'doubt' and then observe these emotions with gentle inner eyes. Nothing needs to be fixed or pushed away. When there is some space again, you can resume the original wish. When you notice that you are daydreaming or lost in thought, you can also acknowledge this with kindness and resume the wish. If you feel overwhelmed by drowsiness you can acknowledge that too; if so it may help to use the phrases a bit more actively.*

8. *At times it may seem that nothing much happens and the practice has no effect at all. This, too, is okay. The kind, compassionate intention to whatever arises is already a healing quality. You may also feel irritated, as if you are brainwashing yourself by repeating these phrases over and over again. An underlying harshness towards yourself or feelings of unworthiness or shame can make it hard to wish something kind for yourself. However, if you give yourself some space and time and do this practice regularly, inner harshness will slowly but surely soften.*

9. *In the beginning it helps to do this practice when you feel reasonably well and relaxed. If in spite of that, there is a lot of resistance, you could also focus the wish on that resistance and wish something for yourself like 'May I be as I am' or 'May I be gentle when there is resistance.' Another option is to bring to mind a person in your life you can easily wish something kind to—somebody who is a great example for you and who symbolises qualities like gentleness, patience, trustworthiness and wisdom, or a relative or friend who means a lot to you. You could first make this person the centre of the kind wish, and after a while you could direct the wish towards yourself. You might even start with a beloved pet.*

10. *Some people think an exercise like this should evoke profound feelings of love and happiness. This may happen, but if it does not it is not your fault. This practice is more about cultivating good will than about creating good feelings. Whatever you experience in this moment is fine. To have the intention to send some kindness to yourself is already beneficial, for every time you send yourself a kind wish you cultivate an inner garden where the flowers of kindness compassion can grow. So don't hesitate to keep offering yourself kind wishes, as long as you want, on the rhythm of the breath or independently from the breath.*

Feedback from a participant:

> 'Many emotions came up during the exercise of wishing something for myself. It felt great to send myself a loving wish, as though I finally arrived home again.'

2.1.11 Nourishing the Soothing System

Most exercises in this training will nourish the soothing system, and practising a soothing breathing rhythm is very basic. We can also nourish the soothing system by mindfully opening the doors of our senses. In this section we offer a number of suggestions that can be helpful throughout the training.

If possible treat yourself regularly to a 'pleasure-walk', preferably in nature.

Find a soothing walking rhythm and pause inwardly at everything you experience as pleasant, like seeing a beautiful flower, hearing a bird sing, feeling the sun and the wind on your skin or the earth that supports you. Acknowledge and savour your experiences, let them sink in your body. Feel your body move, the contraction and releasing of your muscles that make walking possible, allow a smile on your lips and spaciousness in your heart area. Even when it rains you might feel joy for all living beings that benefit from the rain.

Like natural sounds and rhythms, soothing music can induce an atmosphere of calm, peace and safeness. Research shows that the cadence in music affects the breathing rhythm, which in turn affects the heart rhythm. A calm breathing rhythm with a frequency of around five to six breaths per minute appears to be beneficial for the heart rate variability (Brown & Gerbarg, 2012; Servan-Schreiber, 2005; see also 1.6.4). Many of the slow movements in baroque music support this rhythm with the same cadence. Singing mantras or specific recitations can have a similar effect on the rhythms of the breath and the heart. When there are six breaths per minute, one breath cycle lasts on average ten seconds.

You do not have to use a metronome but we would like to invite you to *experience* what music strikes the compassion chord in you. Explore what type of music supports your soothing system, calms your breathing and opens your heart.

There are many ways to experiment. Some people are more attracted to rhythm and sound, others more to shapes and colours. We can open ourselves to visible beauty and soothing colours in nature, decorations, paintings or photographs. We can also work with our imagination.

Allow yourself to arrive at a soothing breathing rhythm and, when you are ready, imagine a colour that you connect with comfort, warmth and safeness. Even if you only experience a fleeting sensation of colour, that is okay. Imagine the colour steadily expanding until it envelops you. Then allow the colour to fill your heart and gradually your whole body. With each breath let the colour flow into you heart and spread from your heart throughout your body. While this happens, allow yourself to feel how the colour supports and nourishes you. Feel how these qualities flow through your body and let your facial expression radiate kindness. You may wish to experiment with several colours that you associate with different qualities of compassion (for instance, patience, gentleness, courage).

Similarly you can explore the soothing effect of scents with actual objects that emit pleasant fragrances, or use your imagination.

Bring yourself into a relaxed state and imagine a scent that evokes a gentle, calm atmosphere. Imagine that this scent envelops you completely and even permeates your skin, like a warm and relaxing bath that you can enjoy. Imagine that you deeply inhale the scent with every in-breath and let it sink in your entire body on the out-breath.

Many know the soothing effect of taste. It is fine to explore this sense with healthy foods. It has a downside, of course, when it leads to comfort eating or drinking too much.

Touch also can be very soothing, so do not hesitate to explore this sense as well. If you find it difficult to have a kind and gentle attitude towards yourself, regularly touching something soft can be a reminder. The experience of physical contact with softness and warmth is how babies, toddlers and young mammals learn to feel safe and secure. When the mother or carer is absent, a teddy bear, for example, might provide this. A case in point is the famous experiment by Harlow (1958) who raised young rhesus monkeys with two kinds of surrogate mothers. He showed that the monkeys preferred to cling to a surrogate mother that was covered in furlike cloth, even though it did not provide milk, than to cling to one that gave milk but was made of cold wire mesh. In human adults touch also remains important. In a group of students, touching a teddy bear mitigated effects of social exclusion and encouraged prosocial behaviour compared with students who just viewed a teddy bear from a distance (Tai, Zheng, & Narayanan, 2011). In a group training in the British mental health care services for people who suffered from strong self-criticism and shame, participants noticed that feeling the contact of the soft surface of a tennis ball supported the experience of calm and safeness (Gilbert & Proctor, 2006).

During this training we would also like to invite you to be mindful of the symbols of compassion. Without desperately searching for them, we would like to ask you to become open to and let yourself be surprised by objects like flowers, incense and aromatic oils or candles and by all kinds of images that evoke feelings of compassion in you. Perhaps there are small objects, cards, sayings, texts and so on that you can keep close at hand to remind you of the values of mindfulness and compassion. Perhaps there is an object you would like to carry with you wherever you go.

2.1.12 Calendar Exercise: 'The Soothing System'

At the end of each session we always advise participants to keep a calendar for daily observations that are focussed on a specific theme as regards living and relating compassionately. Here is the first such exercise.

Recognise moments when you are experiencing the soothing system. An example can be 'I decided to go out of the office and have my lunch in the park. After finishing my lunch I just sat there, enjoying the sunshine and looking around.' Afterward you can reflect on and take notes using the following questions as a guideline:

- *Were you aware of the soothing system while it was happening?*
- *What physical sensations did you experience? For example, 'pleasant', 'warmth of the sunrays on my skin', 'soft belly' or 'relaxed face'.*

- *What emotions and thoughts were accompanying this event? For example, 'I felt peaceful and thought: This is a wonderful way to have lunch.'*
- *What do you feel now, when writing things down or reflecting? For example, 'I feel warm again and happy, now that I am remembering it.'*

Feedback from a participant:

'Evidently I find it difficult to receive compassion. I quickly feel guilty and think I am not worthy of compassion.'

Overview of Session 1: Three Emotion Regulation Systems

Themes

In Session 1 we look at the 'why' of compassion training and show the connection with the evolution of our brain. We deal with the three emotion regulation systems: the threat system, the drive system and the soothing system. We discuss how the regulation systems can get out of balance and how compassion training can have a restorative effect by strengthening the soothing system.

Agenda

1. Introductory meditation: mindfully arriving in the moment; soothing breathing rhythm; reflection on the question 'What brings you here?' followed by a kind wish to oneself.
2. Participant are invited to introduce themselves:
   a. What is your name?
   b. What brings you here?
   c. Mention one or two things you value in your life (people, pets, work, hobbies).
   d. What do you wish for yourself?
3. Explanation of ground rules:
   a. Inform the trainer when you cannot come.
   b. Just join in when you arrive late.
   c. Mobile phones off or in silent mode.
   d. Commitment to safety and confidentiality.
   e. Take good care of yourself and respect your own and other people's boundaries. It is not compulsory to do an exercise or share anything you do not want to share. Adapt your bodily position as needed during exercises.
   f. 'Park' expectations and be open to outcome and experience.

4. Short break with tea or coffee and a paradoxical question to reflect on individually or in small groups: 'Can you think of good reasons *not* to practise compassion for yourself and others?'
5. Sharing what came up. Followed by relevant theory why practising compassion makes sense; evolution of the brain; three emotion regulation systems.
6. Guided meditation 'The safe place', followed by sharing experiences.
7. Handing out course materials and suggestions for home practice for the week after Session 1 (see below).
8. End with 'The Breathing Space With Kindness'.

Practice Suggestions for the Week After Session 1

Formal

- Draw the three circles and reflect on how these developed in your life (2.1.5).
- Practise with the safe place daily (2.1.7).
- Practise 'Kindness Meditation—Yourself' daily (2.1.10).
- Regularly practise a familiar mindfulness exercise (body scan, mindful movement, sitting meditation, walking) with particular awareness of the inner attitude with which you practise.

Informal

- Regularly pause from your daily activities and take a breathing space with kindness (2.1.2).
- Follow the suggestions in 'Nourishing the soothing system' (2.1.11)
- Calendar exercise: 'The Soothing System' (2.1.12).

2.2 Session 2

Stress Reactions and Self-Compassion

Perhaps everything that frightens us is,
in its deepest essence,
something helpless that wants our love.
(Rainer Maria Rilke 1875–1926, from
Letters to a Young Poet, 1929/2002)

2.2.1 Fight, Flight, Freeze

Jon Kabat-Zinn (1991), the founder of the course Mindfulness-Based Stress Reduction (MBSR), reminds us of the saying 'Pain is inevitable; suffering is optional.' This may sound rather bold. Who chooses his own suffering? What he points to however, is the suffering created by our internal stress generator when we get involved in unwholesome stress reactions to life's inevitable pain. As soon as we 'see' our reaction we can choose to go along with it. An unconscious reaction can turn into a conscious response. If we are caught up in resistance to the pain our suffering will only increase. This is reflected in the following formula by Christopher Germer (2009):

PAIN × RESISTANCE = SUFFERING

We could add another formula:

DESIRE × STRIVING = SUFFERING

When the functions of the old brain are dominant and we instinctively avoid pain and chase pleasure, the internal stress generator is going full steam. When there is a physical threat, for example a car heads for us at full speed while we are crossing the road, a quick automatic reaction such as jumping sideways can save our life. It is less obvious when there is a psychological threat, such as experiencing an unpleasant emotion or thought. Yet we often show similar stress reactions to physical and psychological threats. If our body is threatened, we react by fighting, fleeing or freezing. This helps us to survive physically. When we experience emotional pain as a psychological threat, we often react similarly in order to survive psychologically (Germer, 2009; Neff, 2003a, 2003b):

- 'Fighting' comes in the guise of *self-criticism* and *self-blame*: We direct our aggression to that part of ourselves we feel threatened by.
- 'Fleeing' becomes *self-isolation*: we keep ourselves—or the threatening part of ourselves—hidden from others out of fear, shame or distrust and are alone in our suffering.
- 'Freezing' becomes *self-absorption* and *overidentification*: We get imprisoned by our thoughts and beliefs about ourselves and our pain.

These stress reactions to psychological threats seem to be new-brain variations of the instinctive reactions of the old brain. They often are counterproductive. So why are these reactions so persistent? Earlier on we saw how in evolutionary terms, the brain is an organ that evolved for survival. It seems that we have an in-built bias for negativity (Baumeister, Bratslavsky, & Finkenauer, 2001; Rozin & Royzman, 2001). For immediate survival it is more crucial to not miss the negative than to miss the positive, and old brain circuits support this. In neuroscience, the on-going and subconscious assessing by our nervous system whether people or situations are safe, dangerous or life threatening has been called 'neuroception' (Porges, 2007). The *amygdala*, a part of the memory area of the emotional brain, is important for processing incoming information and can act like an alarm system in response to potential threat. When the alarm goes off, our body is immediately aroused into a state of alertness to take us to safety as quickly as possible. When an animal is being hunted, it is better to be safe than sorry. At the *possibility* of danger, a hare prefers to run rather than take the chance—better to miss lunch than to be lunch (see Figure 7).

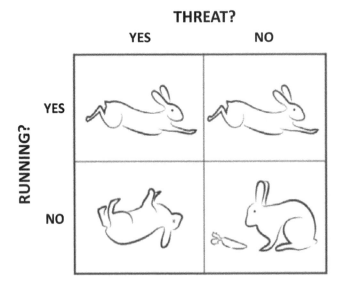

Figure 7 Decision diagram for potential danger.

Our survival instinct gets activated by physical as well as psychological threats. In both cases the amygdala sounds the alarm and our body shows similar stress phenomena. Our 'tricky brain' has difficulty distinguishing between an external and an internal threat and between physical and psychological self-preservation. When the alarm sounds, we often flee before we have had time to distinguish between the two. When there is emotional pain we can automatically act on the decision diagram of Figure 7: When there is *potential* danger . . . RUN! When emotional pain is seen as a threat to our psychological self, we react as if our life was at stake. Instead of being a safe place where we can feel at home, part of our internal world becomes a 'life-endangering area', including areas in our body where the emotional pain is felt. Therefore it is quite understandable that we 'flee' because our survival instinct reacts so quickly, but in the long term there is a high price to pay: We can no longer tend to our emotional pain, and we lose the connection with our body. Often it is 'safer' for us to focus on others' pain than on our own pain, as we see in overinvolved caregivers. We get alienated from one part of ourselves (painful emotions and associated physical sensations) and retreat to another part, namely our rational mind, where we think we are safe. Instead of feeling the experience as it is, we begin to think and identify with a limited view of ourselves and the world, which is like a psychological 'freezing'. We withdraw behind our views and defend ourselves against feelings and thoughts we see as potential threats. We 'fight' against these internal threats and against others who doubt our views and opinions.

At the beginning of Session 2, we guide the following exercise to help participants to become more aware of the inner struggle with their experience.

2.2.2 Exercise: 'Compassionately Dealing With Resistance'

You can start the exercise as described in the introduction in 2.1.7.

In your mind you may then look for a recent situation that was somehow stressful or painful. It may be an emotional, relational or physical discomfort. Choose a difficulty that feels okay to work with. For instance, an argument with a friend, a conflict with a colleague, the loss of a loved one, a power struggle with one of your children . . . It can also be a recurring or chronic physical pain or disability . . . Imagine you are in that situation right now, as if it is happening again. The more you get in touch with the painful charge of the situation, the more you can be aware of the feelings in your heart and body. What do you notice in your belly, chest, throat and the rest of your body? What is it about this situation that evokes the strongest feelings? Perhaps you imagine a scene, you hear the words that were spoken or you recognise a belief you hold about how this situation affects you and what this means for the future . . .

Now we invite you to experiment with responding to all feelings and sensations when you become aware of them with 'no' or 'I don't want this'. So you are saying 'no' to everything you encounter; 'no' to the fear, anger, shame or grief. Let the word carry the energy of 'no', rejecting and resisting everything you are experiencing. If you didn't encounter anything in yourself that was difficult when you were invited to do so, you can perhaps let a stream of 'no' go towards whatever you are experiencing now from moment to moment. 'No' to thoughts. 'No' to physical sensations. 'No' to whatever mental state is there right now. 'No' to sounds you may hear or 'no' to the reactions to this exercise. 'No, no, no'. . . even 'no' to or at the movements of the breath. And while you are embodying this 'no', notice at the same time how this resistance feels physically . . . in your face, your jaws, your chest and stomach, your breath, your muscles . . . What happens in your heart and mind . . . what happens to the experience of the situation as you say 'no'? What happens to the image of the situation itself? Also take some time to reflect on the question of how compassionate it would be if you persisted in embodying 'no' in this particular situation for a longer time.

Now let go of saying 'no'. Take a few deep breaths and see if the body can soften or relax somewhat; if you wish you can open your eyes for a while or you can change your posture a bit.

Then bring to mind again the same painful situation, remembering the images, words, beliefs and feelings connected with it. Let the situation come to life again. Then start a flow of 'yes'. 'Yes' in the direction of the painful emotions. 'Yes' to the physical sensations. 'Yes' to thoughts. And if during the introduction of this exercise you found it difficult to get in touch with a painful or difficult experience, you can perhaps say 'yes' or 'it's okay' to whatever you are aware of from moment to moment . . . to thoughts, emotions, physical sensations, sounds . . . 'yes' to the movements of the breath. Allow everything with a stream of 'yes', even if a wave of 'no' arises in the form of fear, anger or perhaps resistance against doing this exercise . . . You can also meet this with a 'yes' or 'it's okay'.

Notice what you experience as you embody this attitude of 'yes'. What does 'yes' do to your body . . . your heart . . . your mind? What happens to your experience of the situation and the image of the situation itself when you say 'yes'? How compassionate would it be, if you would continue embodying 'yes' in this particular situation for a longer time?

You may end just sitting for another few minutes with the attitude you feel was the most compassionate one, or with whatever ripples on in your mind from this exercise. With kind attention to whatever arises from moment to moment. You can also softly repeat a compassionate wish towards yourself in connection with the painful situation that you explored.

(Adapted, with kind permission, from guided meditations offered by Tara Brach.)

Feedback from a participant:

'Next Saturday I have a date. So far this has caused me a lot of stress. I realised that my inner "no" is exaggerating the stress, so I want to approach this date in a "yes" mood.'

As with any mindfulness practice, there is no right or wrong experience with the above exercise. It may be that taking on an attitude of 'yes' feels better than one of 'no', but it could also be the other way around. It depends on the painful situation you picked. The openness of 'yes' can feel liberating, but the clarity of 'no' can also give the strength you need in these particular circumstances. Be clearly aware of how the experience is as it is, feel and respect your boundaries and limits. You can always play safe, out of kindness for yourself. You may also say 'yes' to your 'no', and the other way around.

Feedback from a participant:

'The effect this exercise has on me is amazing. The "no" gives me power; the "yes" makes me softer.'

2.2.3 Tend and Befriend

Nowadays scientists distinguish a fourth instinctive reaction to stress that evolved in mammals, namely *tend and befriend* (Taylor, 2006). It is characterised by a protective, caring attitude towards offspring and vulnerable members of the species (tend) and by being more focussed on social connectedness (befriend) in situations of imminent danger.

An example of the basic tendency towards tend and befriend is the story of 10-year-old Tilly Smith from the U.K. ('Girl, 10, Used Geography to Save Lives', 2005). She was on a beach holiday with her parents in Thailand in December 2004. She had recently learned about the phenomena and causes of a tsunami at school. When she noticed that the sea withdrew dramatically, she recognised this as a sign of a tsunami. Tilly did not flee to safety but first warned her parents, who notified the hotel. The beach was evacuated and many lives were saved. Another example is a train suddenly coming to a halt for an unknown cause. You often notice how, after an initial sense of threat and insecurity, the atmosphere changes. The passengers, who had hardly looked at or spoken with each other, now become kinder and more caring. People ask each other where they are headed, showing concern and empathy. Sweets are offered and mobile phones handed around to notify the people at home. The tend-and-befriend reaction can be very strong, and because it is so automatic, in some situations even dangerous. In safety instructions on planes, for instance, parents are warned to put on their own oxygen masks first before they help their children.

The tend-and-befriend reaction involves release of oxytocin, which plays a role in social bonding in both men and women. Now the female sex hormone oestrogen appears to enhance the effect of oxytocin, which may be linked to the finding that women show stronger affiliative responses in stressful circumstances. So it seems that women are by nature more equipped to tend and befriend, but this does not mean that men are not able to do this. Compassion in both women and men seems to be the new-brain processing of the old mammalian brain's stress reaction, the conscious choice of tend and befriend aimed at the suffering other and, in the case of self-compassion, the suffering self. Whereas tend and befriend is an instinctive short route reaction from the threat system, compassion is a slower, more conscious response accompanied by the calming influence of the soothing system.

Although tend and befriend may be a less primitive stress reaction than fighting, fleeing or freezing, it can also trigger the new brain into reactions that generate more suffering. An example is the 'caring stress', which may be more prevalent in women than in men. Mothers are usually more worried about the children not finishing their meals than fathers. They also stay awake more often when the children haven't come home yet from a party. They seem unable to stop caring and worrying, as if in their imagination many things could go wrong if they did. What was designed as a reaction aimed at social connectedness and putting each other at ease ends up as compulsive caring behaviour, which may result in exhaustion in the giver and frustration in the receiver. This caring is insufficiently tuned in to what is actually needed. Where self-criticism, self-isolation and self-absorption seem to be the unhealthy proliferation of the old-brain reactions of fight, flight and freeze in the new brain, self-sacrifice and being excessively focussed on the supposed needs of others seem to originate in the tend-and-befriend reaction. We can often recognise the primitive stress reactions in our communication with each other. Fight, flight and freeze reactions to assumed threats can lead to a 'me first' way of communicating where our minds contract around our own needs and remain closed to those of others. Tend and befriend can lead to 'you first' communication by forcefully focussing on the needs of others and ignoring our own. Mindful compassion and equanimity (see 2.6.3 and 2.7.1) can help to restore the balance with openness to both our own and others' needs, leading to more healthy 'we first' communication (Gillis Chapman, 2012).

The Rat Family

When I (Frits) lived and studied as a Buddhist monk in Southeast Asia, I stayed for 3 months in a meditation centre in Thailand during the rainy season of 1986. Near where I stayed, at the edge of the centre compound, was a beautiful small wooden hut surrounded by a stream and an atmospheric bamboo grove. When the monk who had been meditating there during the rainy season left after his retreat, I saw my chance and asked and was granted permission to stay in the hut for a few months. I joyfully moved into the beautiful cabin and at around 11 p.m. I went to sleep. About an hour later I was awakened by an enormous racket going on above my head. The noise went on throughout the night, and I didn't sleep at all. The next morning I went on alms round and came back to eat. From the veranda I looked up and suddenly saw a large rat's tail. I panicked and felt nauseous. All kinds of scenarios went through my mind, and I was already thinking of leaving. Until suddenly there was a different reaction. This rat undoubtedly had lived here longer than I had. If I were to give him food he most likely would not attack me. I picked a piece of meat from the alms bowl. I was shaking when I lifted my arm and with a trembling hand I held the piece of meat close to the hole in the ceiling. After a few seconds a rat's mouth appeared . . . and to my surprise and relief the rat didn't bite! He only sniffed at the piece of meat and went back into the hole.

Although I had always thought that rats preferred to eat (human) meat, this rat didn't like meat. Somewhat relieved, but not relaxed, I picked up a green bean and decided to try again. I was astonished and excited that the second time the rat didn't bite me either. He, or probably she, sniffed the food again, took the bean with her little forepaw from my fingers, and went back. I was very touched.

From then on I fed the rat every day. My fear and repulsion gradually disappeared, and at night I was less disturbed by the commotion that went on above my head. A few weeks later a baby rat came down from the hole and scuttled away across the veranda. That night all was quiet; the whole family had left.

I missed them and have never forgotten that adventure.

2.2.4 Self-Compassion as a Response to Emotional Pain

Self-compassion is the healthier response to emotional pain. Kristin Neff (2003b, 2011) distinguishes three qualities that are the antidote to the psychological equivalent of fighting, fleeing and freezing (see Figure 8):

- The antidote to self-criticism is *self-kindness*, that is, tenderness and loving-kindness towards ourselves.
- The antidote to self-isolation is *common humanity*, an awareness of connection with the whole of humanity. Our suffering may differ in form and detail, but it is part of the universal human condition and we are not alone in our suffering.
- The antidote to self-absorption and overidentification is *mindfulness*, an open and nonjudging attentiveness to the emotional pain and our reactions to it without identifying with our judgments. By mindfully staying present with that which was frozen, we can thaw again.

The following brief exercise we learned from Kristin Neff (2011) and is based on the three qualities of self-compassion as described above.

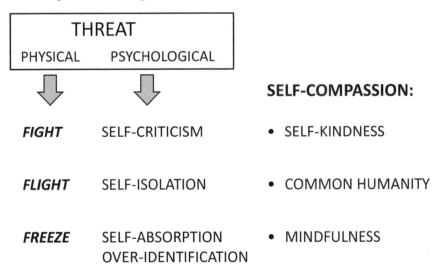

Figure 8 Stress reactions and self-compassion.

Derived from Germer, 2009; Neff, 2011.

'The Self-Compassion Mantra'

Every time we experience emotional pain, we can remind ourselves to have compassion for ourselves by saying the following phrases. When we do this repeatedly they will turn into a kind of mantra. If you wish you can put one or both of your hands on your heart area.

> *'This is a moment of suffering.'*
> *'Suffering is a part of life.'*
> *'May I be kind to myself.'*

The phrases are short and easy to remember and they connect us with all three components of self-compassion: mindfulness, common humanity and self-kindness. 'This is a moment of suffering' supports the mindfulness aspect and helps us to be present with our suffering. 'Suffering is a part of life' reminds us of the imperfection of human existence. 'May I be kind to myself' reminds us of the kindness aspect of self-compassion and helps us feel connected in a warm and caring way to the pain we experience. You could add 'May I give myself the compassion I need' to emphasise that you, just like any other human being, cannot live without compassion. You might think up your own variations of these phrases so that they really speak to you. Make sure, however, that all three components are present.

Practising self-compassion can result in a more wholesome and helpful relationship to our pain. It is not a substitute for effective therapies and treatments, but it may help us to make wise choices in dealing with 'dis-ease'. We mentioned earlier the distinction between cure and care. Cure is what we do when we have a solution for the problem for example by removing the inflamed appendix, splinting the broken leg or destroying cancer cells by radiation or chemotherapy. Care is always an option, even when all possibilities for cure have been exhausted. When striving for a change works against us, a shift towards acceptance can be more beneficial. Whenever there is emotional pain, refraining from trying to fix or 'change' it is often best. Paradoxically, when there is emotional pain, acceptance and care can more likely bring about change and cure (Germer, 2009). Physical pain, too, can become chronic and in turn lead to a lot of emotional pain (Burch, 2008). Physical causes cannot always be found, or even when they are, there is not always a cure. Physical pain itself can also be an expression of emotional pain, caused by higher stress levels and increased muscle tension. Accepting pain is easier said than done. Sometimes all we feel is resistance, and the road to acceptance may look like a long one. Christopher Germer (2009) has distinguished five stages in the process of accepting pain. *Aversion*, which can take the form of actively resisting or anxiously avoiding, can gradually shift to *curiosity* when we begin to turn towards the pain with interest. This can be followed by *tolerance*, peacefully enduring the discomfort, and proceed to *allowing*, letting the painful feelings come and go. Finally this can lead to *befriending*: embracing our pain and recognising the deeper needs and hidden values. 'Com-passion' literally means 'suffering with'. 'Self-compassion' is 'suffering with ourselves' and therefore it is a special form of acceptance, namely acceptance of ourselves as we are, of our pain and of our reactions to the pain. Self-compassion is giving ourselves the care and kindness that we would also give to loved ones. There is nothing artificial about it. It is a deeply rooted natural tendency in the old mammalian brain and the soothing system.

Culture and nature are constantly interacting. In our culture the attitude towards emotional pain seems rather hostile, and therefore our threat system often overrides the soothing system when we are confronted with emotional pain. We forcefully strive for cure, even when care would be more appropriate. And when curing emotional pain is not working, the emphasis is often on our individual responsibility encouraging guilt and shame rather than on self-compassion. Emotional deprivation and psychological trauma should automatically lead to practising self-compassion. Yet we quickly react with self-blame, self-isolation or self-absorption. We experience the problems as our fault, we think we are the only ones, or identify with victimhood. In cultures where compassion for self and others is actively practised, posttraumatic stress syndromes appears to be less prevalent; an example is the remarkable resilience found in Tibetan exile communities (Lewis, 2013). Monks who were tortured in Chinese prisons remained compassionate towards themselves *and* towards their torturers (P. Gyatso & Shakya, 1998). In Western culture there is often more self-pity than self-compassion. When there is self-pity the world contracts around us and we can only perceive our own suffering. Self-compassion, on the other hand, opens us up to the world and to the universal suffering of humanity. Cultivating self-compassion helps us heal ourselves and the world around us, for we develop a caring attitude that not only encompasses our own suffering but any form of pain.

In Chapter 1.6 we reviewed the relevant research that shows how self-compassion is positively correlated with our well-being and health. We summarised the evidence that actively training ourselves in kindness and compassion improves our health on various levels—physically, by balancing out our neurobiological systems; psychologically by improving our flexibility in coping with adversity and emotion regulation; and relationally, by increasing our capacity to help and support each other. It strengthens our capacity for care, even when there is no cure.

2.2.5   Ways to Self-Compassion

Christopher Germer (2009) distinguished five key ways in which we can bring more self-compassion into our lives:

The way of the body: softening. Increased muscle tension is normal when we react to external threat; it enables us to fight or flight. When the threat is internal, softening is what the body really needs. When we become aware of tension in the body, we can allow it to flow away—not by forcefully striving for relaxation, which only results in more tension, but by allowing softness to enter with the breath, in our belly, shoulders, face or any other part of the body. Our body needs attention, care and nourishment to be able to function well. We can practise kindness for the body any time: when going to bed, waking up, taking a shower, getting dressed, going for a walk, cycling, engaging in sport or fitness training or eating.

The way of feelings: soothing. We can befriend our painful emotions instead of fighting or ignoring them; we can hold them like a loving mother holds her upset baby. Seeing ourselves from the perspective of someone who has our best interests at heart may be helpful: How would your best friend support you now? Your ideal mentor, Jesus, Buddha . . .? Naturally we may also allow ourselves to have positive feelings, not as an escape from pain but out of kindness, by engaging in an activity that gives us a sense of well-being, such as listening to music, caring for a beloved pet, going into nature, reading an inspiring poem or book or looking at art.

The way of thoughts: allowing. We can allow our thoughts to behave in whatever way they are behaving in this moment. When our mind is preoccupied or thoughts are racing, or when we are fighting or resisting thoughts, we can take a step back and just look at them. Although we often take the content of these thoughts so seriously, we can also keep them lightly and playfully in our awareness. See how transient they are; it is not possible to hold on to them. Neither can we predict them. Do you know what you will be thinking in the next minute? So let them come and go. They will do that anyway. We can think of helpful metaphors, such as looking at clouds in the sky or at leaves in the river, or standing behind a waterfall or making an acknowledgement such as 'this too is allowed to be here.'

The relational way. Others can cause us pain but also offer us kindness and a sense of common humanity (we are not alone). They can help to loosen our rigid views and opinions. What is essential is *how* we make contact. If our motivation is to wish others well and not to harm them, this in turn will inspire them to be friendly towards us. The Dalai Lama calls this *wisely selfish*, altruism as a wise form of egotism (T. Gyatso, 2003). Research confirms that altruism, happiness and well-being are closely related (Klein, 2014). Caring for animals or plants can also be kind for ourselves. Ellen Langer (1989) did research in a nursing home for the elderly. She compared a group of residents who could choose from a selection of indoor plants to take care of themselves with residents who were simply assigned the plants and were told the staff would take care of them. After 18 months those who were still alive and who had cared for the plants themselves were physically and mentally in better shape than those who did not have any responsibility. Moreover, in the caring group of residents, less than half as many people had died than in the other group.

The spiritual way. There are many religious ways leading to compassion for ourselves and others (Armstrong, 2011). Here we do not imply a formal religion but rather an experiential spirituality that helps us to take ourselves more lightly. This helps us not only to be open to others but also to be open to the mystery of life itself, the miracle of existence and our awareness of that. Having less 'self' to protect is having less 'burden' to carry around and having more space for self-transcending values. Spiritual self-care means being dedicated to those values that touch our heart and give direction and vitality to our life. You may think that you cannot access any of that because of your painful situation. Yet, in every culture, stories are told of how pain reveals our values and how treasures are hidden in that which we fear most.

2.2.6 Exercise: 'A Hand on Your Heart'

There seems to be one common characteristic in all ways to self-compassion: They open 'the heart'. We don't mean the heart as the organ that is pumping blood, but the tangible heart area that sensitively informs us about the quality of connection with what we are aware of, whether it is physical sensations, thoughts, emotions, contact with others or commitment to meaningful values. The heart can be extremely sensitive, and we are able—even when we have learned to close ourselves off from our own heart—to cultivate and deepen this sensitivity through compassion practice. A simple exercise follows.

First of all be aware of your posture as you are sitting now. What do you notice in your body? And what do you notice in the mind? How is the breath? Then place an open hand (or both hands) on your heart area. You can let the breath become calm and soft and breathe consciously through the heart area. Sense the contact and warmth of your hand and feel how this sensation is being received in your heart area. What sensations are you aware of in your chest . . . and what effects do you notice in the rest of your body? How is your mind now? Notice what is happening, without needing to judge it. All experiences are allowed to be there. Also observe attentively what happens when you take your hand away again. Does anything change?

This exercise often stirs up a lot. Some participants indicate that they suddenly become more aware of their body when they place a hand on the heart. Others feel a stronger connection with themselves and with their body. Sometimes participants suddenly discover deeper emotions, such as sadness.

Any time you want to remind yourself in your daily life of the sensitivity of the heart, you could place an open hand on your chest. During formal sitting or lying down practices you can place one or both open hands on your heart from time to time. And observe specific sensations in the heart area during exercise. Most mindfulness practitioners confirm that the practice results in a stronger awareness of the body and the sensory experience of internal and external phenomena, including our heart area. In compassion training we deepen our awareness of the heart area and learn to listen more carefully when it opens up to and closes down from what is present. This sensitivity in turn accompanies us when we do the basic practices from the mindfulness training. Therefore we would encourage you to return regularly to the body scan exercise, the movement exercises or the sitting meditation and to tune in to all the subtle sensations in the heart area as an additional field for mindful investigation. What can be sensed there from moment to moment? Do you experience heaviness or lightness, coolness or warmth, tightness or space? Is there a feeling of contraction or of expansion?

2.2.7   Survival of the Nurtured

It is not the strongest of the species that survives,
nor the most intelligent,
but the one most adaptable to change.
(Leon Megginson, paraphrasing
Charles Darwin, 1963)

Frans de Waal (2009) has argued that the term *survival of the fittest*, coined by Herbert Spencer, does not correspond at all with the original idea of natural selection in Darwin's evolution theory. *Survival of the fittest* quite soon got translated as 'the rights of the strongest', to enable those who lived in better conditions, with more money and more powerful weapons, to exploit the weak, the poor and the voiceless with impunity. Darwin himself was disappointed that others misinterpreted and misused his theory. In nature it is not the physically strongest organisms that have the best chance of survival. Better flight behaviour, better camouflage, better social connectedness and tend-and-befriend reactions can also contribute to survival. In more evolved mammalian species, it is qualities like emotional and social intelligence, empathy and altruism that particularly increase the chances of survival, especially for the species as a whole and in the long term. A motorbike riding participant in one of our MBCL workshops sensed this very clearly; he wanted to get himself a T-shirt with an alternative epigraph: 'Born to be mild.'

We get closer to original Darwinism when we understand the term *fittest* as 'fitting best'. The fittest is the one best adapted to his environment. In accordance with the results of scientific research and to prevent confusion, where mammals are concerned, it might be better to speak of *survival of the nurtured* (Cozolino, 2006) or *survival of the kindest* (Keltner, 2009) because those being able to receive and to give care have the best chances of survival. Those nourished with loving care have the best chances of survival. Obviously this does not mean that a person who did not get the emotional nourishment they needed when they were young no longer stands a chance. The inborn capacity to receive and give care is still present. And even if the capacity is not well developed, compassion training can help those whose needs were not met to become more open and responsive. The following exercise can be helpful to nourish ourselves in difficult circumstances.

2.2.8   Exercise: 'The Breathing Space With Compassion— Coping With Emotional Pain'

This exercise is a variation of the 'coping' version of the Three Minute Breathing Space (Segal, Williams, & Teasdale, 2013). Like the self-compassion mantra (2.2.4) it can be practised in situations where you experience emotional pain or stress. As with the 'regular' breathing space, we mindfully come to a halt, and we distinguish three phases.

Being Present With Open, Kind Awareness

The first phase involves being aware, with an open and gentle attentiveness of whatever is there . . . You open up fully and bring the attention to the experience of this moment . . . Notice what thoughts, feelings or physical sensations are present . . . Acknowledge and name whatever is there . . . For instance, 'There is pain . . . fear . . . sadness . . . anger . . . shame . . . vulnerability . . .' or 'There is tension in my jaw . . . my neck . . . my shoulders . . .' or 'There is self-criticism . . .' Feel and acknowledge . . . whatever is there in this moment . . . Don't exclude anything . . . Open up gently to physical sensations, however unpleasant they may be . . . Allow thoughts to be there in a nonjudging way, whatever their content . . . Kindly embrace emotions, however painful they may be . . .

Allowing a Soothing Breathing Rhythm

The second phase involves bringing your attention back to the breath opening up to receive compassion . . . Attentively follow each in and out-breath with a receptive attitude. Allow the breathing to become calmer . . . and there are several ways to support yourself in this:

If the breath is quick and shallow, you can intentionally slow down the breathing, with kindness, without forcing anything . . . Let the exhalation be complete . . . and allow the inhalation to arise by itself . . . You can adjust your posture and facial expression so that they support a calm breathing rhythm . . . You can follow the breath in your belly and allow it to become softer and softer . . . You can consciously breathe through the heart area and allow feelings of space, light and warmth to be there . . .

You can place one or both hands on your heart area . . . You can bring to mind a soothing image that supports a calm breathing rhythm, for example a safe place, a calming colour, relaxing music, or a benefactor or compassionate companion . . .

Allow Compassion to Flow to the Body and to the Emotional Pain

The third phase involves expanding your awareness and embodying an attitude of being compassionate . . . You can be aware of the body as a whole, the breathing body, in whatever way the body is right now . . . Compassionately acknowledge the pain and suffering that are there . . . and whatever need is most clearly there right now.

Is there anything kind, gentle or supporting that you could wish for yourself in this moment? For example, 'May I . . . be safe . . . be free from pain or discomfort . . . be happy . . . experience clarity . . . be at peace . . .' Use your own words and let them flow from your heart. You can direct them to yourself on the rhythm of the breath. On the in-breath it could be 'May I . . .' and coordinated with the out-breath it can be whatever you wish for yourself. Let the wish flow from your heart through your entire body. If there are areas where you feel particularly uncomfortable, tense, resistant or perhaps numb, you could breathe into those areas and let the wish flow through you.

And if you are in a stressful situation involving one or more people, you can also acknowledge their pain and suffering and hold wishes of goodwill for them. For example, 'May you be safe . . .' or 'May you and I be happy . . .' or 'May we live in peace and harmony . . .' And then continue to repeat this wish silently to yourself, either on the rhythm of the breath or independently from the breath.

2.2.9   Dealing With Obstacles

Just as in a mindfulness course, many participants in compassion training come across obstacles in the first week of practising at home. Loving-kindness and compassion exercises do not always go smoothly. Depending on our learning history, we can encounter various pitfalls and be troubled by misunderstandings. It is helpful to recognise unhelpful motivations, expectations and beliefs.

Unhelpful motivations. Arranging time and space to practise can be difficult. We need the right motivation and the right discipline. Both lack of discipline and the wrong kind of discipline can form an obstacle. When we lack discipline it can be helpful to remind ourselves of our motivation and return to the questions in the introduction of Part 2. Discipline can get in the way, however, when it is forceful and not coming from a kind and caring attitude. Just as in mindfulness practice, a sense of duty (threat system) and striving for results (drive system) can soon become the motivation for compassion practice. Neither is very helpful. We are more likely to cultivate compassion when our motivation connects with the soothing system. To become aware of what drives us, you can think of the example of the cat in Session 1. Can you recognise the energy of one of the three emotion regulation systems in yourself like you can in a cat? You can also ask yourself: 'What *verb* is predominant right now?' Often we are driven by 'shoulds', 'oughts', 'musts' or 'wants', verbs that link to the threat or drive systems. The soothing system involves other verbs such as 'allow', 'may', 'wish' or 'grant'. Whenever you notice you are dominated by verbs with a compulsory character you can remind yourself of the more supportive verbs that are compatible with a kind and caring attitude.

Some participants find it difficult to deal with the many suggestions for home practice and the freedom of choice they are given. Some feel overwhelmed and unable to make choices. They may feel inclined to leave it altogether. Others stretch themselves to explore every exercise in depth and find it too much for the time they have set aside. If either applies it is helpful to remind yourself that making choices also is an exercise in self-compassion. Ask yourself regularly: 'What do I really need?', 'What would be compassionate for myself?' and adjust your home practice accordingly.

Unhelpful expectations. It might be that we expect unpleasant feelings to go away and pleasant feelings to arise. And then we soon think we have done something wrong when we feel restless, tired, irritated, anxious or sad or frustrated and disappointed when positive experiences stay away. Instead of judging ourselves harshly it is more helpful to acknowledge that this is also part of the practice and meet it with a nonjudgmental attitude. It is not evidence of failing but rather an extra cry for self-compassion. Simply start where you are and be present with whatever is there, notice expectations and judgments as thoughts, unpleasant feelings as feelings, restlessness or tiredness as physical sensations. Then we can feed these experiences back into the practice with a connecting wish, perhaps 'May I be calm' or 'May I experience vitality.' A paradoxical wish may also give space: 'May I feel this tension' or 'May I feel this tiredness just as it is.'

Compassion is open to any outcome and welcomes both pleasant and unpleasant emotions as potential valuable messengers. It is true that compassion practice often generates 'positive' emotions, but they cannot be forced. Peace, happiness, warmth and contentment come in their own time and grow on the ground fertilised by practice. As Germer (2009) said, this practice is more about cultivating good will than about cultivating good feelings. It becomes tiring when we try very hard to change what is, to control what is, to get rid of what is or to create something that is not there. If we can kindly recognise what presents itself, the practice turns out not to be tiring at all and can be an oasis of rest. The threat and drive systems consume a lot of energy, but the soothing system is not tiring. If we focus on the outcome of a kind wish and want to make it come true as quickly as possible, the practice becomes forceful and frustrating. When we are less focussed on the results and more on the good intentions of our wishes, paradoxically wholesome effects will follow more likely.

Feedback from a participant:

'I learn that I can water the desert in me.'

When we practise self-compassion, it sometimes seems as if the increased warmth thaws inner ice blocks. This thawing process may unexpectedly give rise to waves of old pain and sadness. We will discuss this phenomenon, which can be a major obstacle, in more detail in 2.2.12. It is good to know that nothing is wrong with you but that this often is the beginning of healing processes taking place. If old painful memories and emotions are quite strong, do the exercises in smaller steps. Remember the five stages of acceptance; you do not need to jump from aversion to friendship in one go.

Unhelpful beliefs. Many associate practising kindness and compassion towards ourselves with being 'selfish'. It is helpful to realise that this practice is about cultivating a sensitivity to give and receive care that will benefit ourselves as well as others. It has long been recognised that we become insensitive to others when we are harsh on ourselves and that we become kind to others when we are kind towards ourselves. This is how we can understand the biblical wisdom 'Love your neighbour as yourself.'

Others may find the practice too 'soft' and fear it will turn them into 'wimps'. It is not about glossing over the reality of life with a sugar coating of sweet words, however. Neither do we need to wallow or drown in self-pity. In fact we become more open to the depth of the human condition, including the inevitable pain. Often kindness expresses itself in gentleness, but it can also express itself in a firm 'no' towards harmful behaviour. Just as it needs tenderness and caring, compassion also demands courage and strength. Realise that compassion is rooted in our survival instinct and is not meant to deal with just small inconveniences but also with severe suffering. Do we have the courage and the confidence not to look away, but to keep watching in a heartfelt way and to do what is needed? Courage and compassion are both qualities of the heart that go hand in hand. The word *courage* has been derived from 'cor' or 'coeur' (= heart). The attitude of nonviolence or nonharming is another aspect of compassion. This is not soft either. It takes courage not to use violence. Violence only increases our suffering. This is not to say that compassion will never result in 'strong' actions and discipline; these will result not from 'should' or 'want', however, but from the wish to alleviate suffering in the most friendly and least harmful way.

Some have the impression that practising with repetitive phrases or wishes is a kind of 'brainwashing'. After all, we soon know intellectually what we are wishing for ourselves, so why repeat it all the time? Yet the gentle and genuinely intended repetition of a wish proves itself to be healing. Daniel Siegel (2010a) stated that contemporary scientific knowledge solidly affirms that kindness and compassion are to the brain what the breath is to life. So instead of brainwashing ourselves with harmful thoughts we practise wholesome brain training. Another misunderstanding is that it is like saying 'affirmations'. Affirmations usually contain an element that does not correspond with the reality of the present moment. You could say for example, 'I feel confident' while you do not feel confident at all. The wishing phrases in the compassion training are more like aspirations: 'Gosh, if this were here, that would be nice. I would really wish this for myself.' Whether it comes true or not is not so relevant; what is already wholesome is the inner attitude and sensitivity to what we really need.

Another unhelpful belief about compassion training is that it is a very serious matter and not meant to be joyful or playful. Even when compassion opens us to our suffering, this does not mean that we cannot be open to enjoyable moments as well. On the contrary, it is part and parcel of the kindness aspect of self-compassion and the intention to relieve suffering that we are open to pleasant sensations and feelings that arise and savour them fully as long as they are there, without grasping onto them. Most of us have experienced the enormous relief of a good laugh in difficult times. So let us not exclude the power of humour and light-heartedness from our practice and from time to time smile about the imperfections of life.

2.2.10   Imagine . . . Imagination as Skilful Means

Imagination is your greatest gift,
for it allows you to participate
in the act of creation itself.
   (Sister Stan, *Day by Day*, 2013)

In compassion training we make good use of our new brain capacity for language and imagination so that it will work for us. We make use of the fact that our emotional brain and our body react in the same way when a stimulus arises, whether externally or internally from our imagination (see Figure 9).

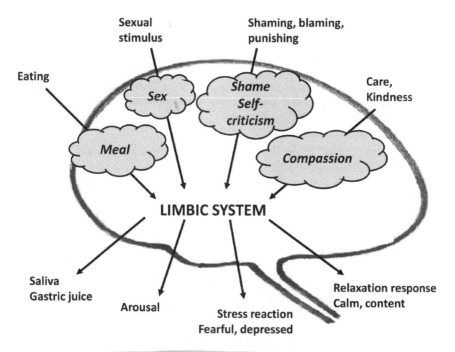

Figure 9 The same reactions to real and imagined situations.

Reproduced and adapted with kind permission from *The Compassionate Mind* by Paul Gilbert, London: Robinson, 2009.

When we are eating a tasty meal the body reacts physiologically, producing saliva and digestive enzymes. Just imagining a nice meal has the same effect on the body. Just thinking of food makes us salivate. When we are totally absorbed in sexual activity, the body shows all kinds of arousal phenomena. The same things happen just thinking about sex, and the more vivid our imagination the stronger the body reacts. If we are experiencing an event where others shame or punish us, our body shows a whole range of stress reactions. Thinking back to this event, the same reactions happen in our body. If we think repeatedly about a situation or imagine that it will reoccur, the stress reaction becomes triggered again. In fact we do not need the outside world at all to become stressed. The stress reaction occurs whenever we criticise ourselves, and if we do this often enough, our body will end up chronically stressed. This is how the new brain can work against us.

When we are in a warm, safe environment with caring people around us, our body reacts with feelings of calm, contentment and well-being. In this state there is space for recovery, growth and potential for change. The body reacts in the same way when we only imagine this situation. Even if we have only experienced a few caring and calming situations we can still use our imagination to train our soothing system. However, this is not always so easy. It may be difficult to imagine a situation with caring others when we received little or no loving care from our parents or carers or when their love turned out to be unreliable because they were unpredictably aggressive or they abused or abandoned us. If we do imagine a situation with caring others, our threat system may be triggered instead of our soothing system. The exercise 'The Safe Place' (2.1.7) or 'Nourishing the Soothing System' (2.1.11) would be a more suitable starting point because it does not involve others. In any case, we take to heart the advice from Compassion Focused Therapy to always start with a soothing breathing rhythm as an introduction to guided compassionate imagery (Gilbert, 2009a, 2010). Slow breathing will induce a parasympathetic tone and calm the body, which will make it easier for our mind to create soothing images. Obviously it works both ways as soothing images also slow down the breathing.

There are many ways to use our imagination to practise compassion, so we can find exercises that suit us. This is an area where Western and Buddhist psychology can benefit from each other (Gilbert & Choden, 2013; Ringpu & Mullen, 2005). We can do guided memories, for example, remembering moments of giving or receiving compassion, or guided fantasies, such as imagining a compassionate person or a compassionate self. If we don't get clear visual images, it doesn't matter. It is quite normal for mental images to be fleeting impressions, changeable from moment to moment. Sometimes sensory impressions other than the visual are more prominent (hearing, smelling, feeling). The key is to have the intention to be open to feelings of compassion, even if they are not immediately evident. Getting distracted is also normal; observe it without judging or condemning and then return with kindness to the chosen theme of imagination in the exercise. The accompanying instructions of the imagery exercises, as described in this book or as can be downloaded from www.routledge.com/9781138022157 often contain more text than is usual in the basic mindfulness practices. In the initial phase this can be helpful. However, as

soon as you notice that you no longer need the instructions or th
practice, you can continue to practise without them. It is an ar
guided by the instructions that are helpful and to just let pass by
are not. We hope you will eventually internalise the helpful *i*
them less and less, but of course you can continue to use them ...
The next exercise, taken from Paul Gilbert (2009a), is another example u.
power of the imagination.

Feedback from a participant:

'It is wonderful to realise how good I am at imagining disastrous scenarios and how challenging it is to imagine something wholesome. But
it is more relaxing!'

2.2.11 Exercise: 'The Compassionate Companion'

Don't walk in front of me. I may not follow.
Don't walk behind me. I may not lead.
Just walk beside me and be my friend.
                    (Anonymous)

The next exercise may start as described in the introduction in 2.1.7.

*You can let yourself be inspired by people whom you consider embody compas-
sion. It may be people you know from the past or from the present, from history
or from your personal life, or from stories, books or films that appeal to you. You
can give your fantasy free reign. It is essential that you create your own image of
a compassionate companion, one that is completely free from threatening projec-
tions. If you choose an image from the religion you grew up with, and associations
of threat or compulsion arise, it will be your threat system that is triggered rather
than your soothing system. Let your image be one where there is no threat at all,
but where all the qualities of compassion are present. It can be a human being but
also a supernatural or a celestial being, or something from nature like the sea, a
mountain, a tree or an animal, as long as it is an image that makes sense to you
and that you can relate to.*

What this image can express is

- *true commitment: it cherishes the deep wish to help you, as well as others, to
  carry your suffering and to cope with it;*
- *strength and courage: it is not overwhelmed by your pain, can always carry
  it and never shirks away from it, whatever or however it may be;*
- *wisdom: it deeply knows from experience what you are going through, has
  also been through this and understands your pain and struggle like no other;*
- *warmth: it is kind, gentle, caring and involved;*

acceptance: it does not judge or criticise you and accepts you unconditionally as you are.

You can allow a soothing breathing rhythm and, if you wish, you can imagine you are in your safe place . . . This can be a suitable place to bring to mind your compassionate companion.

You may find the following questions helpful:

- What would you wish your compassionate companion to look like: old/young, big/small, male/female, human/nonhuman? What would be its colour(s), external characteristics, visual aspects?
- What other sensory qualities would your compassionate companion have? What kind of voice? What rhythm? What tone of voice? How would it feel to be in the presence of your compassionate companion?
- What would help you to see that your compassionate companion expresses commitment, strength, wisdom, care and acceptance?
- How would you like your compassionate companion to relate to you? How would you yourself like to relate to your compassionate companion?

Getting a clear visual image is not the point of this exercise; a relaxed and playful attitude can be very helpful. The image may be vague, fleeting, changing, that doesn't matter. Whenever you imagine your compassionate companion, it is a practice in allowing a caring attitude of another being towards you . . . an exercise in receiving compassion . . .

While we imagine an ideal compassionate companion we can focus our attention on how it feels when another being cares about us unconditionally . . . Imagine how your compassionate companion cares for you with warmth and benevolence . . . truly wishes you to be safe . . . to be free from fear and pain . . . to be happy and contented . . . What physical sensations and emotions do you notice? What do you notice about your bodily posture . . . your facial expression? The essence of this practice is that you learn to feel how your compassionate companion has your best interests at heart and is devoted to your well-being . . .

Perhaps you think, 'All this is very nice but it is not real. I don't want a fantasy image but a real person who cares about me!' During this exercise the lack of such a person in your life may be felt even more strongly. If this is the case it's good to realise that we don't need to deny that we long for people who care about us. We can mindfully acknowledge that we have this longing. At the same time it is important that we can allow feelings of close connectedness in those moments when no actual caring person is there for us, particularly if we are frequently tormented by our inner bully. This we usually do consider real, even though it is not really there either. We are always better off with self-compassion than with self-torture. The advantage of the compassionate companion is that we can call on it whenever we need compassion . . . And the more we practise imagining a compassionate companion, the easier it will become to receive compassion from real people . . .

The compassionate companion is your unique creation and you can imagine how it rejoices to be in your presence . . . Allow yourself to feel that joy . . . And allow yourself to feel grateful for the presence of your compassionate companion . . . And for the capacity to evoke it whenever you want . . . The following poem beautifully reflects the atmosphere of how a compassionate companion can be experienced:

> I am not I.
> I am this one
> walking beside me whom I do not see,
> whom at times I manage to visit,
> and whom at other times I forget;
> who remains calm and silent while I talk,
> and forgives, gently, when I hate,
> who walks where I am not,
> who will remain standing when I die.
>   (Juan Ramón Jiménez, 1973)

2.2.12   Backdraft—How Self-Compassion Can Evoke Old Hurts

Stray dogs that had a hard life of neglect and abuse can react viciously and mistrustfully when approached with kindness. Neglected and traumatised children can be very mistrustful when adults with the best intentions try to befriend them. Similarly we must not be surprised to meet resistance when we offer kindness to parts in ourselves that have been hurt and rejected.

It is not uncommon that participants experience adverse reactions while practising compassion and kindness. Paul Gilbert (2010) emphasises how psychotherapy clients may experience compassion as threatening and resist experiencing warm feelings. Research done by his team shows that people with low levels of self-criticism reacted to compassionate imaging with increased heart rhythm variability and decreased cortisol production, which are signs of a soothing reaction. Highly self-critical people reacted with decreased heart rhythm variability, which is a sign of threat, and no changes in cortisol levels (Rockliff, Gilbert, McEwan, Lightman, & Glover, 2008). In another study magnetic resonance imaging scans showed that highly self-critical people who were asked to self-soothe had more response patterns consistent with threat than the less self-critical subjects in the control group (Longe et al., 2010). Christopher Germer (2009) has used the term 'backdraft' to refer to a strong adverse reaction to the practice of self-compassion. Fire fighters are familiar with this phenomenon. When there is a fire in, say, a large high-rise building with many apartments, several rooms may be on fire whereas in others the fire is just smouldering. When a window breaks or someone inadvertently opens a door, a wave of oxygen comes in and there is suddenly an explosion of fire.

This is a metaphor for what can happen during kindness meditation. If we have not been used to looking at ourselves with kindness it can act as oxygen for those areas in ourselves that were previously closed off. There can be difficult moments, when out of the blue a lot of sadness and old, unprocessed pain surfaces. It is good to know that there is nothing wrong with you. On the contrary, it is quite normal and a sign that you are healing by connecting more intimately with areas in yourself that were previously inaccessible. Here, too, being familiar with mindfulness practice is extremely helpful, so that you can deal with this more easily by noting it; you can allow the fire to simply burn itself out, being present as the witness. The phenomenon of backdraft does not occur in everyone; it depends on the person, their history and their familiarity with self-inquiry. However, if it does occur it is important to realise it is a normal phenomenon and that we can adjust the dosage of kindness to the amount that can be handled. Some participants find the image of 'backdraft' a bit scary and relate easier to another metaphor. Many of us have had the experience that as children we played in the snow and did not notice that our hands got nearly frozen. When we warmed them up near the fire they first started to hurt and glow strongly and we cried with pain. This intense pain was a healing pain, however, because it was a sign that the warmth came back into our fingers, which kept them alive. It was only compassionate however to prevent these extreme pains and let the warming up process happen slowly. Similarly it can be compassionate to ourselves to let kindness in slowly.

If our upbringing consistently lacked kindness and compassion, we simply have not learned to let it in. If the soothing system has been underdeveloped, every time we begin to experience kindness our threat system can be activated, and this might stop us from practising. Reasons for this might be that no secure attachment was formed with our parents or carers, that we didn't know and internalise compassionate role models, that we have memories of traumatic experiences without having been supported compassionately and that situations that initially seemed safe turned out to be unreliable after all. We might have become allergic even to just the words 'compassion' and 'loving-kindness' and feel resistance to accepting warm feelings. We have identified with an unloved self and have learned to survive without compassion and an adequate soothing system. We react from our threat system with aversion, fear or aggression whenever care is offered. Even a small amount of care can feel like an overdose. When we experience emotional pain, a (form of) inner bully promptly shows itself, whereas what we actually need is an inner helper. However, the soothing system only works as another trigger for even more threat because it is associated with yet more emotional pain.

Figure 10 shows a diagram of the mechanisms that are involved when we experience emotional pain as an inner threat, the soothing system is underdeveloped and the inner bully is dominant. The result is that we reject the experience of the moment, look back at the past with resentment and look to the future with suspicion.

Figure 11 indicates what experiences feed the soothing system and how compassion practice and an inner helper can make emotional pain feel less threatening and help it to subside by activating the soothing system. If we experienced

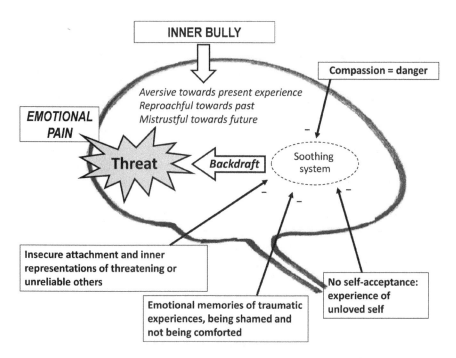

Figure 10 Threat from emotional pain and increasing threat because of an underdeveloped soothing system.

Adapted with kind permission from Gilbert, 2010.

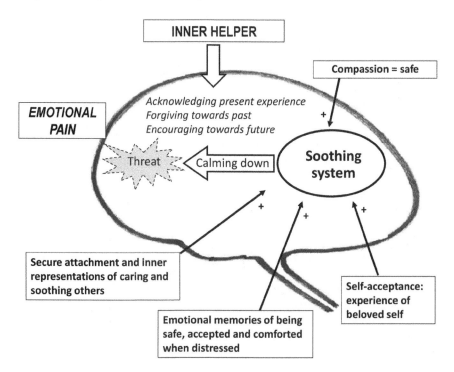

Figure 11 Threat from emotional pain and diminishing threat because of a well-developed soothing system.

Adapted with kind permission from Gilbert, 2010.

secure attachment as a child, internalised compassionate role models, have memories of being accepted and comforted when things were difficult and identify with a loved self our soothing system may be better developed. Fortunately our brain is flexible enough to develop a stronger soothing system even if we had a disadvantageous start in life. Understanding these mechanisms motivates us to practise patiently and with respect for our inner pain and the resistance we feel when we allow compassion. Think of how we would approach an abused dog living on the street. We would do it slowly and gently to gain its trust. We cannot set the pace ourselves, we can only let the dog decide when it feels ready to receive more of our kindness. This image may help us to treat the suffering parts in ourselves. We can only give more kindness to a hurt or neglected part in ourselves when this part is ready to receive it.

We have given the theme of backdraft quite a lot of space here. It depends on the participants in the group when and how much time is given to this theme. During the course of the programme we will always give some explanation at some stage; more often sooner rather than later because in most groups in our clinic we meet backdraft in the first sessions.

When we started guiding MBCL to groups of people outside a psychiatric setting, like trainers, health care professionals and others wishing to deepen their mindfulness practice, we saw similar backdraft phenomena in a less intense way. Usually the practice of mindfulness and compassion makes us more aware of inner feelings and needs that were ignored or neglected before. Some mention becoming more aware of how demanding they are for themselves and how tired they actually are. Others become aware of sorrow that has had little space so far. It may be compared with growing pain as we experienced it as a child, when our teeth started to grow. It is a healthy process that we can trust to find its course in an atmosphere of patience, understanding and compassion.

2.2.13   Calendar Exercise: 'The Threat System'

Pay attention to the moments when you notice an experience of threat. An example could be that you are walking in the park and you meet a man you don't know. Suddenly this man starts talking to you. Afterward you can reflect on this and take notes concerning the following questions:

- *Were you aware that the threat system became activated?*
- *What physical sensations did you experience? For example, 'tension' or 'my heart started racing'.*
- *What emotions and thoughts accompanied this event? For example, 'I felt unsafe and thought, what does this man want? What's up? I hope someone is around' or 'relief when it turned out he was only asking for directions.'*
- *What could a compassionate response be now, looking back? For instance, 'Good that I could help him. I don't need to judge myself that my threat system sounds the alarm. I can congratulate myself that I could stay present. By being mindful of myself and the situation, I discovered that the man was friendly.'*

Overview of Session 2: Stress Reactions and Self-Compassion

Themes

In Session 2 we discuss the instinctive stress reactions of *fight, flight and freeze* and the lesser known *tend and befriend* reaction. We show how physical and psychological threat can cause the same stress reactions. We reflect on how we can develop self-compassion and how we can use our imagination to do this. We discuss pitfalls and misunderstandings in the process of developing self-compassion, including the 'backdraft' phenomenon.

Agenda

1. Short landing exercise and round, invite participants to give an 'inner weather report' and share what they wish for themselves in this moment.
2. Guided meditation 'Compassionately Dealing With Resistance', followed by sharing experiences, first in pairs, then in the group.
3. Inquiry about formal and informal home practice done in the week after session 1.
4. Short break followed by some (standing) mindful movement exercises.
5. Theory: stress reactions and components of self-compassion; pitfalls and misunderstandings; backdraft; the use of imagery. These themes can often be braided into discussions on what comes up in exercises.
6. Guided meditation 'The Compassionate Companion', followed by sharing experiences.
7. Suggestions for home practice for the week after Session 2 (see below).
8. Ending with an introduction of the informal exercises for coping with stress or emotional pain: the self-compassion mantra and the breathing space with compassion.

Practice Suggestions for the Week After Session 2

Formal

- Practise 'The Safe Place' (2.1.7) and/or 'The Compassionate Companion' at least every other day (2.2.11).
- Practise kindness meditation to yourself at least every other day (2.1.10).
- Do the exercise 'Compassionately Dealing With Resistance' (2.2.2) with different stressful situations.
- Regularly practise a familiar mindfulness exercise (body scan, mindful movement, sitting meditation, walking) with particular awareness of the inner attitude with which you practise.

Informal

- Use the self-compassion mantra (2.2.4) as needed.
- Practise 'The Breathing Space With Kindness' (2.1.2) regularly and 'The Breathing Space With Compassion' (2.2.8) as needed when there is stress or emotional pain.
- Calendar exercise: 'The Threat System' (2.2.13).

2.3 Session 3

Inner Patterns

It is not the perfect, but the imperfect,
who have need of love.

(Oscar Wilde, 1899)

2.3.1 Exercise: 'Compassionately Dealing With Desire'

The exercise from the previous chapter 'Compassionately Dealing With Resistance' (2.2.2) is very much linked to the threat system and a way to explore our reactions to experiences and situations we rather do not want and that we tend to avoid or resist. In this session, we first invite you to explore some difficult aspects of the drive system and how we can deal with this in compassionate ways.

Start the exercise as described in the introduction in 2.1.7.

Then you are invited to reflect on an area in your life where you feel controlled by desire and attachment. It might be as regards food, cigarettes, coffee, alcohol, sex, surfing the Internet, e-mail or computer games, work, buying things, habitual social behaviour like expressing favourite opinions or criticisms . . . It may be a slight urge or a strong pattern that confirms and reinforces feelings of guilt, shame and unworthiness. Choose an area that you feel capable of working with at this moment.

Allow yourself to think of a recent situation when this desire or urge was predominant and imagine you experience this situation right now. Explore the physical situations, emotions and thoughts that are linked to this urge. Let it be your intention to pause inwardly as you feel the urge without fighting or giving in to it, even if it gets stronger and stronger.

When you pause, observe with interest the nature of desire and attachment. What does your body feel like when wanting is strong? Where do you feel these physical sensations most clearly? What do you feel in your chest, your belly, your face, your arms and legs? What do you observe in your mind? Is it tight or dull, are your thoughts racing or sluggish? What emotions are there? Notice if the sensations change whilst you observe them. 'Surf' as it were on the wave of your desire, stay intimately connected with it, however it may be, without letting yourself be dragged away or submerged by it.

Then allow a number of questions to be asked. Do not force any answers; there are no good or right answers, and if no answer comes up, that's fine too. 'What lies underneath this desire?' Is there perhaps an emotion that was overruled by the desire before? Or is there a deeper need underneath this desire? Listen with your heart to the answers. You can let this question or variations of it resonate deeper and deeper in your heart and mind. 'What is really missing?' 'What do I really need?' 'What is my deepest longing?' Let yourself be surprised by the answers that arise. When there is an awareness of a deeper longing, then you can wish for yourself that which you genuinely need—for example, 'May I experience connectedness, rest, calmness, inner peace' or another kind wish towards the desire, the emotion or deeper need you discovered or towards yourself as a vulnerable human being.

(Adapted with kind permission from guided meditations offered by Tara Brach.)

Feedback from a participant:

'Urge-surfing makes me aware of what I lack and connects me to my deeper feelings and vulnerability.'

The exercise 'Compassionately Dealing With Desire' is meant as an exploration of a field in our life where we can easily get stuck. You can do the exercise with the same or different desires at different moments. Sometimes the pause and the awareness may result in just observing the urge and not acting on it. If after a short pause you do decide to follow the urge, then that's fine too; do so slowly and mindfully. What do you feel? Is there tension or excitement, self-judgment or fear? Notice the physical sensations, thoughts and emotions with a clear and compassionate awareness when they arise. In people with addiction problems 'urge-surfing' has proved a helpful practice in the phase of abstinence. Mindfully riding the wave of the urge until it gradually subsides is a form of exposure exercise, in this case not to what is feared but to what is desired (Bowen, Chawla, & Marlatt, 2011).

2.3.2   Which Mode Is Predominant?

Two Wolves

An old American Indian teaches his grandson about life. 'A struggle is going on inside me', he says to the boy. 'It is a terrible fight between two wolves. One wolf is bad—he is anger, envy, sorrow, regret, greed, arrogance, self-pity, guilt, resentment, worthlessness, lies and false pride.

The other wolf is good—he is joy, peace, love, hope, serenity, humility, kindness, benevolence, empathy, generosity, truth, compassion and trust. Inside you the same struggle is going on—and it is the same for everyone.'

The grandson thinks about this for a while and asks his grandfather, 'Which wolf is going to win?'

The old man smiles and simply says, 'The one you feed the most.'

Mindfulness training (Mindfulness-Based Stress Reduction/Mindfulness-Based Cognitive Therapy) distinguishes two basic attitudes: the 'doing mode' and the 'being mode'. In this session we will look at the competition mode and the threat mode, which are particular forms of the doing mode, and introduce the 'compassion mode', a special form of the being mode. First of all we want to give a balanced view of the different modes, mentalities or inner patterns.

We have many inner faces that become more or less predominant, depending on the amount of 'feeding' they get. Buddhist psychology argues that we are in essence 'self-less'. What we call our 'self' is the part of us we identify with in any given moment, and it is impermanent. This corresponds with insights from evolutionary psychology (Gilbert, 2009a). As social connectedness became more important for survival and the relationships in a social group became more complex, it became very helpful to have an image of the other and to imagine how the other viewed us. Different 'social mentalities' developed, roles or patterns that were needed to give stability to a group and so increase the chances of survival. Some of these are so general that they appear as 'archetypes' (ancestral patterns or blueprints for society) in almost every culture: dominance and power, submissiveness and obedience, rivalry and social rank, giving care and receiving care, male and female role patterns. Apart from archetypical mentalities, many other patterns can be distinguished that can be more or less present in a culture or an individual, depending on how much they were 'fed'. In certain situations we behave according to such a mentality. This can be recognised by where we put our attention, by what feeds our imagination, occupies our thinking and reasoning, guides our motivation and behaviour and colours our emotions. Rigid patterns can cause a lot of problems because they limit our adaptability to new circumstances. The flexibility to adequately change between different mentalities is a sign of psychological health.

We do not want to burden you with difficult theories but to offer a language that can be helpful when describing our complex experiences. Do not let the theory distract you from the experience itself. Mindfulness practice can help you recognise patterns in the moment they are occurring, in all their idiosyncrasies. It may help to put words to them so as not to get too entangled. All elements of a pattern can be attended to in therapy. Because you are your own therapist in this training, we give the basic structure of a mental pattern in Figure 12, which is at the same time a model for self-therapy.

New-brain functions are important to forming social mentalities, but the more instinctive old-brain functions still are a driving force. The emotion regulation systems and stress reactions that were described in Sessions 1 and 2 are anchored in our old brain and can function perfectly well without the new brain. The more complex inner patterns, which are discussed in this session, arise from the interaction between the functions of the old and new brain. It is not always easy to understand the manifestation of such a pattern. We will gain more insight when we recognise the deeper layer, the old-brain component, of the pattern. From the old-brain perspective life is relatively simple: We are busy avoiding the unpleasant, grasping the pleasant or resting and feeling contented. Think of the mule that loves to graze peacefully in the meadow. The mule's boss knows it will only do

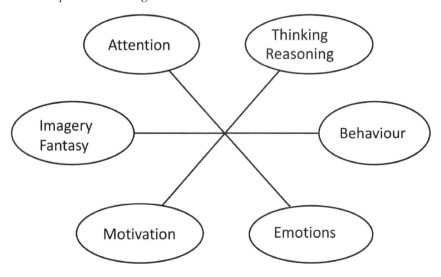

Figure 12 Structure of a mental pattern.

Adapted from Gilbert, 2010.

work for him when he beats it with a stick (threat system) or lures it with a carrot (drive system). It becomes more complicated in humans when the new brain creates stories around the instinctual motives of the old brain that keep us busy in the doing mode. In many new-brain stories, 'avoiding sticks' or 'chasing carrots' are still the main theme, albeit in disguise. Neuroscientists discovered that particular regions in the brain, called 'the default mode network', become active when the mind has nothing in particular to be engaged with (Raichle et al., 2001). When our mind is no longer focused it begins to wander. This wandering provides us with associations, linking past and future, and with a sense of self. Experienced meditators seem to be able to turn down the default mode so that their minds wander less (Brewer et al., 2011). The function of this default network is still unclear, but from an evolutionary perspective it is likely to have survival value and provide us with a kind of radar to be alert to potential threats and gains. In that case the associations may naturally gravitate towards these signals and stimulate the threat and drive systems. When mindfulness practice calms the wandering mind, we are more likely to settle into the soothing system and prepare for affiliation, kindness and care (D. J. Siegel, 2010b). When our mind wanders it most likely dwells in the trodden paths of our most familiar mental patterns.

Below, three basic mental patterns connected to the three emotion regulation systems are listed (adapted from Gilbert, 2009a, 2010; we have decided to use the more neutral term 'mode' instead of 'mind'):

- The *threat mode* is dominant when we view the world as a dangerous place full of 'sticks' we must avoid, where we have to be constantly on our guard and defend ourselves against others. Self-protection is the primary concern.

- The *competition mode* is dominant when we view the world as a place full of 'carrots' we want to have, where we want to achieve success and prove that we are better than our rivals. Here it is all about self-improvement and moving up the social rank.
- The *caring mode* is dominant when we view the world as a place to feel at home with ourselves and others, where we can be sensitive to both our own and others' needs and feel committed to each other's well-being. This mode focusses on social bonding and well-being.

We schematically present these three mentalities in Figures 13, 14 and 15. Which of them looks the most and which one the least familiar to you?

A mentality, pattern or mode can become more persistent each time it is repeated. What is a healthy adaptation and increases our well-being and our chances of survival in one context can be unhealthy and maladaptive in another. A particular mode can be predominant, not only in our relationships with others but also in dealing with ourselves. Whether we have experienced our relationships with our parents and those close to us as mainly caring and appreciative or as neglectful, abusive or hostile, this will have a significant impact on how we experience ourselves. Our learning history determines which becomes predominant, and this makes a huge difference to our feeling of well-being. If we are trapped in the threat mode we are mainly focussed on 'sticks', and we usually feel ill at ease with others—and with ourselves, because thoughts and feelings associated with ourselves also form threats. If the competition mode is predominant and we feel attracted by the 'carrots' of success, we often feel tense in the company of others as well because they may grab 'our' carrots, and we feel urged to compete and improve our position on the social ladder.

Figure 13 Threat mode.

Adapted from Gilbert, 2010.

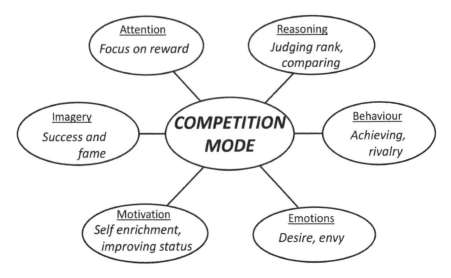

Figure 14 Competition mode.

Adapted from Gilbert, 2010.

Figure 15 Caring mode.

Adapted from Gilbert, 2010.

2.3.3 The Hunger for Self-Esteem

Somehow it is not so difficult to believe that a strong threat mode does not make us happy, but in our culture it is much more difficult to accept that a dominant competition mode also affects our well-being. The message that we lack all kinds of things comes from all directions, suggesting that we can only be happy when we buy certain products and achieve certain goals. This might be good for the economy but not for our well-being because when one desire has been satisfied the next already presents itself.

The competition mode evolved to regulate social relationships but is not always aimed at real relationships, because we also get competitive with imaginary others. We would like to live up to the demands we think others put on us; if we don't, we expect to miss out on their appreciation, which we need to feel accepted.

A way to get caught up in the competition mode is the search for self-esteem. Kristin Neff (2011) gives a scientific overview of how for a long time Western psychology was obsessed with the idea that thinking positively about ourselves (self-esteem) was important for our well-being and that this resulted in better achievements. Consequently many subsidised educational programmes for children and adults were focussed on improving their sense of self-worth. Later, researchers found that self-esteem was not the cause of better achievements but the result. Striving for self-esteem as an end in itself encouraged unnecessary social competition and resulted in a continuous comparison with others, which actually hindered achievements.

The craving for self-esteem is like an addiction: Every time the desire for self-esteem has been fulfilled, the satisfaction only lasts for a short time and we want more. This produces stress rather than happiness, and a lot of energy that is needed for improving our achievements gets spent on improving our ego. It seems that our drive system (the desire to be superior to others) and also our threat system (the fear of inferiority and social isolation) are working overtime and that we do not give ourselves the time for nurturing our soothing system.

Research (see also 1.6.1) shows that self-compassion is more important for our well-being than self-esteem (Neff, Kirkpatrick, & Rude, 2007; Neff & Vonk, 2009). When self-esteem is highly valued, it encourages narcissism, and our ego is easily threatened. We constantly worry whether we are good enough. It inhibits social connectedness because we tend to compete with others. Self-compassion on the other hand promotes a more lasting sense of self-worth that is independent from the esteem of others. It is nurtured by a sense that we are okay as we are, including our vulnerabilities. Self-compassion is accompanied by the acknowledgment that none of us is perfect and that in our imperfection we all need recognition and compassion. This understanding of our common humanity increases social connectedness. And it is significant that we more easily achieve results because of self-compassion than by chasing after self-esteem, precisely because we accept that it is okay to make mistakes. Making mistakes is part of being human, and it is how we make new discoveries. Or in the words attributed to Albert Einstein, 'Anyone who has never made a mistake has never tried anything new.'

The competition mode can be overactive in such a way that we are only preoccupied with working our way up the hierarchical ladder to be 'seen'. On the other hand, we could also be preoccupied with constantly working our way downward into submission. In both instances we seek a secure place in the group we want to belong to. For it is crucial for our survival that we are accepted by our species, and our position in the hierarchy offers security, whether that position is high or low.

2.3.4   The Inner Bully

A self-critical mentality can be developed when our threat system is frequently triggered because we fell short in others' or our own opinion and there was a threat of aggression, rejection or abandonment (Gilbert, 2009a, 2010; Gilbert & Irons, 2005). In this training we speak of 'the inner bully', but you can give it other names, such as inner critic, tormentor, cynic, tyrant, antagonist, controller, doubter, busybody or whatever name you think will help you to recognise it. The inner bully can control and poison our lives; it can create a lot of suffering. When we practise mindfulness and compassion, the inner bully is quick to comment, 'Don't you have something better to do?' or 'If you really want to do this, at least try harder'; 'Now you are distracted . . . striving . . . judging . . . again'; 'The others are doing much better than you'; 'Oh, you're hopeless.' And so on.

It is difficult to observe ourselves from the position of the nonjudging witness in formal practice, and in daily life this is even more difficult. The inner bully often raises its ugly head automatically and controls us without us being aware of it. The wider the gap between the picture we have of the person we are (actual self) and the person we think we should be (ideal self), the more our inner bully has to comment on, either by humiliating our actual self ('You're no good!') or whipping us up to our ideal self ('You must do better than this!'). Thus the inner bully fuels our threat and drive systems. Even if we are aware of this inner tormentor, how can we deal with it? We can bully back, but then we are only feeding this destructive tendency by doing more of the same. We can also 'watch' the inner critic . . . with compassion. Can we see the suffering and the needs behind it?

If we can acknowledge the inner critic as an expression of our deep longing for psychological survival, we may understand the 'good intentions' behind it—for example:

- rejecting unacceptable parts of ourselves;
- disapproving of ourselves may urge us to behave better and escape disapproval by others;
- honouring the view that punishing and shaming ourselves keeps us under control;
- preventing ourselves from making (even more) mistakes;
- keeping us on our toes and prompting us to strive for more achievements;
- protecting someone else by directing our anger at ourselves;

- staying loyal to our parents by treating ourselves in the same way they treated us;
- maintaining a familiar habit and a self-image, because it gives support and security and relieves us of the responsibility to make changes.

The reasons for maintaining an inner bully correspond with the reasons for not practising compassion, which we discussed at the beginning of Session 1 (see 2.1.1). If this kind of reasoning dominates strongly, we should not be surprised that the inner bully speaks loud and clear as we take the first steps on the path of compassion training. The self-critical mentality is mainly fed by shame and guilt, emotions that arose later in evolution in higher developed self-conscious mammals. We are born with the need to receive care from others. To increase our chances for that care we developed the capacity to constantly evaluate the image that others might have of us. Because social connectedness is crucial for our survival, we have developed a strong self-consciousness and need for others to see us in a positive light. When that is not the case, we feel unsafe and the threat system is triggered. Shame and guilt are self-conscious emotions (Tracy, Robins, & Tangney, 2007); they are the messengers that indicate that the way others see us could be disturbed and that we might be ostracised. In compassion focused therapy (Gilbert, 2010, 2014) much attention is given to these emotions. Excessive shame, guilt and self-criticism are correlated with many mental health problems such as depression, paranoid ideation and social anxiety (Kannan & Levitt, 2013; Kim, Thibodeau, & Jorgensen, 2011; Matos, Pinto-Gouieva, & Gilbert, 2013). A better understanding of these emotions can help us in the practice of self-compassion.

> Feedback from a participant:
>
> 'I have learned that I can view the inner bully with kindness, and then I notice that it is bothering me less.'

2.3.5   Shame and Shyness

Shame feels very unpleasant, but even this emotion can be a useful messenger. Just imagine a 'shameless' person. They are generally not very popular. Shame protects us against excesses and antisocial behaviour and against being excluded from the group. But when others try to shame us when there is not really a whole lot wrong with us, it can become a destructive emotion—particularly if this happens when we are young, vulnerable and dependent. Shame memories have characteristics similar to those of traumatic memories and correlate with shame and depression in later life (Matos & Pinto-Gouveia, 2010). If we have experienced many situations where others criticised us and we were shamed, we can become overly sensitive to negative attitudes of others, real or imagined. Shame and everything that evokes shame triggers our threat system. When we place high demands on ourselves it is usually caused by shameful experiences and the fear of not living up to expectations and of not being accepted. Making high demands in turn leads to increased sensitivity to shame, and this is how the vicious circle starts. The greater the distance between our actual self and our ideal self, the easier we will feel shame.

Being sensitive to others' negative attitudes towards us can manifest as a tendency to externalise and to internalise. When we externalise we easily feel humiliated and hurt by others. The shame is projected outward ('the other is bad'), we look for justification or even retribution and revenge. Our threat system primarily reacts to external signals that could indicate that others think negatively about us. Externalising happens especially when our competition mode has been well developed. We cannot bear to be dominated and humiliated, and we attack the other. When we internalise, the shame goes inside ('I am bad') and we have a negative view of ourselves. We even exaggerate and start to attack and humiliate ourselves. Our threat system reacts not only to external but also to internal signals. Any of our views, feelings, actions or physical characteristics that we only suspect might lead to being viewed negatively by others can become a threat and a target for self-criticism. Internalising especially happens if we are not very competitive. When we externalise excessively we start to bully others, and when we internalise excessively we develop an inner bully.

Shame can in turn lead to fear of shame. Erythrophobia, the fear of blushing, is an example of this. It is actually quite brave to admit that we feel shame. Brené Brown (2010, 2012) is a researcher and well-known author on this subject. She writes that where there is no room to face shame, there is no room for vulnerability. Vulnerability is not the same as weakness. Vulnerability is common humanity, and to be open about shame is to take the courage to be vulnerable and embrace our imperfections.

An emotion that is very much related to shame is shyness. Whereas shame is linked to fear of falling down the social ladder, shyness is linked to fear of moving up the ladder. Clinical psychologist Lynne Henderson (2010) developed a compassion-focused programme for people suffering from social anxiety and low confidence. She has described how we can feel shy when we meet new people, get a new job, get a sense of being observed or are being praised. This feeling comes along with unpleasant physical sensations, such as blushing and feeling weak and shaky. In essence it is a very healthy and useful emotion, linked to social sensitivity and social intelligence, wise prudence and altruism. However, especially in Western culture, where the emphasis is on individualism, self-esteem and competition, we easily interpret it as a sign of weakness. From an evolutionary perspective shyness is very important for survival in groups because social functioning is simply more efficient when a group has more followers than leaders.

2.3.6   Guilt

Guilt is a younger emotion in evolution than shame, when not only receiving care but also giving care became increasingly important. Whereas shame is mainly concerned with 'What do others think of me', guilt is linked to empathy

('What have I done to the other?') and a sense of responsibility ('How can I make amends?'). Shame is feeling 'I am bad', whereas guilt is feeling 'What I did was bad'. Guilt can help to mend social relationships and is a very useful emotion when it is embedded in a caring mentality. However, guilt can also become destructive when it repeatedly triggers the threat system. This happens when we have learned to be afraid of our mistakes, which many of us have through our upbringing or education. Then harmful behaviour towards others becomes shameful behaviour. Instead of judging our behaviour as a rectifiable mistake, we judge ourselves as being a bad person. Instead of seeing a mistake as a challenge to learn from, we see it as proof that we are not good enough and as a good reason to turn the inner bully on ourselves. If small mistakes get blown up into big ones, it becomes more likely we fail to repair the damage. In this way we give the inner bully plenty of ammunition to fire away on us.

When shame and guilt are no longer the useful messengers they were originally meant to be, they can become very destructive. When the alarm bells go off repeatedly, rubbing it in that we are not okay, life can become hell. Self-criticism can grow into self-hatred. It is not easy to erase a self-critical mentality. But what we can do is to observe it with compassion—observe the suffering from which the inner bully developed as well as the suffering it causes. Just as a self-critical mentality unintentionally developed through practice, we can develop a caring and compassionate mentality through consciously practising the compassion mode. In this way we begin to grow an inner helper.

A specific form of guilt is so-called survivor's guilt, or feeling guilty about causes that were beyond our control. A survivor of a disaster feels like a failure because others died, or an employee feels guilty because colleagues lost their job in a reorganisation despite the fact that they could have done nothing to prevent it. Survivor's guilt might be considered as a frustrated tend and befriend reaction (see 2.2.3). Paul Gilbert has been working with people who suffered badly from guilt and shame for years. One of the strategies he uses to deprogramme the brainwashing of their inner bully is to simply repeat the phrase 'It's not your fault.'

It is worthwhile to remind ourselves of this phrase not only after surviving disasters that we couldn't do anything about. Like no other species, we human beings criticise ourselves for events that are beyond our control. It is not our fault that we are a complex organism, evolved over millions of years, with a layered brain, which is far from perfect for dealing with the tangle of largely unconscious internal and external processes; that we are the result of a complex coming together of genetic and environmental influences; that our automatic reactions to stimuli are the result of endless conditionings; that we simply cannot control the reactions of and the interactions with others, who are in the same boat and who are just as complex as we are. All of this . . . *is not our fault*.

It can be very healing to frequently repeat this in the moments we want to blame ourselves for things we have no control over. At the same time it may help us to improve our power of discernment and to recognise the areas where we are responsible, where the light of mindfulness has shone and our automatic patterns and reactions become visible. We may have more freedom to replace an auto-matic reaction by a conscious response. But then how are we to deal with every-thing that is ungovernable, uncontrollable and unpredictable in life? The answer is simple—with self-compassion. It is much healthier than self-blame.

In the next session we will offer a special compassion mode exercise, although in fact all exercises and practices in this course are aimed at training us in the compassion mode, including the exercises that help us become aware of inner pat-terns, resistance and desires. These will open the door to healing old wounds by compassionately embracing the pain that is at the root of the old patterns as well as the pain that is still arising from these patterns.

2.3.7   Exercise: 'Recognising Inner Patterns'

Before you read any further we would like to invite you to complete the following exercise. To do this you can read the sentences in Table 2, 'Inner Patterns', one by one and in the column 'Recognisability', with pen or pencil, give a score between 1 and 5 (1 = 'I don't recognise this at all in my life'; 2 = 'this I recognise some-what'; 3 = 'this is reasonably recognisable for me'; 4 = 'this I recognise well'; 5 = 'this I completely recognise'). In giving a score it may be worthwhile to pay more attention to the sphere around these sentences than to the words.

After having scored the recognisability of all the sentences, we may select one sentence, namely the one that has a higher score and resonates the most (other inner patterns may be explored a next time you do this exercise). We then invite you to read this sentence again, close your eyes, allow mindful awareness and a soothing breathing rhythm and connect with a recent situation where this pat-tern was clearly predominant. Imagine the situation comes fully alive again and explore the physical sensations, emotions and thoughts that are part of it. What do you do or try to avoid, what do you say or keep inside, what do you long for, what do you resist?

You may then allow a further inner exploration by reflecting on each of the following questions regarding this inner pattern you selected. You don't need to try and get answers, but you may just see what kind of emotional, physical or mental responses arise by themselves. You may be surprised by the answers that come up; if no answer arises you may acknowledge that too. The questions are the following:

- *Can you remember when this pattern arose in your life? Is it recently or were you still a child? Is there a specific situation or period that you remember? Or are there specific persons who are somehow connected to this pattern?*
- *How has this pattern evolved in your life? How and when does it manifest itself clearly?*
- *Which of the three emotional regulation systems can most clearly be sensed here? The threat system? Or the drive system? Or the soothing system?*
- *This may be a strange question, but did you purposely develop this pattern? Or was it basically an attempt to cope with a difficult situation?*

- *Has the inner pattern **helped** you in your life? And if so, how?*
- *How many other people on this planet do you think you share this pattern with? Ten? Hundreds? Millions?*
- *To help you recognise this pattern next time it comes on stage, could you give it a playful nickname? Just see what arises. Let it be a name that evokes an inner smile.*

Table 2 'Inner Patterns'

	Recognisability
1. My close relationships will end because people are unreliable and unpredictable.	1 2 3 4 5
2. I expect that others will hurt me and take advantage of me.	1 2 3 4 5
3. I can't seem to get what I need from others (warmth, attention, understanding, protection, support).	1 2 3 4 5
4. I'm defective, bad, not okay, and don't deserve to be loved by others.	1 2 3 4 5
5. I'm alone in this world, different from others, I do not belong.	1 2 3 4 5
6. I'm boring and totally uninteresting to other people; they don't want me in their company.	1 2 3 4 5
7. I'm not capable of living my life; I need help to take care of myself and to make decisions.	1 2 3 4 5
8. A disaster might happen any moment, and I won't be able to cope.	1 2 3 4 5
9. I feel empty, confused, lost without guidance from my elders.	1 2 3 4 5
10. I'm a failure, I'm stupid, inept, and will never be successful compared to others.	1 2 3 4 5
11. I deserve whatever I can get; others need to take my wishes into account.	1 2 3 4 5
12. I'm easily frustrated, react impulsively or throw in the towel.	1 2 3 4 5
13. I adapt to what others want from me, out of fear for their anger or rejection.	1 2 3 4 5
14. I suppress my own needs and emotions in order to be of service to others.	1 2 3 4 5
15. For me everything revolves around getting recognition and appreciation from others.	1 2 3 4 5
16. I presume that whatever can go wrong will go wrong, and that my decisions will not work out.	1 2 3 4 5
17. I prefer not to show my feelings (positive or negative) to others and would rather take a more rational approach.	1 2 3 4 5
18. I'm a perfectionist, need to spend my time efficiently, and abide strictly by the rules.	1 2 3 4 5
19. I'm impatient with others and with myself, and insist that people should be punished for their mistakes.	1 2 3 4 5

(adapted from 'My schemas'; Germer, 2009)

The fact that these 19 sentences are formulated for general use may already show that we all develop inner patterns. We can consider them our enemy but we may also be compassionate towards them. Therefore, this may be a good moment to bring kindness to the (carrier of the) pattern you have explored. The inner pattern may limit you in many ways but it may also have supported you. Therefore, you may say and dwell on the next three sentences of the self-compassion mantra (2.2.4), maybe with a hand on your heart:

> *'This is an example of suffering.'*
> *'Inner patterns are a part of life; we all experience them.'*
> *'May I be kind to myself and with this inner pattern; may I compassionately name it.'*

You may end with gently repeating a kind wish to yourself or towards the inner pattern you have explored, or with just being mindful of whatever is predominant.

2.3.8   Naming Inner Patterns

Various therapists have combined mindfulness practice with schema therapy (Bennett-Goleman, 2003; Germer, 2009; Van Vreeswijk, Broersen, & Schurink, 2009). Schema therapy was developed by Young and colleagues (Young, Klosko, & Weishaar, 2003). Schemas are the patterns that were already formed when we were still quite young and that unremittingly continue into adulthood. In the previous exercise (2.3.7) you may have recognised some schemas that are particularly relevant to you. Below we give a more detailed list of old maladaptive schemas to help you recognise them. In order to become less identified with them it is important to recognise such a schema and to name it.

Recognising a schema is mindfulness. To look at a schema with friendly eyes is self-compassion. We have given the 19 inner schemas nicknames, to make it all a bit less serious. For example, at the moment you are about to explode with irritation, you could say, 'Ah, Short Fuse is here again. Good morning.' Feel free to give your own names to all these schemas or tendencies, preferably names that evoke some kindness or an inner smile!

Some of these schemas may be easier to recognise than the inner bully, or they are part of it. Notice what emotions and physical sensations you feel when the schema presents itself, and what your thoughts are and what is your tendency to do next. It may be helpful to recognise the underlying emotion regulation system(s) too. Is the schema a manifestation of an overdeveloped emotion regulation system? Or is the schema, on the other hand, an expression of an underdeveloped regulation system? Usually it is a combination of overdeveloped and underdeveloped systems, like the combination of an overdeveloped threat system and an underdeveloped soothing system in Schema 1. If one system is excessively activated this obviously is detrimental for the development of another system.

Remember that the schemas are not 'truths' or immutable characteristics of yourself but mental constructs that originated as survival strategies in difficult situations. Perhaps they came naturally at the time and helped you to survive in difficult situations, but it is debatable if this is still the case. They are contractions from a long time ago that still remain in place, and you could gradually soften and loosen them in the light of your mindfulness and the warmth of your compassion.

1. ***Abandonment/instability:*** *You expect that eventually everybody will abandon you. Other people are unreliable and unpredictable in their support and commitment. Fear, sadness and anger alternate when you feel abandoned.*
   Nickname: Everyone-Abandons-Me.

2. ***Mistrust/abuse:*** *You are convinced that others will eventually take advantage of you one way or another, or cheat or humiliate you. Your feelings are changing all the time and you are constantly vigilant.*
   Nickname: Mrs/Mr Suspicious.

3. ***Emotional deprivation:*** *You expect that your basic emotional needs, such as support, care, empathy and protection, will not be met or will insufficiently be met by others. You feel isolated and lonely.*
   Nickname: Deprived *or* Outcast.

4. ***Unworthiness/shame:*** *You see yourself as defective and bad. As soon as others get to know you better they will discover this and reject you. Feelings of unworthiness often lead to shame.*
   Nickname: Mrs/Mr Not-Good-Enough.

5. ***Social isolation/alienation:*** *You feel isolated from the rest of the world and different from other people.*
   Nickname: Loner *or* Alien.

6. ***Social undesirability:*** *You are convinced that socially you are inadequate and unattractive. You see yourself as boring, stupid and ugly.*
   Nickname: Ugly Duckling.

7. ***Dependence/incompetence:*** *You feel helpless and dependent on others. You cannot make decisions about simple daily problems and are often tense and anxious.*
   Nickname: Mrs/Mr Helpless.

8. ***Vulnerability to illness and harm:*** *You presume that any moment a disaster will befall you and your loved ones and that you won't be able do anything to protect yourself.*
   Nickname: Doom Thinker *or* Misfortune Teller.

9. ***Enmeshment/tangle/underdeveloped self:*** *You are excessively involved with and attached to one or more carers so that you can't develop your own identity.*
   Nickname: Mommy's Child *(or* Father's Pet*)*.

10. ***Failure:*** *You are convinced that you are not able to achieve to the same extent as your peers. You feel stupid and inept.*
    Nickname: Loser *or* Good-for-Nothing.

11. ***Entitlement/self-centeredness/self-aggrandisement:*** *You think you are superior to others and entitled to special treatment. You can do what you*

want without consideration for others. Your life centres around wanting to have power and control over people and situations.
Nickname: Centre-of-the-Universe.

12. **Lack of self-control/self-discipline:** *You don't have any tolerance for frustration and can't control impulses and feelings. You can't tolerate dissatisfaction and discomfort (pain, arguments, effort).*
Nickname: Mrs/Mr Intolerance *or* Short Fuse.

13. **Subjugation:** *You subject yourself to the will of others to avoid negative consequences. You suppress your own needs for fear of conflicts and punishment.*
Nickname: Adaptor *or* Self-Effacer.

14. **Self-sacrifice:** *You voluntarily sacrifice yourself for others whom you view as weaker than yourself. When you pay attention to your own needs you feel guilty and you give precedence to others' needs. Eventually you get irritated by the people you care for.*
Nickname: Helpaholic *or* Saviour-of-Humankind.

15. **Approval-seeking/recognition-seeking:** *You look for approval, appreciation and attention in an exaggerated way, to the detriment of your own development and needs.*
Nickname: Attention Freak.

16. **Negativity/pessimism:** *You always see the negative side of everything and you ignore or undervalue the positive. You worry most of the time and are on high alert.*
Nickname: Pessimist.

17. **Emotional inhibition:** *You always suppress emotions and impulses because you think that expressing them will hurt others or result in shame, punishment or distraction. You never react spontaneously, and you emphasise rationality.*
Nickname: Mrs/Mr Bottling-Up.

18. **Unrelenting standards/excessively critical:** *You believe that you are never good enough in what you do, and that you should try harder. You are highly critical towards yourself and others, perfectionist, rigid and overly efficient. This is detrimental to pleasure, relaxation and social connectedness.*
Nickname: Control Freak *or* Mrs/Mr Perfect.

19. **Punitiveness:** *You're of the opinion that people should be severely punished for their mistakes. You are aggressive, impatient and unforgiving.*
Nickname: Little Prosecutor.

Feedback from a participant:

'When I can give my reaction patterns a humorous or playful name, they recede more easily.'

2.3.9   Exercise: 'Kindness Meditation—A Benefactor'

We would like to invite you now to resume the practice of kindness meditation.

1. *The exercise may start as described in the introduction in 2.1.7. You can then silently repeat a kind wish for yourself, something that arises spontaneously. If you don't know what you can wish for yourself, you can use the traditional phrases: 'May I feel safe and protected'; 'May I be healthy to the extent that is possible'; 'May I be happy'; 'May I be at peace or live with ease'. . . gently repeated. . . if you like, flowing on the rhythm of the breath.*
2. *We are now going to expand the field of kindness. First of all we invite you to bring to mind somebody you unreservedly consider an example. Somebody, who embodies warmth, stability, wisdom, kindness and an open, nonjudging attention. Perhaps you know someone like that in your family, or it could be a teacher you may have had. Or somebody who inspires you and whom you deeply respect for their generous heart, a benefactor. It can be an inspirator from a religious tradition, a historical or contemporary person who changed the world for the better.*
3. *If you find it helpful you can visualise this person and imagine them in front of you. If joy or gladness arises you can be aware of this and then reflect as follows: 'Just as I want to be happy and live in harmony, may you too be happy and live in harmony.' Then continue repeating silently a kind wish for this person who inspires you and let it flow through you, on the rhythm of the breath or independently from the breath. What would you like to wish for this person? Perhaps a wish that arises spontaneously and is appropriate for this embodiment of compassion and wisdom, or else you can use one of the traditional phrases: 'May you be free from danger'; 'May you be free from illness'; 'May you be happy'; 'May you live with ease and experience good fortune in your life.'*

2.3.10   Calendar Exercise: 'The Drive System'

Pay attention to the moments when the drive system clearly manifests itself. For example when you are at work and you notice that you do your utmost best to do the job as perfectly as possible. Later on you can reflect and make notes with regard to the following questions:

- *Were you aware that the drive system got activated?*
- *What physical sensations were there? For example, 'leaning forward' or 'somewhat contracted.'*
- *What emotions and thoughts accompanied this event? For example, 'I felt aroused and noticed I was forcing myself. I thought, I need to get it finished by tonight!'*
- *What is present now? And what could be a compassionate response, while reflecting? For example, 'I realise I am trying to prove myself and looking for recognition from my colleagues. It would be more caring to listen to my body and allow myself some rest. Good enough is okay too.'*

Overview of Session 3: Inner patterns

Themes

In Session 3 we deal with the three fundamental patterns that are rooted in the three emotion regulation systems: the threat mode, the competition mode and the caring mode. We discuss the 'inner bully' and self-conscious emotions like shame, shyness and guilt. We investigate which inner patterns dominate us most and how we can recognise, name and compassionately deal with them.

Agenda

1. 'Inner Weather' check-in and 'What Do You Wish for Yourself?'
2. Guided meditation 'Compassionately Dealing With Desire', followed by sharing experiences, first in pairs, then in the group.
3. Inquiry about formal and informal home practice done in the week after Session 2.
4. Short break and reflecting on the possible *advantages* of the inner bully, individually or in small groups. Follow with a few mindful movement exercises and/or self-massage.
5. What came up as possible advantages of the inner bully? What are disadvantages?
6. Theory: three modes (threat, competition and caring mode), self-conscious emotions (shame, shyness, guilt).
7. Filling in the form 'Recognising Inner Patterns', followed by a guided meditation on a chosen dominant pattern. Sharing about the exercise.
8. Suggestions for home practice for the week after Session 3 (see below).
9. Close with a short kindness meditation for oneself and a benefactor.

Practice Suggestions for the Week After Session 3

Formal

- Regularly practise 'The Safe Place' (2.1.7) and/or 'The Compassionate Companion' (2.2.11).
- Regularly practise kindness meditation and extend with a benefactor (2.3.9).
- Practise 'Compassionately Dealing With Desire' (see 2.3.1) with different desires.
- Read the paragraphs on inner patterns (2.3.7 and 2.3.8) and explore other dominant patterns by doing the exercise 'Recognising Inner Patterns'.

Informal

- Practise the breathing spaces with kindness (2.1.2) and compassion (2.2.8) or the self-compassion mantra (2.2.4) as much as you need.
- Calendar exercise: 'The Drive System' (2.3.10).

2.4 Session 4

The Compassion Mode

Last night as I was sleeping,
I dreamt—marvelous error! —
that I had a beehive
here inside my heart.
And the golden bees
were making white combs
and sweet honey
from my old failures.
                    (Antonio Machado, 1983;
                    excerpt from 'Last Night as
                    I Was Sleeping' translated
                              by Robert Bly)

2.4.1 The Circle of Compassion

In Session 4 we present the *circle of compassion* as shown in Figure 16, which is central in the work of Paul Gilbert (2009a, 2010) and offers a helpful model of the compassionate mind or compassion mode.

The two circles represent the two psychologies of compassion (Gilbert & Choden, 2013). The first psychology is based on the sensitivity to suffering of oneself and others, requiring a number of key attributes for engagement, shown in the inner circle. The second psychology is based on the commitment to do something about it and alleviate this suffering. This requires a number of skills, which we can train, shown in the outer circle. The more we train these skills, the more the attributes of compassion begin to flourish. The circles 'float' in an atmosphere of warmth, calmness, kindness and playfulness, the feeling tone that is characteristic of the soothing system. It is after all quite difficult to practise compassion while the threat or drive systems are active.

Attributes

We will list the attributes of the inner circle; they are interdependent, and one needs the support of the others:

- *Care for well-being*: The first attribute and starting point for compassion is always motivation—the deep desire and commitment to alleviate suffering and promote well-being and happiness, for ourselves and others.

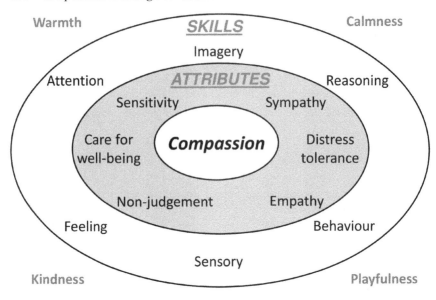

Figure 16 The circle of compassion.

Reproduced and adapted with kind permission from *The Compassionate Mind* by Paul Gilbert, London: Robinson, 2009.

- *Sensitivity*: Compassion needs the capacity to be sensitive to pain and suffering, including their subtle gradations, and a careful 'reading' of the needs and wants of others and ourselves.
- *Sympathy* or 'feeling with': Once we are in contact with suffering we require the ability to be emotionally connected. Sympathy is the capacity to emotionally resonate with the ups and downs in each other.
- *Distress tolerance*: When suffering touches us and moves us, we need to be able to tolerate the distress it may cause and hold the pain and our reactions into mindful awareness. Being caring and sensitive to suffering asks for resilience to stress; otherwise we get overwhelmed and swept away. It also calls for patience and perseverance.
- *Empathy* or 'feeling into': When we are able to engage, sympathise and tolerate the suffering, we then are able to develop insight into what goes on in our inner worlds. Empathy is the capacity to step in others' shoes and mentalise and understand the interaction between motives, thoughts, feelings and behaviour. We can also empathise with our selves, with our different ways of being, for example with our angry self or our sad self. Whereas sympathy is predominantly a feeling quality, empathy involves both feelings and cognition. Many think empathy and compassion are quite the same, but empathy without the motivation to care for well-being may also burden us. For instance when we can no longer watch the news without getting nauseous, or in the case of 'empathy fatigue' (see 1.6.4) in self-sacrificing caregivers.

Empathy may also be employed to manipulate others for our own gain. For example, a criminal can use his capacity for empathy to force parents to give him money by threatening their kidnapped child. Here, of course, there is no compassion because the motivation to care for others' well-being is lacking. Compassion gives a wholesome twist to empathy because it also includes the other qualities of the inner circle. The opposite of empathy is projection: We don't see the other as they are, but we only see the image that we have constructed ourselves and project onto them.

- *Nonjudgment*: the capacity to meet others and ourselves with an *open mind*, unprejudiced, and respectful of the complexities of life deepens compassion with wisdom. This does not mean that we should not have preferences—our preference could be determined by the care for well-being. But we make wiser decisions if we first look at a situation from a nonjudging perspective, including our own likes and dislikes, so that we are not unconsciously carried away by them. Being nonjudgmental also means that we are open to outcome and not attached to results. A light, playful touch and humour can help to open the mind when it is contracted with heaviness and overinvolvement.

Skills

As regards developing skills, we focus on the aspects of our functioning in the outer circle:

- *Compassionate attention.* This not only involves the kind, nonjudging attitude of mindfulness (the *how*) but also the field of mindfulness we choose (the *what*) and the intention with which we do so (the *why*; Shapiro & Carlson, 2009). We direct our attention in a compassionate way when we 'treat' ourselves, a benefactor, a good friend or loved one, other people or animals to a kind and compassionate wish. Compassion expresses itself in the kindness towards ourselves when we recognise that we have wandered and in the patience with which we bring our attention back to a compassionate focus. We refocus our attention with kindness (soothing system), not out of greed (drive system) or fear or compulsion (threat system).
- *Compassionate imagery.* This refers to consciously calling on our imagination to evoke images that have a wholesome effect (Lee, 2005), like 'The Safe Place', 'The Compassionate Companion' and other kindness and compassion meditations in this programme.
- *Compassionate sensation.* When we focus on compassion we can also explore the experience of our body and senses. It is a very powerful way to help the experience of compassion sink in. Remember that our memory for the positive needs more practice than our memory for the negative (Hanson, 2013). It is therefore particularly important to savour pleasant sensory experiences, which gradually will rewire our brain and increase our sensitivity to the positive.
- *Compassionate thinking and reasoning.* Cognitive therapy (Beck, Rush, Shaw, & Emery, 1979), dialectical behaviour therapy (Linehan, 1993) and

mentalisation-based therapy (Fonagy & Target, 2006) have developed interventions for healthier thinking and reasoning. Mindfulness-based approaches (Hayes, Follette, & Linehan, 2004; Segal, Williams, & Teasdale, 2013) accept that we cannot directly control our thoughts but we can 'observe' our thinking mind and notice the effect of our thoughts on our well-being. We can distinguish between helpful and unhelpful thoughts. We can choose to what extent we connect with certain thoughts, from what perspective we look at a situation, and let compassionate values motivate our choice. Table 3 shows the differences in reasoning from the perspective of an inner helper and that of the inner bully. We often reason on automatic pilot. Earlier we saw how our old brain can hijack our new brain, even during elaborate deliberations or discussions. Are we reasoning from the threat system, the drive system or the soothing system? You might also go over the schema exercise 'Recognising Inner Patterns' (2.3.8) again. Are there perhaps old maladaptive schemas from which your reasoning unconsciously arises?

- *Compassionate feeling.* Apart from being mindful of the whole spectrum of emotions, pleasant and unpleasant, from moment to moment, we can also consciously practise generating a warm emotional tone and creating the right

Table 3 Self-Correction Versus Self-Attack.

Self-correction from the inner helper	*Self-attack from the inner bully*
• Desire for improvement	• Need for condemnation and punishment
• Growth and development	• Mistakes and shortcomings
• Focussed on the future ('what is possible?')	• Focussed on the past ('what went wrong?')
• Kind, supportive, encouraging attitude	• Harsh, impatient, humiliating attitude
• Builds on what is already good ('glass is half full')	• Attacks what is wrong ('glass is half empty')
• Focusses on specific aspects of self ('this behaviour has that effect')	• All of self is targeted ('you're a bad person')
• Hope for success	• Threat of failure
• Being concerned for others	• Avoiding others
When things have gone wrong . . .	*When things have gone wrong . . .*
• Feeling guilty out of involvement with other(s)	• Feeling ashamed and fearful of rejection by other(s)
• Remorse, concern for the consequences for the other	• Collapse, ruminating about the consequences for self
• Understanding for self and other; taking responsibility for making amends and repair of relationship	• Aggression towards self (and/or other), avoiding (or irritable towards) other, self-punishment and resisting contact
Metaphor: kind, patient teacher who helps and supports a child who is having difficulty learning.	*Metaphor*: critical, impatient teacher who humiliates and punishes a child who is having difficulty learning.

(adapted from Gilbert, 2009a and 2010).

conditions for feeling positive emotions (Fredrickson, Cohn, Coffey, Pek, & Finkel, 2008). If we consciously choose a kind, caring and nonselfish attitude, it will be easier to feel the corresponding emotions of warmth and connectedness in our heart area than when we are caught up in fight, flight, freeze (threat system) or the pursuit of short-lived pleasures (drive system). When we are mindful of these compassionate emotions and acknowledge and savour them, we train our capacity to be sensitive to compassionate feelings. We also become aware of the direction in which compassion flows: from others to self, from self to others, and from one part of the self to another part. Compassion does not exclude unpleasant emotions; when faced with injustice, for example, it can be very compassionate to turn anger into assertiveness.

- *Compassionate behaviour (speaking and acting).* What we say and what we do, or don't say and don't do, have consequences that can be wholesome or harmful. Religions often emphasise what we should *not* do, which is essentially don't harm (don't lie, steal, kill, harm sexually, drug or numb ourselves). Compassionate behaviour, however, is not the same as being a 'goody-two-shoes' or behaving in a subservient manner in order to be accepted or rewarded. It is behaviour that alleviates suffering and promotes well-being and growth. This means having the courage to live a valuable life, letting what we say and do be in the service of the values that touch our heart. In that case nonharming comes from an inner motivation. We will revisit this in Sessions 6 and 7.

2.4.2   Exercise: 'The Compassion Mode'

As the inner bully gets activated more easily, calling on a caring attitude towards ourselves becomes more difficult if it has not been developed well because of lack of training. We can do an exercise to encourage this development by imagining that we embody compassion in all its qualities. In doing so, we feed the inner helper instead of the inner bully. Here is an exercise to help you imagine yourself in the compassion mode:

The exercise may start as described in the introduction in 2.1.7. Allow the breath to calm and excessive tension to flow away . . . First of all connect with your safe place . . . Then let your compassionate companion appear . . . Now imagine how you yourself become a person who embodies compassion, just like your compassionate companion . . . Be aware of all the qualities you would show . . .

Imagine . . . that you are calm and wise through experience . . . that you are sensitive to everybody's needs and wants . . . that you have the strength and the courage to acknowledge and tolerate pain and suffering . . . that your deepest wish is to alleviate suffering and to enable living happily and meaningfully . . . that you show tender and kind feelings . . . that you are nonjudging and forgiving . . . that you are playful and open-hearted . . . Let your eyes, mouth, face express compassion . . . let your physical posture express compassion . . . let the feelings of compassion flow through your heart and your entire body . . . allow compassion to extend beyond the boundaries of your body and radiate to the world around you . . . And mindfully explore what it does to your body. . . to your face, heart, belly. . .

Focus on your wish to express compassion and all its attributes . . . in your thoughts, feelings, words, actions . . . to whomever needs it . . . don't exclude anyone . . . not yourself either . . .

Now look at yourself as you sit here . . . with the pain you may be carrying . . . with all the memories . . . of small pain . . . of big pain . . . your deepest pain . . . of difficult situations, alone or involving others . . . in recent times, in the past . . . And also with all your insecurities about the future . . . your fears, your hopes, your desires and needs . . . with all your possibilities . . . known and unknown . . . your wishes and dreams for yourself and the world around you . . . your deepest and most heartfelt wish . . . And while you embody compassion, focus your compassion on the part of yourself that is now showing itself to you . . . and now . . . and now . . . Let compassion flow from your heart to the suffering part of yourself . . . and continue as long as you feel it benefits you . . . Let compassionate wishes flow towards yourself on the rhythm of the breath, like you practised in the kindness meditations. 'May I . . . experience rest . . . be safe . . . feel accepted . . .'

Of course you can also practice embodying compassion while you let it flow to another person you bring to mind . . . to whomever you wish . . . no need to exclude anyone . . . As in the kindness meditation, you can let compassionate wishes flow to the other.

In this way we can alternate between letting it flow towards ourselves and towards the other . . . Continue as long as you feel it is beneficial.

As with all exercises, respect your limits, don't force anything and be kind. This in itself is already an expression of the compassion mode. You can practise the exercise in parts, you can divide the parts over several sessions, you can return to it in formal and informal practice, in moments in your daily life. Remember that training in compassion involves progressing in mindfulness as well. Be aware of what sensations are there from moment to moment. Sometimes you may experience the practice as purifying and enjoyable, other times as heavy and difficult. In both cases you can note this with a nonjudging attitude. It does not mean that you are doing better in one than in the other. Your experience is your experience. Insight and compassion can grow in pleasant as well as in unpleasant experiences, and with continuing practice you will make new discoveries.

And remember, you don't need to achieve anything! Compassion can be given unconditionally. When the practice is accompanied by forceful striving for results, you are trapped in the pitfall of the drive system and in the doing mode. Realise that the compassion mode is a particular form of the being mode. You hold the suffering in the clear light of your awareness; you are present for it with an open attentiveness, not with a cold, sterile, distant gaze but with the kind, warm glow of compassion. This involves not only seeing with the physical eye but more importantly seeing with the heart as well, a way of 'being' with presence of mind and caring connectedness. The two wings of mindfulness and heartfulness keep you balanced, so that you can make wiser choices as regards what needs 'doing' or not.

2.4.3 Just Fooling Ourselves?

Yesterday I was clever, so I wanted to change the world.
Today I am wise, so I am changing myself.

(Rumi)

An untrained soothing system can only become stronger through repeated practice. We do this through mindfulness exercises where we apply our imagination in a wholesome way. We already have become familiar with exercises like 'The Safe Place' and 'The Compassionate Companion', and in this session 'The Compassion Mode' is introduced. In all these practices we use our imagination to activate the soothing system and cultivate the qualities of compassion, and mindfully notice what happens when we do so. Some may wonder whether this is just a way of fooling ourselves with unreal images.

Our motivation to do these exercises can easily be undermined by the thought that mental images are not real. You may think your imagination is definitely not capable of changing anything. Do realise, however, that our imagination is active a lot of the time and mostly on automatic pilot or in default mode (see 2.3.2). By believing your imagination is meaningless or powerless, you are already giving a lot of power to your imagination; however not for it to work for you but against you. For you *imagine* that your imagination cannot change anything. And this is not supported by clinical practice and research (Brewin et al., 2009; Gilbert & Irons, 2004, 2005; Gordon, 2008; Lee, 2005; Longe et al., 2010; Singer, 2006; Rockliff, Gilbert, McEwan, Lightman, & Glover, 2008; Rossman, 2000). Our imagining mind does influence our brain, our body and our well-being to a great extent, for better or for worse. And how our brain works in turn affects our mind. With the aid of imagery exercises we train certain neural networks, and as they get stronger, it becomes more probable that certain patterns begin to arise spontaneously, even when we don't really 'unlearn' the old patterns (Brewin, 2006). In the beginning we have to make a lot of effort; later on it becomes easier.

We are not asking you to believe in miracles but only to act 'as if' there is a tiny miracle, namely the miracle of an inner state, a way of being that has a beneficial influence. There is little to lose. You only need to imagine a desired reality without being concerned whether that image will ever become reality. Don't let the drive system ensnare you by chasing after results. You cannot fail at this, for you only do 'as if'. Don't let yourself be caught by the threat system, either, by interpreting the image as dangerous. What is not familiar is not per definition dangerous, as long as you remember that it is only a visualisation. Don't let yourself be carried away by what you want or by what you fear, but investigate mindfully what these particular exercises evoke in you. When you pretend a wholesome inner state is present, chances are that something will change in the desired direction, even if that state is not (yet) real. If you pretend that this wholesome inner state is not possible, you are also doing 'as if', but then in the direction that works against you. More than likely you will continue to feel dissatisfied.

A Dutch research team found that brief exercises in imagining a 'best possible self' (just 5 minutes daily for 2 weeks) improved levels of optimism, which correlate well with psychological and physical well-being (Meevissen, Peters, & Alberts, 2011). No matter what the reality of the image, the effects are real. Pretending has beneficial effects in itself, psychologically and physiologically. These are real, in the sense that they are experiential as well as measurable. Even though you might notice very little, your new brain is already forming new circuits that favourably influence the emotional systems in your old brain. We don't want to suggest that imagery can cure serious physical ailments and replace other treatments. However, we do ask you to investigate, like a scientist, your inner processes and see if these exercises have a soothing impact on your emotional pain and suffering.

Perhaps you could be open to the following 'pretend' experiment, seeing it as a mindfulness exercise to explore what imagery does to you.

Exercise: 'Doing as If'

What do you notice when you pretend to be angry for a while, say for 5 minutes? Make an angry face and adopt an angry posture. Embody the anger as best as possible. You really need to try hard. How does that feel in your facial muscles, and what do you notice in your body, your mind?

Then pretend that you are joyful for 5 minutes. Bring a smile to your face and adopt a posture that expresses joy. Embody the joyfulness as best as you can. Totally surrender to it. What do you notice now in your face, your body, your mind? Then reflect on this exercise and write down what you noticed.

Feedback from a participant:

'When I bring a little smile to my lips while I am cycling, I often automatically begin to feel less harshness, more lightness and eventually more calmness.'

2.4.4   Exercise: 'Kindness Meditation—A Good Friend'

It can be helpful to expand the field of kindness further, training the mind in friendliness and compassion. At this stage in the training many participants are still content to radiate kindness only to themselves. Other participants, on the other hand, prefer to extend the circle of compassion and bring other people into the field of kindness. What follows are a few elaborations you can practise on your own.

1.   *The exercise may start as described in the introduction in 2.1.7. Then start repeating silently a kind or gentle wish for yourself—a wish that arises*

spontaneously as something you would really like to wish for yourself. If you don't quite know what you can wish for yourself, you could use one of the four traditional phrases: 'May I be free from fear or danger', 'May I be as healthy as possible'; 'May I be happy'; 'May I be at peace or live with ease.' Repeat the wish gently, the whole sentence or just a keyword, if you like, synchronised to the rhythm of the breath.

2. Then you can expand the field of kindness further and bring a good friend to mind, and in a playful way wish something kind or gentle for them. It may be someone who means a lot to you and brings a smile to your face—someone you trust, someone dear to you and who opens your heart. It can be somebody in your family: one of your parents, a brother or sister, a grandparent, a good friend, perhaps one of your children, a beloved colleague . . .

3. If you find it helpful you can visualise the person you chose and imagine them in front of you. Then you can reflect as follows: 'Just as I want to be happy and live in harmony, may you too be happy and live in harmony.' What would you like to wish for this person? Perhaps there is a wish that spontaneously arises, or otherwise one of the four traditional phrases: 'May you be free from danger'; 'May you be free from illness'; 'May you be happy'; 'May you live with ease.'

4. You can stick to one person, but if someone else comes to mind who is also dear to you, you can include them as well and radiate a kind wish to them. You could just stay with one wish, but if after a while another wish arises spontaneously that is slightly more suitable, continue with the new wish. And if you find it tiring to keep repeating the complete phrase, you can also shorten the wish to one or two words and silently repeat them, on the movements of the breath, or independently from the breath. Or you could stop the phrases for a while and just sit, the mind filled with kindness and gentleness. When you notice that the mind becomes restless again, you can resume repeating the wish or meaningful keywords quietly.

5. If you find it difficult to find an appropriate person, you can also think of a pet, your dog, cat or horse, and let the kindness flow to this beloved animal. Whether the wishes are received by and have an effect on the chosen person or animal may remain an open question. In any case the kind intention of wishing well is beneficial in itself. For at that moment there is a state of mind that is free from resentment and aversion, a mind that is open and generous. You don't need to judge yourself when you notice that you have wandered or that the attention has been drawn away from the wish by a thought, sound or something else. You can note it with kindness as 'thinking', 'hearing' or 'feeling' and with the same patient attitude let this wish flow through you again in the way that connects most in this moment.

2.4.5   Exercise: 'Kindness Meditation—A Neutral Person'

1. If you like you can return to yourself as the centre of the kind wish . . . and then bring someone to mind towards whom you have a fairly neutral attitude.

Somebody you may know only superficially, a passer-by in your life, whom you don't strongly like or dislike. Perhaps someone who lives on the same street as you but with whom you have little contact. Or somebody who works in the supermarket where you go shopping from time to time. Or a colleague you sometimes meet at work. See if there is such a person in your life.

2. *If you find it helpful you can visualise the chosen person and imagine them in front of you, and reflect: 'Just as I want to be happy and live in harmony, may you too experience happiness and harmony.' Then repeat silently a wish that arises spontaneously or one of the four traditional phrases, letting them flow naturally, coinciding with the movements of the breath or independently from the breath.*

3. *After some training you could also invite a few other neutral people, and animals if you like, into your practice and treat them to a kind wish. As you repeat these wishes you develop or cultivate four healing qualities. There is a wholesome intention in the form of benevolence. There is also attention or mindfulness to bring the wish back, again and again, in a gentle, calm way when the mind has wandered. The positive emotions that are being developed bring relaxation, light-heartedness and joy, and the deep connectedness with ourselves and others brings us peace and safeness. People and animals that were previously neutral take up a bigger space in your heart after regular practice. So continue this practice with neutral beings for another few minutes.*

Feedback from a participant:

'I notice that the practice gets more into my system, and that this ripples out to my surroundings. As long as I can continue to practise . . . '

2.4.6   Exercise: 'Kindness for the Body'

1. *You are invited to lie down and make yourself as comfortable as possible; you are allowed to be kind and compassionate towards yourself. And there are all sorts of reasons for this. For example, it is not easy to live in a hectic society like ours. An awful lot is demanded of our brain when it is barely equipped to process all stimuli. Besides, it is really an art to deal with all those basic instinctive emotions and impulses that can arise in us. And to live with a body that can show all kinds of discomforts and limitations we usually did not choose consciously . . . There are plenty of reasons to be compassionate to yourself.*

2. *Just like all beings want to be happy and free, you can wish this for yourself as well . . . and be kind to yourself, and to your own body. For kindness and compassion can also be directed at our body. Perhaps you can let a soft smile be on your lips . . . and let the breath find a soothing rhythm, allowing your body to soften and surrender to the gravity and the ground that carries you.*

3. *Now make contact with a part of your body you can easily look at with sat-isfaction, because you find it a good-looking part, or because it is a faithful companion through life that so far has never let you down . . . look at it with friendly eyes and connect with a wish, for example, 'May you be healthy', 'May you be soft or beautiful' or 'May you be relaxed.' Choose a suitable wish. The content of the wish does not need to be realistic, but it can express something of kindness towards this part of the body. You can also direct such wishes to other parts of your body with which you have a good relationship.*

4. *Then connect with a part of your body that is neutral for you, because you barely feel or see it or because it doesn't let you feel pain or pleasure very often . . . This part, too, you can approach with a kind wish, for example, 'May you be accepted and belong.' You can attend in the same way to other parts of the body you have a neutral relationship with.*

5. *Next bring a part of your body to mind that you consider difficult to deal with. Perhaps because you usually view it as ugly, perhaps because it often is painful and rather vulnerable, perhaps because it lets you down now, or did so in the past, by not functioning well. Continue by gently repeating a kind or compassionate wish to this less loved part of your body on the rhythm of the breath or independently from the breath. You can direct these compassionate wishes to other parts as well that you have a difficult relationship with.*

6. *If you notice that there is resistance or sadness, you can acknowledge this and label it and continue again once there is more space, or go back to a part of your body that is less challenging if you wish. Eventually you may place your whole body as it were under a shower of warm, kind wishes: 'May you be in peace'. . . 'be healthy'. . . 'be energetic and joyful'. . . 'be in harmony with your surroundings.' Use wishes that connect well.*

7. *There are several healing components in this simple exercise. It has a compo-nent of giving or open-heartedness, wishing something for yourself. Another aspect is whether you can receive it, allow and appreciate it. Sometimes the first aspect is more evident, sometimes the second. But both components are hidden and overlap in this exercise, which has been practised for centuries. Evidently practising this meditation for a few minutes as a regular training is conducive to concentration and for the soothing system. It adds to a greater tenderness and tolerance for ourselves and those around us. So continue for a while to lightly repeat the wish and let it flow through you, on the rhythm of the breath or independently from the breath . . . as long as you like.*

2.4.7 Movement Exercises With Kindness

We deal with this issue relatively briefly here but wish to emphasise that move-ment exercises are an important and integral part of a Mindfulness-Based Com-passionate Living training, just as they are in a basic mindfulness course. We often do short mindful movement exercises before starting a guided meditation exercise, or when the energy level is low, or whenever there is a need to reconnect with the body and revitalise it.

Mindful movement exercises as we already know them from Mindfulness-Based Stress Reduction and Mindfulness-Based Cognitive Therapy are a valuable way of learning to take care of our body and mind. We generally make use of these exercises, which are derived from Hatha Yoga, and do not describe them here because they can be found in the basic manuals (Kabat-Zinn, 1991; Segal et al, 2013). We emphasise more explicitly, however, that movement exercises can also be a gateway to the cultivation of an inner attitude of kindness and compassion. We gratefully integrated the subtle adaptations for mindful movement from the Breathworks programme (Burch, 2008; Burch & Penman, 2013). This mindfulness-based programme was developed particularly for people with chronic pain and physical restrictions. These adaptations also are very helpful in awakening tenderness and kindness for the body for those who are physically healthy.

Another possibility is to introduce gentle Qigong or Tai Chi movements if the teacher feels competent to do so. These have been demonstrated to contribute significantly to physical and psychological well-being (for a review of controlled studies, see Jahnke, Larkey, Rogers, Etnier, & Lin, 2010). We also often include simple movement exercises derived from Dru Yoga, also known as 'the yoga of the heart' (Barrington, Goswami, & Jones, 2005). A controlled study of the efficacy of this form of yoga amongst university employees showed that participants who attended a yoga session at least once a week for 6 weeks (they also received a 35-minute CD to practise with at home as they saw fit) considerably improved in mental well-being, contentment and self-confidence in stressful situations (Hartfiel, Havenhand, Khalsa, Clarke, & Krayer, 2011). A number of movement exercises can be downloaded from www.routledge.com/9781138022157

2.4.8   Exercise: 'Walking With Kindness'

1. *You can also develop kindness while you walk or go for a stroll. Choose a place where you have a stretch to walk to and fro or in a round. First of all be aware of the standing posture. Make sure that you are standing comfortably, feet hip width apart, the knees soft at the back, not locked. The body relaxed upright, arms alongside the body or the hands folded in front of the belly or behind the back. The head is up straight. The eyes are open and the gaze is about 3 to 4 metres ahead of you on the floor or on the ground, but there is no need to be focussed on anything in particular.*

2. *You can be mindful of the standing posture. Pay particular attention to your mind state as you are standing like this. Whatever is there, it's okay . . . Then start walking slowly and calmly. Allow the body to find a soothing walking rhythm by itself, a rhythm that makes you feel at ease . . . After walking for a few minutes, resume a standing posture . . . Then ask yourself the following question, 'Could I offer myself in this moment a kind wish? What would I wholeheartedly grant myself?' Observe what answers arise. Perhaps kindness, trust, courage, calmness or space . . . If there is no clear wish then you could use one the four traditional phrases: 'May I feel safe'; 'May I feel healthy'; 'May I be happy'; 'May I live with ease.'*

3. *Then again start walking in a soothing rhythm. Just as you can let the wish correspond to the movements of the breath in the sitting posture, now you can let it flow with the movements of your walking body. So as you move your left foot you can synchronise the wish, for example, 'May I be happy.' And next let the same wish flow with the placing of the right foot, and so on. In this way you repeat, step by step, a wish that you feel is appropriate. Or you can place one word of the wish on each step: 'May' (right foot) 'I . . .' (left foot) 'be . . .' (right) 'safe . . .' (left). Or you let a key word of the phrase coincide with every step: 'Ease . . .' (right) 'ease . . .' (left) 'ease . . .' (right) 'ease . . .' (left). If you feel it is too complicated to let your chosen wish coincide with the movements of the feet, you can quietly repeat it independently from the steps.*

4. *Sometimes you feel closely connected to the feelings involved in the wish; then you can decide to repeat the wish less frequently. When the connection disappears again you can softly resume the wish or the word. Here, too, keep it simple by sticking to one wish, and you don't need to continue looking for a new wish. But when another wish arises spontaneously that is more appropriate, you can continue to use that.*

5. *Whichever way you feel, it is fine. It can feel peaceful, or touching, irritating, sad or boring. Acknowledge it as it is; you don't need to feel anything specific. There is something valuable in the compassionate intention, and through regular practice, this will establish itself more and more inwardly. You can continue to repeat the wish quietly and let it coincide with the moving feet and body.*

6. *If you walk to and fro in a room, you can also let the wish flow with the turning movements at the end of every stretch, being mindful of standing, and then start a new stretch, continuing to repeat the wish and, if you want, letting it coincide with the movements of the feet.*

7. *You can freely practise walking with kindness at different speeds. You can also practise it when you are walking at a normal pace, in the woods, or in a shopping street . . . You may also vary with the person you direct the kind wish to: Apart from yourself, it can be a person who is dear to you, or someone who is just passing by. Whoever crosses your path can be a person to silently offer a kind wish. In this way a walk in stressful surroundings can become more joyful. It can be a playful way to practise kindness to neutral persons. Try it out and observe how it affects you.*

Feedback from a participant:

'From time to time "secretly" wishing myself and others something kind when I walk down the street is fun and can make me joyful, even on a day when I feel bad.'

2.4.9   Calendar Exercise: 'The Inner Bully'

Notice the moments when the inner bully is clearly there. An example could be that you get a compliment from a colleague about something you did well according to them, and immediately the inner bully reacts. Afterward you can reflect on it and make notes as regards to the following questions:

- *Were you aware that the inner bully was triggered?*
- *What physical sensations were there? For example, 'blushing', 'I held my breath' or 'physical tension'.*
- *What emotions and thoughts accompanied this event? For example, 'I felt uncomfortable and thought, he cannot be serious. He is only mentioning it to compensate for something I messed up.'*
- *What is present for you now? And what could be a compassionate response? For example, 'I think it is difficult for me to receive and allow compliments. Great that I recognised the inner bully. That is worthy of a compliment! If I wish for myself to be happy, perhaps I may also be able to receive a compliment from someone else.'*

Overview of Session 4: The Compassion Mode

Themes

In Session 4 we give an overview of the attributes and skills of compassion, using the model 'The Circle of Compassion'. We explore how we can learn to embody kindness and compassion and how basic mindfulness exercises can be deepened with these qualities. We explore how 'doing as if' can have real effects and support the cultivation of an inner helper.

Agenda

1. 'Inner Weather' check in and 'What Do You Wish for Yourself?'
2. Guided meditation 'The Compassion Mode' and sharing about the exercise first in pairs, then in the group.
3. Inquiry about formal and informal home practice done in the week after Session 3.
4. Short break followed by mindful movement and/or self-massage.
5. Walking with kindness, offering kind wishes to oneself, a good friend and a neutral person. Sharing about the exercise.
6. Theory: the circle of compassion, attributes and skills,'doing as if'.
7. Suggestions for home practice for the week after Session 4 (see below).
8. Ending with 'Kindness for the Body'.

Practice Suggestions for the Week After Session 4

Formal

- Regularly connect with a safe place and/or a compassionate companion.
- Regularly practise 'The Compassion Mode' (2.4.2).
- Regularly practise kindness meditation and extend to a good friend (2.4.4) and a neutral person (2.4.5).
- Try the exercise 'Doing as If' (2.4.3).
- Vary this week and the following weeks with 'Kindness for the Body' (2.4.6), 'Movement Exercises With Kindness' (2.4.7) and 'Walking With Kindness' (2.4.8).

Informal

- Practise the breathing spaces with kindness (2.1.2) and compassion (2.2.8) or the self-compassion mantra (2.2.4) as much as you need.
- Calendar exercise: 'The Inner Bully' (2.4.9).

2.5 Session 5

Self and Others

I'm nobody! Who are you?
Are you nobody, too?
Then there's a pair of us—don't tell!
They'd banish us, you know.
How dreary to be somebody!

How public, like a frog
To tell your name the livelong day
To an admiring bog!

(Emily Dickinson, 1891)

2.5.1 Compassion Practice: Self-Transcendent and Relational Aspects

Even when we practise mindfulness and compassion while we are alone, we are still dealing with relationships. We not only look at the content of our mind but also at how we relate to that content, to those thoughts or feelings as mental or emotional phenomena. We look at how we feel, physically and emotionally, at how we judge that and at the tendencies that arise. Do we feel attraction or aversion, a loving connection or angry resistance? We develop a sense of self through our experience of others from a very young age. If we had not met any others, there probably would not be a self either. Daniel Siegel (2010b) has described how we use our new brain to constantly take mental pictures of ourselves and of others. We might call them me-pictures and you-pictures, and also us-pictures and them-pictures. During the course of our life we create a whole album of such pictures. Just like photographs are representations of the world but not the factual world itself, these mental images are not facts either but impermanent constructs of the mind. They may temporarily offer us shelter on our way through life, but when they become our prison it feels extremely liberating when we realise they are just the creations of our imaginative mind.

Through our capacity for imagery, language and communication, the mental images of ourselves and others and the relationships between them have become numerous and complex. Even though we usually think of ourselves as one 'self', we are made up of many 'selves', parts of ourselves that relate to each other and to others, and with which we temporarily identify. From which 'self' do we look at which other 'self'? Do we look *from* a critical self, an indifferent self, a loving self? Do we look *at* an inadequate self, a boring self, a successful self? The quality of the relationship changes with the part we look *from* and the part that is looked *at*. And our emotions and thoughts are floating along in this process and feel pleasant or unpleasant, depending on the emotion regulation systems and mental patterns involved. In mindfulness practice we learn to look from an 'aware' self, from the perspective of the 'neutral observer', even though we can easily create another concept of 'self' from that as well.

Perhaps this view evokes feelings of confusion and threat. Who are we then, really? Only awareness, only bare mindfulness, which itself is invisible? Are we like a lamp that never sees itself but only sees what comes into its beam of light? This is an understandable reaction when we strongly identify with our psychological self, our 'ego', which we believe we have to defend at all costs, in the same way we would protect our body against physical threat. But actually this view only wants to liberate us from the illusion that our ego is a fixed entity and from the irrational fear that we are in grave danger when we 'lose' it. The ego is without substance, unlike our body. We don't 'have' an ego like we have a body. We 'construct' an ego, and it is impermanent, just like other mental constructs. It is a useful tool as long as we can use it skilfully, but it becomes an obstacle if we hold on to it too tightly. Letting it go can indeed help us survive. The following story might illustrate this.

The Castaway

A castaway fights for his life in rough seas. He grabs the first bit of driftwood that he finds. He considers himself fortunate; the driftwood helps him to keep his head above water and to catch his breath. When the sea calms down, he sees a large barrel floating by. He immediately lets go of the driftwood, swims to the barrel and can lift most of his body onto it. Only his legs are still in the water. He has forgotten about the driftwood and considers himself fortunate; now he can dry off and he is less cold. After a long time he spots an empty lifeboat that must have become dislodged from the ship before it sank. Without deliberation, he lets go of the barrel and swims in the direction of the lifeboat. He already has completely forgotten about the barrel when, exhausted, he seizes the boat and climbs on board. He considers himself fortunate; the oars are even in the boat as well as a small parcel of emergency provisions. He eats and drinks and his strength returns. He starts to row in the direction where he suspects he will find land. After a long time his exertions are rewarded; he spots dry land! He pulls the boat that saved him onto a beach, abandons it and starts walking in the direction of a village he sees in the distance. He deeply longs for human contact and has already forgotten about the boat . . .

The piece of driftwood, the barrel and the boat are metaphors for the various forms our ego can take: useful for the time being, perhaps even lifesaving, but obsolete as soon as another situation presents itself. It can then be lifesaving to let it go. The support has served its purpose and is left behind for another one. The function remains the same—it remains a tool that helps us survive—but the content changes. Ultimately we don't survive by grasping onto one particular 'self'; we survive because of our ability to adapt to new situations and let go of redundant self-constructs. The mind does not like to be unemployed, however, and when we do not give it a task it switches to default mode (see 2.3.2). Identifying with its own constructs is a favourite pastime of the mind, enabled by our new brain; it is something we can't help, and it can be useful for our survival. However, as we saw earlier, our new brain can also work *against* us. It is important not to 'overidentify' and to 'dis-identify' when needed. If because of our learning history the threat and competitive modes become dominant, we easily develop a fixed image of ourselves and of others, which we find hard to let go of. Being stuck in old schemas means there is no flexibility to loosen our identifications; we continue to overidentify. We are *fused* with mental content, as it is called in Acceptance and Commitment Therapy (Hayes, Strohsal, & Wilson, 1999). Mindfulness helps us to be more flexible around identifications and *defuse*. We learn to witness the *process* of identification and learn to recognise whether it has beneficial or harmful consequences in a particular situation. This gets easier as our mind gets calmer. When our threat or drive systems are activated, there is restricted view and little flexibility; we cling to mental images in the same way as we would to a piece of driftwood. Our perspective can widen in the relaxation of the soothing system, and we can allow old images to dissolve and new ones to emerge. We can follow the process without clinging or pushing away.

Other people, too, are part of our mind. We 'see' the others as mental representations and they, too, show themselves in various guises, attractive and less attractive. The nature of the relationship with a mental other depends on *which part of ourselves* we look *from*, and *which part of the other* we look *at*. Do we look from uncontrived mindfulness, from the compassion mode, or from a piece of driftwood, a barrel or a lifeboat? Are we looking from a certain mentality or an old schema? Is our threat, drive or soothing system dominant? In addition, do we see in the other only their piece of driftwood, their barrel or lifeboat? Do we see a certain mentality or an old schema in which the other person is stuck? Or do we also see an imperfect human being, like us, who wishes happiness and freedom from suffering with potential to change? Do we look at a projection of the image we have of the other or do we look with empathy and compassion?

The quality of the relationship between the part of ourselves that is looking and the part of the other we are looking at determines the emotions we feel. As already mentioned, from an evolutionary point of view emotions are messengers that help us survive. They let us know whether we are on the right track to survival. In the course of evolution, social connection has become increasingly important for survival, and many of our memories concern relationships with others in the external world as well as the mental others in our internal world. If there is a lot of conflict and disconnectedness in a relationship, we feel unpleasant emotions; if there is a harmonious connection we feel pleasant emotions. The relationship between (parts of) ourselves and (parts of) others in our mind can be a source of pain as well as joy, just like the relationships we have with real people. If the relationship with another in our inner world mainly evokes painful emotions, it is unlikely that the relationship with this person will be harmonious in real life.

As we become less controlled by our threat and drive systems and our maladaptive patterns and can rest in our soothing system, our learning ability increases and we become more flexible in how much we are attached to our self-image and the image of the other. We also become more sensitive to the relationship between (parts of) ourselves and (parts of) the other. We reach across the boundaries of our self-image and the image of the other from the compassion mode, and we begin to see our common humanity. The accompanying emotions are the messengers that let us know that we are on the road of social connection. In compassion practice we look at our emotional pain, which indicates a nonharmonious connection. We watch with mindfulness, from a nonjudging awareness as well as with warm connectedness, from the wish to alleviate the pain. Compassion practice is self-transcending and relational. Martin Buber (1937) wrote in his famous book *I and Thou* 'All real living is meeting.' It is not the content of 'self' and 'other' that is important but the relationship between self and other. It concerns connection and healing of that which has become separate. The next exercise can contribute to feeling wholeness and connection between the various parts of ourselves.

2.5.2   Exercise: 'A Compassionate Letter'

Mind creates the abyss,
the heart crosses it.
(Sri Nisargadatta, from *I Am That*, Acorn Press, 2012)

In this exercise, adapted from Paul Gilbert (2009a), you are invited to write a letter to yourself whilst experiencing a difficulty in your life (either recent or from long ago). Choose a situation that involves emotional pain, a feeling of shame or inadequacy or a tendency to self-criticism. You write the letter from the compassion mode. If right now it feels difficult to connect with the compassion mode, you could do the exercise from the previous session first (see 2.4.2).

Imagine how you embody compassion and how you grow in wisdom and loving-kindness. From the compassion mode, you know from your own experience how difficult life can be, and you look at the suffering part of yourself from a deep caring, a profound wish to offer understanding, tenderness, comfort, strength and support. From this connectedness you take pen and paper and you write a letter to your suffering self. The 'I' in the letter is the perspective of your compassionate self. The 'you' in the letter is your suffering self that you can call by your own name. Let the words be as they arise. When you notice that you are in doubt about how compassionate you are—'Am I doing this right? I can't seem to put a lot of feeling into it'—then just be mindful of it and remember that it is an exercise. There is no right or wrong here; all that matters is your intention to be kind to yourself. You can practise this exercise as often as you like, and gradually you will become more familiar with the perspective of the compassion mode.

After you have written the letter we suggest that you read it with attention and curiosity and ask yourself whether the letter really expresses compassion. Therefore also switch to your suffering self who receives the letter. Are the words well chosen? Is the tone warm, kind, patient and playful? Or did perhaps criticism and judgment sneak in here and there; subtle insinuations that you should have known better, patronising advice, wagging fingers? If so, congratulate yourself; that's the way to learn. Just recognising the inner bully or critic in its various guises is valuable, as is learning to discern what might be a compassionate alternative. You can also ask your 'compassionate companion' to read along with you for support. Don't hesitate to change your letter. Is there anything you want to add that really wants to be said? What is the core message to your suffering self?

Also practise reading the letter with compassion, out loud (when alone) or in silence (when with others). Again, switch back and forth to the listener (your suffering self) and the reader (your compassionate self). Is the opening okay? How are you treating your suffering self? Does your tone of voice correspond to what you want to convey? Is there warmth and kindness? Is the pace calm and patient? Do you pause? How is your breathing? How is your physical posture, your facial expression, your gaze? Do they express kindness and concern? Is there a smile on your lips? Do the words emanate from your heart, and are they true? Do you feel what you want to express? Is your attitude a genuine, authentic expression of your compassionate self? And can your suffering self really receive the message?

Issues to be aware of when practising the compassionate letter:

- Acknowledge the pain of your suffering self, respect the complexity and the details of what you are aware of (recognition, sensitivity)—for example, 'I see your anger and frustration . . . in your eyes, your mouth, your shoulders, your hands . . . I notice you have trouble swallowing . . . your tight fists . . . the tension in your posture. . . .'
- Show acceptance and understanding of the circumstances for why it feels like this (nonjudgmental, empathetic): '. . . and that is understandable considering the disappointment you felt, when you heard that . . .'
- Why your suffering self thinks like this: '. . . and these dark thoughts are part of it. I can imagine you experience the event as threatening . . . For it has happened to you before that . . . and it reminds you of . . .'
- And why your suffering self behaves like this: 'I recognise that you need a warm, safe place and that you prefer to stay in bed in the morning . . . have cancelled that appointment . . . never opened those letters . . . there is so much going on for you already and you need some rest . . .'
- Show that you really feel connected with your suffering self (sympathy) and that you are not turning away from the pain (distress tolerance): 'I feel how awful about . . . you must feel . . . I want you to know I'm there for you . . . you're not alone . . .'

- And that you are committed to alleviating the suffering and want to look for resources for support and strength (care for well-being): 'Do you remember last time you did yourself a big favour by . . . taking a warm bath . . . giving (person) a call . . . visiting (person, place) . . . going for a walk . . . watching that film . . . listening to that music? Do you remember how those words touched you . . .? I sincerely wish that you are now going to do what you really need . . . Perhaps you need . . . Perhaps you could . . .You may try . . . even though it is difficult . . . We'll find out if it helps . . .'

If you find it difficult to sense a connection with yourself as a compassionate being, you can also write the letter from the perspective of your compassionate companion. When you read the letter out loud you can pretend that you play the role of your compassionate companion in your posture and facial expression, in the tone and warmth of your voice. And remember that acting is a powerful method to get your new-brain functions to work *for* you, as long as you play the correct role.

It might be tempting to rush through this exercise. Perhaps it feels unfamiliar and intimidating, or strange, silly or childish. Yet we invite you to just do the exercise, several times. It can be a powerful practice for becoming more familiar with the compassion mode and to become aware of your automatic self-critical tendencies. This exercise is not only about the words and reasoning with compassion, but it trains all the other skills as well. Observe and train your voice, your facial expression and physical posture when reading the letter out loud and feel the emotional tone while expressing compassion.

In the beginning it may be worthwhile to write your suffering self an actual letter, about various difficult situations (current or a long time ago). Afterward you can also do the exercise in your mind.

Variations:

- You can write a letter to your inner bully or to yourself in one of your dominant patterns, for example in the schema of unworthiness, isolation or being highly demanding: 'Dear Not-Good-Enough . . .', 'Dear Outcast . . .' or 'Dear Centre-of-the-Universe . . .' Humour can help when the atmosphere is heavy. Compassion can be light and playful.
- If you are used to keeping a journal you could also introduce the format of the compassionate letter here and practice writing from the compassion mode.
- Informal practice: continue the practice of looking at yourself from the compassionate mode during your daily activities, in quiet moments and in stressful moments. Remember that it concerns mindfulness practice; the field of awareness you choose is 'yourself as a compassionate being', with all physical sensations, feelings, thoughts, actions and reactions that present themselves, pleasant or unpleasant.
- As an extended exercise you may write a compassionate letter to another person, somebody who is dear to you and you feel worried about or somebody with whom you have a troublesome relationship. You write the letter from

the compassion mode (or if you wish, from the perspective of your compassionate companion) to the other as a fellow human being. There is no need to actually send the letter. It is first of all an exercise in connectedness with yourself and between yourself and the other in you. When you need more self-compassion because emotional pain arises, you can lead the exercise back to yourself.

Earlier we mentioned that allowing compassion can cause backdraft for those who have not received sufficient tenderness, love and care or for whom these experiences were abruptly and unpredictably cut short (see 2.2.12). One person may find the giving aspect of self-compassion challenging, another may have that experience with the receiving aspect. Allowing tenderness can evoke feelings of pain, lack, fear, rage and grief. Here, too, practise mindfulness: Feel the emotions, feel them in your body, notice the images, the reactions, your inclination to fight or to run . . . and be present, respecting the limits of what is bearable for you.

We cannot gauge the progress we make in compassion training by the extent to which we feel positive emotions. We can get very frustrated by this mistaken view when no positive emotions arise, and that in turn can cause us to blame ourselves, to lose heart and quit. Progress on the path of compassion shows itself in *the willingness to feel painful emotions* (Germer, 2009). Western psychology increasingly acknowledges that the avoidance of painful emotions plays a central part in many mental health problems (Hayes et al., 1999; Kashdan, Barrios, Forsyth, & Steger, 2006), whether it is mood swings, anxiety and panic, impulsivity, addictions or eating disorders. Whatever external form your suffering takes, compassion training evolves from this central principle: from *avoiding* to *feeling* what is painful here and now.

Feedback from a participant:

'While I was writing the compassionate letter I realised how much love I lacked in my life. Now is the time to start relating to myself and others with love and respect.'

2.5.3   Practising Kindness for Others

In the first session we started with exercises in kindness meditation aimed at ourselves, and then we gradually extended them to include others: a benefactor, loved ones, family and friends and neutral people. In this session we broaden the practice further to include people with whom we have an uneasy relationship. We can even include people we consider our enemies, and then groups, nations and eventually all living beings. This is done in a way comparable to the traditional Buddhist practice of loving-kindness or *metta* (Salzberg, 1995).

This practice is not about having to make progress through all these levels with, as a final test, a performance of unconditional kindness for *all* living beings. It is about choosing the pace and the way of practising that we feel comfortable with. We also don't need to magically try and bring about results in those we include in the practice. What is important, however, is the intention to mindfully develop our capacity for loving connectedness with others. We cannot be sure that the relationship with the person we bring into our practice will actually change. But the place where change *is* possible is inside us and in how we relate to the other within ourselves. This *may* affect that particular relationship favourably; in any case, it can affect many other relationships, including the one with ourselves. Furthermore, we can expand these exercises to include people who live far away or those who have died. Mother Teresa said, 'One of the biggest human limitations is that we often interpret the concept of "family" so narrowly.'

The least complicated start for kindness meditation towards others, and therefore a suitable one, is aiming the loving wishes to a *benefactor.* This is someone who has our best interests at heart (or had, if the person has passed away), who supports us with wisdom and kindness, causes us to smile and fills us with tender feelings. If it is difficult to visualise such a person, you can start with a beloved pet or an innocent child.

Complications may arise when we include a *family member* or *friend* in the practice. 'Difficult', in the sense of unpleasant, emotions can easily surface. If a family member is vulnerable we can become anxious that they might be unsafe when we wish 'May you feel safe.' If we wish happiness and well-being for a friend, and we think that he has a better job or a more loving partner than us, we might feel jealous. If the person concerned is less fortunate than we are, arrogance or *Schadenfreude* can arise. When such emotions distract us, we can mindfully acknowledge them and return to the loving wishes for the other. When we notice that we are constantly preoccupied with emotions that stay in the foreground, then this is a good opportunity to practise more self-compassion and to direct the kind wishes towards ourselves. 'May I be free from jealousy, pride, arrogance . . .' Difficult emotions are a sign that there is insufficient connectedness in the relationship with the person in question. Then what matters first is to connect with ourselves and to acknowledge and name these emotions, and to *feel* them mindfully as long as they are present.

When a *neutral* person is introduced we expand the exercise to people we are less closely connected with, such as acquaintances and people we barely know or people that 'just' come to mind. Perhaps boredom, lack of interest or sleepiness may arise. Here again there is the choice between 'noting and returning' *or* switching to self-compassion—for example, 'May I be clear and alert'—and reminding ourselves of our intention.

Whereas sending wishes of good will to neutral people is a practice in 'breadth' (every person on the planet is suitable), we begin to practise in 'depth' when we direct our wishes to a *person we experience as difficult, obstructive or hostile.* This is a person with whom our personal connectedness is broken or disturbed. It is common to feel resistance when practising with the difficult person. Thoughts may arise like 'I don't want her to be happy because she bullied me', or 'He deserves his suffering, he should have listened to me.' Keeping awake is usually not the problem here because unpleasant emotions show themselves very easily. Out of compassion with ourselves, it is better not to start with a person with whom the relationship is very complex and challenging. We can always gradually increase the level of difficulty as we feel more space for this practice. When we do this practice we do not condone someone's unskilful behaviour. As the saying goes, 'Hate the sin, not the sinner.' Can we be aware of the person behind the harmful behaviour as well as our personal reaction (pain, rage, grief) and what impact it has on us? Just as we are more than our reactions, that person is more than their actions. Just like us they are not perfect and make mistakes; just like us they want to be happy and free from suffering. To acknowledge this common humanity, it can sometimes be helpful to formulate a wish in the we-form.

In the practice of loving-kindness to *groups* we can visualise all people we have included in the practice so far in a group around us and direct our wishes towards them all. We can expand the wishes 'horizontally' to other groups, nations, continents and eventually *all living beings.* Here, too, we may find it challenging to 'stay present', and we can easily get distracted or unconsciously drift off in thought or boredom. When we notice this happening we can mindfully bring the attention back. We may also feel overwhelmed by the emotions that arise when we get a sense of the immense suffering of everyone affected by wars or natural disasters. Again, self-compassion is vital if we are to feel compassion for all those other people. Only from being connected with ourselves can we make the right decisions about what we can do about all this suffering.

2.5.4   Exercise: 'Kindness Meditation—A Difficult Person or Inner Difficulty'

1. *The exercise may start as described in the introduction in 2.1.7, followed by repeating quietly a kind wish to yourself, a benefactor, one or more good friends or neutral persons—a spontaneous wish or one of the four traditional wishes for safeness, good health, happiness or peace.*
2. *Bring someone to mind you feel ill at ease with and whom you find it unpleasant to relate. Choose the one you feel you can practice with right now; it does not have to be your biggest enemy. You can choose someone who has hurt or bullied you, or a neighbour who makes too much noise, or a colleague who tries to outdo you . . .*
3. *You can visualise this person in front of you, on a distance that feels safe for you. You may then look at this person and see his or her face and eyes. Realise that this person is trying to find a way in life, just like you and other people, makes mistakes or does stupid things at times, like imperfect human beings do, and . . . wishes to be happy. Reflect in the following way: 'Just as I want to live in peace and freedom, may you, too, live in peace and freedom.' Then begin to silently repeat a kind or wholesome wish to this person, on the*

rhythm of the breath or independently from the breath. The exercise is not to condone disrespectful or destructive behaviour but simply to allow a kind attitude towards an imperfect human being.

4. *Initially all kinds of emotions may arise, just as when on opening the cover of a sewage tank unpleasant smells waft out. If old suppressed pain is unleashed, there is nothing wrong with you. It may be the release of hidden anger, disgust, shame, remorse, disappointment or grief. Name these emotions compassionately and then return temporarily to a kind wish for yourself, for example, 'May I feel safe' or 'May I feel inner spaciousness.' When you feel room, you can return to the 'difficult person', possibly via the route of one or more people who are dear to you. A wish in the 'May we . . . ' form may sometimes be more connecting: 'May we feel free from suffering . . . ' or 'May we live in peace . . . '*

5. *There is no need to force kindness. If you feel a lot of resistance you can also stop the exercise for now and return to wishing something kind for yourself, or bring to mind a person who is less difficult. If you cannot easily find a 'difficult person', as an alternative you could also visualise an inner bully or another difficult part of yourself: an addiction you are struggling with, an emotional vulnerability such as depression or anxiety, an unwanted habit or tendency, excessive harshness towards yourself or others . . . and let the wish meet the need of this inner difficulty. You can softly soothe this tendency or vulnerability by repeating a tender, kind wish, as if rocking a small baby or stroking a little kitten. Use a wish that speaks to you, for instance 'May I accept myself as I am'; 'May I be kind to myself'; 'May I take good care of myself.' Let the wish coincide with the movements of the breath or repeat it independently from the breath. In this way you gradually learn to be with yourself as your best friend.*

Feedback from a participant:

'It was good to focus on the demon of depression and look at it with kindness. Particularly the phrase "May I accept myself as I am" was helpful.'

If a lot of resistance arises when we practise compassion for a difficult person, it might be better to return to someone towards whom we find it easier to adopt a kind attitude, or to return to the practice of self-compassion. We agree with Germer (2009) that in the beginning our compassion practice for others comes down to 95% self-compassion, because it is natural that painful emotions come up. We can't simply ignore these emotions; we can only repair the broken connection—first of all with ourselves—by allowing them in, feeling them and letting them be until they subside by themselves. We might even think, 'I want to forgive and forget . . . it's all in the past . . .' but this could be an effort to avoid our emotions and obstruct the connection with ourselves and the other. We cannot rush forgiveness. Real forgiveness is only possible when we make room in ourselves for the emotional pain and accept that it is there.

Practising compassion for others is at the same time practising compassion for ourselves, and the opposite is also true. If this does not go hand in hand, 'compassion fatigue' can develop (Figley, 2002). In fact, this term is confusing because compassion itself does not cause fatigue; there are even different brain regions involved (Klimecki, Leiberg, Ricard, & Singer, 2013; see 1.6.4). As suggested by Matthieu Ricard (2010), it can better be called 'empathy fatigue' because it arises not as a result of too much compassion but from a lack of it. Empathy fatigue happens when we have become exhausted by being too involved in the pain of others and don't get around to giving compassion to ourselves. This is prevalent amongst professional caregivers and other people with a lot of care duties.

Perhaps it would be easier for you
if you could remember people
back as children
for whom and for whom
once a mother lay awake
a father proud as a peacock
took them for a walk
whose little finger
got caught in the door
and who cried over a grazed knee
and that once
they sat in the first class
a pencil far too big
in their little fist
            (Trinus Riemersma, 1973)

I (Erik) have this poem by the Dutch-Frisian poet Trinus Riemersma on a poster up on the wall in my office. Patients sometimes ask me if that poem helps me to deal better with difficult clients like them (so their 'inner bully' is talking). I usually answer something like 'This poem is there for everyone who reads it.' Also for them, to see the challenging people in their lives with different eyes, like their inadequate psychiatrist (my 'inner bully' is talking). It can be extremely helpful to imagine the people we have difficulty with as the innocent children they once were.

In compassion practice it is common for resistance to arise because we are so busy preserving our ego. Our threat system gets triggered as soon as we feel threatened in our ego through our own pain or that of others. An ego-threat is mistakenly interpreted by the brain as a physical threat to our survival. An effective way of alleviating the suffering arising from ego-attachment is the meditation we have called 'Compassionate Breathing'. It may seem that this practice works against the ego. Yet, surprisingly enough, resistance increasingly dissolves as the ego is transcended.

2.5.5   Exercise: 'Compassionate Breathing'

You can develop the compassion mode further through a form of meditation that is called *tonglen* in the Tibetan Buddhist tradition. This practice has been taught by—amongst others—Pema Chödrön (2001, 2003), a female American Buddhist teacher, and it is also recommended by a number of Western psychotherapists (Germer, 2009; Gordon, 2008). *Tonglen* could also be called 'compassionate breathing'. It means literally 'giving-and-taking'; actually the sequence is '*len-tong*': 'taking-giving'. In this practice you visualise breathing in suffering ('taking') and transforming it into something wholesome that you breathe out ('giving'). This might feel contradictory because normally we want to get rid of our pain and let ease in. Yet for centuries practitioners of *tonglen* have acknowledged its wholesome effects. We introduce this form of meditation, just like the other forms in this course, as a suggestion for practice. Use it when it suits you. Some people feel it is confusing to introduce this method alongside the kindness meditations and prefer to limit their practice to these. That is fine. Others, on the contrary, see it as an accessible and supporting method that they can integrate into their practice. The 'Compassionate Breathing' exercise can help us feel physically and emotionally more closely connected to the pain as well as to the stream of compassion because it does not make use of words. As with all exercises, practise with mindfulness and discover what works for you.

You can begin by sitting in a relaxed way and let your mind be like a crystal-clear mirror reflecting whatever presents itself just as it is. Give yourself time to find a calm breathing rhythm . . . You can imagine the breath flowing through the entire body and how all pores open up on the in-breath and out-breath . . . Every breath is a cycle of receiving and giving between the inner world and the world around; every breath shares in the complexity of life . . . Then you can start focussing on an area of actual pain or suffering in yourself. This can be a physical or emotional pain; choose a form of suffering that is manageable for you.

You are then invited to be sensitive and open to the quality of the pain as you are breathing it in. How does the pain feel? Is it sticky, heavy or coarse; dull or sharp; hot or cold? What is the emotional tone? Does the pain feel like gloominess, fear, despair? What do you imagine the pain would look like if you could see it? You can imagine the pain as, for instance, a dark, heavy substance or as black smoke that you inhale from the area in your body where the pain is located . . . You inhale the pain deep into your inner being and you imagine how this undergoes a healing transformation in your heart on the changeover from the in-breath to the out-breath . . . Then you visualise how you breathe out an opposite quality as a result of this transformation, for example a white or golden light, or a stream of healing energy . . . On each inhalation you breathe in the pain as dark smoke, and on each exhalation you breathe out healing golden light . . . If the pain feels hot on the inhalation, breathe out coolness. If the pain feels hard and cold on the inhalation, breathe out softness and warmth. If you breathe in fogginess, breathe out clarity. In the beginning you can consciously take deeper breaths; then let a calm and natural rhythm develop by itself.

Please do not force yourself with this practice. Allow a playful and light-hearted attitude with an inner smile. If it helps you may also use the arms and hands, bringing them to your heart while breathing in and bringing them out from your body while breathing out.

In this way you can also take on the pain of others with each in-breath and give back an opposite wholesome quality with each out-breath. You can visualise how you inhale the pain of the other as a sticky, dark substance or black smoke, then let the pain undergo a wholesome transformation in your heart, and from your deepest being you exhale a stream of white or golden light or healing energy to the other . . . As the practice progresses you could keep to the same sequence of bringing in others as in the kindness meditation: a benefactor, one or more loved ones, neutral people, people with whom you have a difficult relationship, groups and finally all living beings. You can also let the wishes go out to the others on an exhalation, as in the kindness meditation. Find out what works for you.

'Compassionate Breathing' is a powerful exercise for experiencing our common humanity at a deep level; the pain we feel is not only our pain, it can just as easily be the pain of others. For when we feel pain, there are countless others feeling similar pain in this moment. *Tonglen* practice helps us to let go of the identification with pain; we simply breathe in pain—whether it is our own pain or that of others is less important. We breathe out light and love, and it is not so relevant whether that is to ourselves or to others. What matters is that we learn not to reject what is most difficult and not to keep for ourselves what is best. Completely against the logic of the ego, we take in the most difficult and we give away the best! In this way the practice of compassionate breathing can help us to share with each other what is most painful and most precious, in deep connectedness.

2.5.6   Calendar Exercise: 'The Inner Helper'

Notice the moments when an inner helper manifests itself. An example could be that you kindly correct yourself after having made a mistake. Afterward you can reflect on and take notes about the following questions:

- *Were you aware of the arising and/or the presence of the inner helper?*
- *What physical sensations were there during this experience? For example, 'At first some tension, later on more relaxation.'*
- *What mood(s) and thoughts accompanied this experience? For example, 'I felt calm, full of confidence. I thought "Never mind. I made a mistake but we all make mistakes. I can learn from my mistakes so as not to repeat them." '*

- *What is going through your mind now, afterward, while writing or reflecting, and what could be a compassionate response? For example, 'Whereas before I would feel angry and misunderstood, now I can feel more tenderness and understanding.'*

Overview of Session 5: Self and Others

Themes

In Session 5 we reflect on the self-transcending and relational qualities of compassion and address the phenomena of overidentification and dis-identification. We introduce writing a compassionate letter and discuss how we can practise kindness and compassion for different parts in ourselves and different categories of others.

Agenda

1. Reminder that the course is halfway through. 'Inner Weather' check in and 'What Do You Wish for Yourself?'
2. Compassionate letter writing, introduced with guided meditation: Via imagining a safe place and a compassionate companion, participants are invited to embody compassion. A letter is written to a suffering part of oneself from the compassionate mode. Sharing about the exercise.
3. Inquiry about formal and informal home practice done in the week after Session 4.
4. Short break followed by some mindful movement exercises.
5. Guided kindness meditation to a 'difficult' person or an inner difficulty. Introduction to 'Compassionate Breathing'. Sharing experiences first in pairs, then in the group.
6. Theory: identification processes, kindness and compassion practice for 'difficult' parts in oneself and various kinds of persons, including the 'difficult' ones.
7. Suggestions for home practice for the week after Session 5 (see below).
8. Ending with a breathing space with kindness.

Practice Suggestions for the Week After Session 5

Formal

- Regularly connect with a safe place and/or compassionate companion and /or the compassion mode.
- Spend time writing and elaborating one or more versions of 'A Compassionate Letter' (see 2.5.2).
- Extend the kindness meditation to a difficult person or inner difficulty (2.5.4).

- Practise the exercise 'Compassionate Breathing' (2.5.5) a few times or more if this form of practice suits you as an alternative to the kindness meditation.

Informal

- Practise the breathing spaces with kindness (2.1.2) and compassion (2.2.8) or the self-compassion mantra (2.2.4) as much as you need.
- Calendar exercise: 'The Inner Helper' (2.5.6).

2.6 Session 6
Happiness for All

Before you know kindness as the deepest thing inside,
you must know sorrow as the other deepest thing.
You must wake up with sorrow.
You must speak to it 'til your voice
catches the thread of all sorrows
and you see the size of the cloth.

Then it is only kindness that makes sense anymore,
only kindness that ties your shoes
and sends you out into the day to mail letters and
purchase bread,
only kindness that raises its head
from the crowd of the world to say
it is I you have been looking for,
and then goes with you everywhere
like a shadow or a friend.

(Excerpt from 'Kindness' from *Words Under the Words: Selected Poems* by Naomi Shihab Nye, copyright © 1995. Reprinted with kind permission of Far Corner Books, Portland, Oregon.)

2.6.1 Common Humanity

Practising compassion for others can make us more conscious of our *common humanity*, our shared human condition. The Fourteenth Dalai Lama has based his religion of kindness on the principle that all beings want to be happy and free from suffering (T. Gyatso, 1984).

To reinforce the sense of connectedness with others it is helpful to formulate wishes that go as follows: 'May *you and I . . .*' or 'May *we . . .*' or 'May *all . . . and I . . .* be happy, free from suffering' and so on—especially when we practise with people with whom we are in conflict. It can be extremely healing if we also feel, in spite of the problems with them, that we are the same on a deeper level. When we touch our own pain and grief, it 'catches the thread of all sorrows', all pain, and we know we are connected with the 'size of the cloth', as the Palestinian-American poet Naomi Shihab Nye puts it so beautifully. Nobody chose their parents and the country of their birth, the more or less fortunate circumstances of their youth, the uncontrollable windfalls and setbacks, the traumas life had in store for them. The people with whom we have a difficult relationship are responsible for their harmful words and actions, just as we are for ours. But they, just like us, did not have a choice in the design of the complex systems that evolved over millions of years in our brains and bodies. They also struggle with the functions of the old and new brain, with stress reactions designed for survival of the body that are deployed for the survival of the ego.

We usually hurt one another from a survival instinct; we feel our ego is threatened and we want to escape from whom or what endangers us. We cut the connection with each other and we withdraw behind real and imaginary walls that, so we think, guarantee our safety. We retreat to our cities, villages, houses and offices, in stories about ourselves and the world, in our ideologies, religions and philosophies. We fight or flee or freeze in our frames of reference and overidentify with them. We overtrain our threat and drive mode to the detriment of our caring mode. Yet ultimately our chance of survival only diminishes when social isolation overrules social connectedness, whether we view it on a small scale (family, community) or on a larger scale (nationally, internationally, globally). Practising compassion for others is a contribution to that connection between ourselves and others, friend *and* enemy. In doing so, we work on our intention and commitment to alleviate our pain and that of others and the pain in the world. Healing our own emotional pain affects our relationships with others, and that in turn influences their relationships and the world as a whole. Albert Einstein once wrote in a letter to a bereaved father who had lost his son (quoted in Calaprice, 2005):

> A human being is part of a whole, called by us the 'Universe', a part limited in time and space. He experiences himself, his thoughts and feelings, as something separated from the rest—a kind of optical delusion of his consciousness. The striving to free oneself from this delusion is the one issue of true religion. Not to nourish it but to try to overcome it is the way to reach the attainable measure of peace of mind. (p. 206)

Here follows a challenging way to expand the circle of compassion, namely towards rejected parts in ourselves and rejected others.

2.6.2   Exercise: 'Forgiveness'

Forgiveness is giving up the possibility of a better past.
(Unknown source)

Forgiveness has long been praised as a virtue in many religions, but in recent decades it has also entered the domain of psychology (McCullough & Witvliet,

2001). Forgiveness has been described as an important psychological strength, contributing significantly to healthy emotion regulation and well-being (Breen, Kashdan, Lenser, & Fincham, 2010; Toussaint & Friedman, 2008). Although in the scientific literature interpersonal forgiveness has received more attention than self-forgiveness, it has been argued that the latter is no less important (Hall & Fincham, 2005). Forgiveness is a deed of goodwill to a person who has harmed another person. Whether we forgive another or ourselves, we do not have to condone the transgression or forget about it; on the contrary, we are willing to learn from it and give space to the potential to do so.

You might feel no inclination to do a forgiveness exercise right now. Or perhaps you already noticed forgiveness in yourself when you did previous exercises such as the compassion mode or writing a compassionate letter. Softening and opening our heart cannot be forced. The next exercises, however, adapted from Tara Brach (2004), can nurture a willingness to forgive at some stage. We distinguish three aspects of forgiveness: namely, forgiving ourselves, asking others for forgiveness and/or forgiving someone else. You don't need to do the exercises in any particular order, but they are aimed at various areas in life where forgiveness can bring space and softening. You can choose what aspect appeals to you most at this time. If you meet resistance, can you be present with this resistance? Resistance can be allowed in your awareness too, and can be kindly noted as 'resistance'. Respect your limits. If the resistance is strong, just do that part of the exercise that is accessible right now. Or leave the exercise for now and return to it another time when the inner compassion mode is stronger and you feel safe enough; it doesn't need to go smoothly and easily immediately.

Forgiving Ourselves

The exercise may start as described in the introduction in 2.1.7.

In this exercise we're asking you to do something that requires courage, namely to connect with an area in your life where you encounter inner harshness or rigidity. Perhaps something arises by itself, or we can give some examples. Maybe you did something you feel guilty about or ashamed of. Or you hurt someone, or you look back with bitterness and regret to a conflict where you acted tactlessly and disrespectfully. Perhaps there is an inner rage and disillusionment about a habitual pattern you are ashamed of, or you disappoint yourself because you lack courage or perseverance.

If you cannot find such a painful area right now, you may congratulate yourself. But otherwise, we invite you to make contact with this inner area that is surrounded by harshness. It doesn't need to be the most painful area in your life but one that in this moment feels accessible and manageable. What physical sensations do you notice here? And what kind of emotions? What kind of thoughts? It is as if you are exploring an inner landscape.

Then ask yourself a question; let this resonate in you and notice what comes up. There are no wrong answers. The question is, 'Where did this come from and how did it develop?'

It probably didn't develop or happen intentionally, but you possibly acted while you were experiencing strain, insecurity, powerlessness or fear. Sometimes it seems you did something deliberately, but when you look back objectively you will probably realise that your mind wasn't clear but clouded by rage, jealousy, desire or another emotion. And that there are various causes behind your strong reaction that were not your choice. And what about the results that came out of this? Were you able to envisage them beforehand, and did you choose them consciously?

We don't usually cause harm deliberately, and we are far from perfect human beings; we all make mistakes at times.

That is why we wish to invite you now to an act of peace, namely making peace with yourself as a human being. You can do this in various ways. For some people it may feel appropriate to silently repeat words of forgiveness. For example, 'I see how I have caused myself or another harm, and I forgive myself for this now.' Or you could simply repeat the following words to yourself: 'You are forgiven.'

This might be asking too much because you feel you simply cannot forgive yourself. In that case it may be possible to silently repeat a forgiving wish, on the rhythm of the breath or independently from the breath. For example, 'May I in time forgive myself for this hurtful behaviour.' Or, 'I wish for forgiveness for myself.' You might like to put a hand on your heart . . . in this way you can symbolically take your wish to heart as a gesture of forgivingness.

Sometimes a word like 'forgiving' or 'forgiveness' doesn't resonate. You may even be 'allergic' to it. In that case it might be better to use a wish that is focussed on reconciliation or acceptance with regard to what is hard to come to terms with in yourself. See what is possible without needing to force anything. For some, a wish in the 'May we . . .' form can also be very healing.

Remain sitting for another moment, expressing a kind, compassionate, forgiving or reconciliatory wish towards yourself, as long as you like.

Asking for Forgiveness

Then bring to mind a situation in which you have hurt another person. Perhaps you intentionally insulted someone or hung up the phone in a fit of anger. Or you might have caused pain unintentionally by ending a romantic relationship, or by being unnecessarily harsh while not realising your son or daughter actually needed some special attention. Maybe you feel you have been causing harm to someone repeatedly by flaring up in a temper or through lack of care and concern.

Take some time to remember the circumstances of when and how you hurt someone and imagine feeling the pain, disappointment or betrayal that person might have felt. Now, holding this person in your awareness, begin asking for forgiveness. Mentally whisper his or her name and say, 'I understand the hurt you have felt and I ask your forgiveness.' Or 'I am really sorry; may you forgive me.' Repeat this request for forgiveness, with a sincere heart. Then take some moments of silence and let yourself be open to the possibility of being forgiven.

Forgiving Others

Out beyond ideas of wrongdoing and rightdoing, there is a field.
I'll meet you there.

(Rumi, from Barks, 1996, p. 36)

Resentment is like drinking poison and then waiting for the other person
to die.

(Unknown source)

There is a third area of forgiveness, namely as regards the pain others consciously or unconsciously caused us. We will now give the instructions, but it may be quite possible that you are not ready yet to offer forgiveness to another. In that case, leave it until later, when you experience more space. However it can be worthwhile to carefully investigate what happens when we look at someone who has hurt us in a more gentle way. As Fred Luskin (2003) has said, forgiveness is for you and for nobody else. And Archbishop Tutu (2009) confirmed that forgiving is not just being altruistic but is the best form of self-interest. There can be reconciliation, or you can forgive and never again speak to the person concerned. Perhaps you only notice resistance, or bitterness and pain. You can observe this with self-compassion and repeat the exercise at a later stage.

In the same way that each one of us has intentionally or unintentionally hurt others, all of us have been wounded in our relationships with others. Reflect on an experience in which you were disappointed, rejected, abused or betrayed. Without judging or condemning yourself, notice if you are still carrying feelings of blame and anger towards the person who hurt you. Have you banished this person from your heart?

Remember in detail the specific situation that most reminds you of how you were hurt. For example, you might remember an angry look from one of your parents, harsh words from a friend, the moment you discovered that a trusted person had deceived you, your partner leaving you . . . Be aware of the feelings that arose and arise now, the resentment, shame, anger or fear. Feel the pain as it expresses itself in your body, thoughts or emotions with tolerance and gentleness.

Now in your mind look more closely at this person and sense the fear, the pain or the neediness that might have caused them to behave in this hurtful way. Experience this person—just like yourself—as an imperfect and vulnerable human being. While you feel the presence of this person, mentally whisper their name and offer a message of forgiveness: 'I feel the pain that has been caused by you, and to the extent that it is possible for me, I forgive you.' Or if you are not yet able to say this, you might say, 'I feel the pain that has been caused by you; it is my intention to forgive you.' This exercise is not to condone disrespectful or harmful behaviour but to be compassionate and forgiving towards the imperfect, vulnerable person behind this behaviour. Stay connected with your own feelings of vulnerability, and repeat the message of forgiveness as often and as long as you like.

(Adapted, with kind permission, from guided meditations offered by Tara Brach)

Feedback from a participant:

'Since the forgiveness exercise I had a reconciliatory talk with one of my sisters. And I made an appointment with another sister.'

2.6.3   Four Friends for Life

A valuable aspect of realising our common humanity is the cultivation of four emotional qualities that are boundless in their scope and exclude no one: namely, loving-kindness, compassion, sympathetic joy and equanimity. In Buddhist psychology they are traditionally called the Four Boundless States (Immeasurables, Illimitables) or *Brahmaviharas*; in our programme we call them the Four Friends for Life. They are indeed 'boundless' because

1.   they are not restricted by the narrow perspective of our ego;
2.   they do not exclude anyone;
3.   they can be practised without limit.

Until now our emphasis has been on compassion, and we have also become familiar with loving-kindness in the kindness meditation practices. Our practice can deepen further when we include all four Friends. These wholesome 'selfless' emotional qualities are the antidote to all types of unwholesome self-centred states of mind (De Wit, 2008; Wallace, 2010). The Four Friends are a great support when developing openness, sensitivity, receptivity and generosity of the heart. Self-transcending does not mean we have to exclude ourselves from the practice; we *are* included, just like anyone else.

Until recently Western psychology paid little attention to these self-transcending qualities, but it is realised increasingly how important they are for our well-being and for a healthier society. Of course, they are extremely valuable for therapists, too, and are explicitly recommended by some colleagues in the discipline (Bien, 2008). Although they are antidotes for unwholesome mental states, they can also have their pitfalls. They can be distinguished as follows:

*   *Loving-kindness.* Here we are focussed on promoting the happiness and well-being of ourselves and others. You could say that our intentions are aimed at that part of the 'happiness thermometer' that is above zero. Loving-kindness is the opposite of—and the antidote to—hatred and resentment. The pitfall can be that the practice can degenerate into attachment, dependence and

sentimentality. This may seem self-transcending but is in fact motivated by self-centredness.

- *Compassion.* Here we are focussed on the alleviation of pain and suffering. Our intentions are aimed at the part of the happiness thermometer that is below zero. Compassion is the opposite of—and the antidote to—nastiness and cruelty. A pitfall can be that compassion turns into pity: The pain and the sadness of the other become the focus of our sentiments whereas in fact we are afraid to actually connect with the other's and our own pain. We can also become exhausted when we focus excessively on the suffering of others to the detriment of ourselves.
- *Sympathetic joy.* This refers to a straightforward sharing in joy and good fortune. Here we celebrate the warm, positive end of the happiness thermometer. Being joyful with and for the other is the antidote to envy and jealousy. We can develop sensitivity to the joy and happiness of others just as we do to their suffering and needs. The pitfall here can be that we chase after excitement and euphoria. The true aim is to genuinely share in small and big moments of happiness that arise spontaneously and to be grateful, complimentary and appreciative.
- *Equanimity.* This last Friend refers to an open-minded and warm-hearted state of mind that is free from judgment, preference or aversion. We can compare this quality to the holder of the thermometer that protects it against extreme circumstances. Equanimity is the antidote to conceit, arrogance and overinvolvement, which means excessive identification with our attributes, possessions, views and opinions. The pitfall here is indifference: We simply don't care. Equanimity is, just like the other three Friends, a quality of heart. It is not characterised by distancing ourselves but by an 'unbiased connectedness', being open to the other without attachment or aversion. Equanimity or 'equal-mindedness' means our mind and heart are equally open to what presents itself, and there is a balanced attitude in pleasure and pain, in success and failure, in fame and blame and in health and illness.

Cultivating all four of these emotional qualities can give meaning and depth to our practice. Practising one quality can protect us from the pitfall of another, and during the practice we can allow ourselves to be supported by the Friend for Life that is most helpful in that moment. Our ego can rebel when we cultivate qualities that are self-transcending. When the threat or drive systems kick in, the limitless perspective easily contracts again to a self-centred perspective.

We give a few examples of how we can adjust the practice to keep a good balance. Practising compassion while ignoring the other three qualities can result in heaviness and becoming discouraged as we focus only on the painful aspects of life. Perhaps suffering makes us anxious, or feelings of shame and guilt arise; or the enormity of all the suffering in the world makes us feel powerless and hopeless; or on the other hand we wallow in our own suffering and identify with being a victim; or we focus mainly on the pain of others out of self-protection, so as not to feel our own pain. When fear, sentiment and egocentrism creep into the practice, compassion can turn into pity, or even to *Schadenfreude*, when we secretly think that the person in question has only him- or herself to blame for having a hard time. When these feelings arise, it can be beneficial to shift the attention to one of the other Friends, for example to loving-kindness.

In the practice of loving-kindness we can become caught in striving for desirable results. Our intention can be clouded by clinging to a positive feeling. In that case, shifting to the practice of equanimity might be more helpful. The practice of equanimity might turn into indifference and boredom when our heart is no longer open but becomes insensitive. We can then shift our practice to sympathetic joy by sharing in the spontaneous joyful moments we notice in others or ourselves. When this practice slides into attachment to excitement and euphoria, that in turn can cause suffering because we cannot hold on to what inevitably slips away. We can then return to the practice of compassion.

In this way we can deepen our formal practice as well as our everyday practice aided by these Four Friends for Life. Every time, we can ask ourselves, 'What attitude is being asked of me here: kindness, compassion, sympathetic joy or equanimity?' The beauty of these Four Friends is that we can actually invite them quite easily by simply letting a kind, compassionate, congratulatory or equanimous wish resonate in ourselves whenever and wherever we are.

2.6.4   Discovering What Contributes to Happiness

The foolish man seeks happiness in the distance;
the wise man grows it under his feet.
(James Oppenheim)

Alleviating pain and promoting happiness can go hand in hand and reinforce each other. Compassion practice is aimed at relieving suffering, but it would be incomplete if we did not pay attention to the more specific qualities that contribute to happiness in life. Whereas compassion is more focussed on the area of the happiness thermometer that is 'below zero', loving-kindness and sympathetic joy are aimed at the 'above-zero' part. Positive psychology (Seligman, 2002) distinguishes three sources of well-being and happiness:

1. Pleasant life: experiencing positive emotions and sensory pleasure.
2. Engaged life: experiencing social involvement and connectedness.
3. Meaningful life: feeling connected with core values and life-purpose.

Research (Lyubomirsky, 2007) shows that positive circumstances are only minimally responsible for happiness. It is not so much what happens to us but our attitude towards what happens that determines our happiness. It is crucial that we are able to see the sunny side of difficult situations, be grateful for what we have, are not continuously comparing ourselves with others, be kind to ourselves and others, live mindfully and relish wholeheartedly the joyful moments that present themselves. Barbara Fredrickson's (2009) work shows how positive emotions broaden cognition and behavioural repertoires. Positive emotions build durable resources that support coping and nourish mental health. They are an antidote against the dysphoric, fearful or anhedonic states characteristic of many psychiatric disorders (Garland et al., 2010). Hedonia (seeking pleasure and comfort) and eudaimonia (seeking to use and develop the best in oneself) are often seen as opposing pursuits. Yet each may benefit well-being in different ways, hedonia in the short term and eudaimonia in the long term (Huta & Ryan, 2010). Neuropsychologist Rick Hanson (2009, 2013) has argued that our brain works like Velcro for negative experiences and like Teflon for positive experiences. From an evolutionary point of view this is understandable. Remembering experiences where our life was at risk so that we won't be taken unawares by them again is a very old survival mechanism. Because of this inner magnet for negative information and the hard-to-penetrate armour for positive information, we need to intentionally look for, appreciate and cherish moments of happiness to train our brain to 'take in the good'.

In the next section we offer a number of exercises that can specifically contribute to enjoying and savouring moments of happiness consciously, derived from various sources (Germer, 2009; Hanson, 2013; Hayes & Smith, 2005; Neff, 2011). If you would like to follow this up, we can recommend works like *Awakening Joy* by James Baraz and Shoshana Alexander (2010) and *Hardwiring Happiness* by Rick Hanson (2013).

2.6.5   Exercises for Sustainable Happiness

Enjoy, it's later than you think.
        (Chinese proverb)

Taking in the Good

Research by Bryant and Veroff (2007) showed that walking 20 minutes every day for a week with the instruction to consciously enjoy all pleasant experiences along the way was enough to enhance the well-being of the participants. In the follow-up interviews they also showed more appreciation for the world around them. The group scored very positively in comparison with a group that had been given the task of noticing negative experiences during their walks but also in comparison with the control group that had not been given any specific instructions.

Regularly going for a 'pleasure-walk' like we suggested in the first session (2.1.11) is therefore a valuable practice to take in the good. We can enjoy taking a walk, feeling the warmth of the sun, looking at a piece of art, listening to music, smelling a delicious fragrance or eating a delicious meal. We can savour and celebrate these experiences by consciously pausing when they occur, exploring them curiously and letting them sink in and fill our being. We can mindfully explore all the sensations that occur in a joyful moment. At other moments, we can 'remember' these experiences again with the help of our imagination and continue our practice in savouring.

Many moments of joy and happiness in daily life go unnoticed or are easily lost because our minds are preoccupied with other things. However we can train ourselves to savour these moments again and again.

Savouring and Revisiting the Good

You may look for a comfortable posture and allow yourself some time to mindfully deepen and slow down the breathing movements, softening physical tension. You may allow muscles that do not need to work now to have a holiday. And you invite a little smile to appear on your face.

Now bring to mind a memory where you saw something that gave you joy. It may have been a beautiful landscape or a flower, a picture or painting . . . maybe you remember looking at a smiling face or in the eyes of a beloved one . . . Imagine and bring to mind all that you saw and experienced. What kind of visual details do you notice? What kind of colours, shapes and light did you see or look at? And while you are visualizing, what gave you a sense of joy or gladness, what kinds of effects do you notice now in your body? What kinds of sensations do you experience in your face, in your heart, and in your belly? What kinds of emotional effects do you experience? Allow yourself some time to notice whatever you experience while you gently return to the image that gave you joy, savouring it again at this very moment.

Similarly you may explore a memory of hearing a beautiful sound or piece of music, of smelling a fragrant smell, of tasting something delicious, of a comforting feeling of touch and bodily contact with something or someone. So revisit the good that you received through all your five senses that connect us with the external world and the body, one by one, and explore what it evokes in you right now. You can also revisit moments of joy that came to you through what is called the 'sixth sense', your mind. Reconnect with a moment when you rejoiced in a deep insight or revealing metaphor or when you were moved by wise words or a line of poetry and explore what that does to you right now.

At the end of the exercise you may return to being mindful of whatever is clearly perceived, or return to some of the pleasant moments and experiences in this exercise . . . and mindfully appreciate, rejoice or allow gratitude to whatever you experience, if you wish with a hand on your heart.

Feedback from a participant:

'I notice that when I savour enjoyment and happiness, I also become kinder to others.'

Gratitude

> *Gratitude is the memory of the heart.*
> (French proverb)

Gratitude contributes to happiness and health. Interesting research by Emmons and McCullough (2003) took place amongst students who were randomly assigned to three groups and were asked to write a short weekly report about their lives at that moment for 10 weeks. Group A was given the task of writing about things they were grateful for; Group B about things they didn't like or found annoying; and Group C about things that had made an impression on them, positively or negatively. It turned out that the gratitude group was not only happier but also reported fewer signs of illness and more often practised fitness or sport than the people in the other two groups. Before deciding to start a gratitude calendar, you could first connect with gratitude by doing the following exercise.

- *Bring to mind three things in your life you are grateful for (circumstances, events, people, pets; present or past). Describe as specifically as possible the experiences that evoke gratitude or a positive feeling.*
- *Then describe three of your own qualities (talents, skills, characteristics) that you are grateful for. Again, be as specific as possible.*

Many learned as a child to say grace before meals or a short prayer before they went to sleep but lost this practice when they grew older. It can still be very wholesome to spend some time before a meal or at the end of the day bringing to mind three or more things you received that day for which you feel grateful.

'The Silver Lining'

Since my house burnt down, I have a better view of the rising moon.
(Japanese saying)

This exercise may help to shift to Stage 5 in the acceptance process (embracing your pain; see 2.2.4) and to see 'the silver lining' of a dark period in your life or hidden treasure in your suffering. Every time we have gone through or are going through a difficult episode in our lives, we can ask ourselves the following important questions:

- *Remember a challenge or crisis you were faced with in the past. When you look back on this episode, did anything good come out of it? What did you learn from this experience that you would not have learned otherwise? Is there a little lotus flower that grew out of that mud?*
- *Now think of the biggest challenge or difficulty you are faced with right now. What good would you wish yourself that would come out of it, and what do you hope you will have learned from it when you look back on it later?*

Write down what these questions evoke in you.

Discovering Your Core Values

We are shaped and fashioned by what we love.
(Johann Wolfgang von Goethe)

In Acceptance and Commitment Therapy (ACT), commitment to what you really value is seen as an important condition for psychological flexibility and health

(Hayes & Smith, 2005; Hayes, Strohsal, & Wilson, 1999;). You can call something a 'core value' when it really matters to you, not only today but also in the long term. A core value gives direction to your life, over and over again, through life's ups and downs. A core value is not an end in itself that needs to be achieved but a signpost that indicates the direction to proceed in, both when you have reached a goal and particularly when you don't know what your next goal should be. In general people are happiest when they align their lives with their core values and when the goals they set themselves are based on these. A core value is like a lighthouse that shines on the horizon while you go from buoy to buoy. Sometimes in stormy weather you can no longer see the buoys and fear that you are lost, but you can still see the beams of the lighthouse. When you live with commitment to your values, you will detect a trail that runs like a *Leitmotif* through your life. Core values give you vitality, make you open your heart and cause your whole being to resonate when you align yourself to them. If you ignore your core values, you lose the connection with these sources of vitality. Commitment to your core values goes hand in hand with joyful moments and more profound feelings of peace, as well as with pain. There will always be obstacles. You need the willingness to accept the pain that you will inevitably encounter so that you can maintain the connection with your values. Hence, ACT therapists say, 'In your pain you meet your values; in your values you meet your pain.' And of course, we also meet our joy while following our values. Examples of core values are love and friendship, good parenthood, good mentorship, social justice, care for animals and nature, good health and spiritual care.

Reflect on the following questions:

- *What are my core values? You can discover them by asking yourself questions like: What do I wish my life to stand for? How do I want to look back on my life in, say, 10 or 20 years' time? What would I want people to say about me when I am no longer here? What would I wish my epitaph to be?*
- *What obstacles do I encounter on the way towards my values?*
- *How can self-compassion help me to deal with these obstacles?*

Write down what these questions evoke in you.
The practice of kindness meditation can also contribute to happiness and connection with your core values. The last part of this meditation is kindness for all living beings.

2.6.6   Exercise: 'Kindness Meditation—All Beings'

1. *The exercise may start as described in the introduction in 2.1.7.*
    We then wish to invite you to silently repeat a kind or compassionate wish for yourself. You can use one of the four standard wishes or a wish that arises spontaneously, a wish that is appropriate in this moment. Then extend the practice to radiate a wish to a group or groups of people, for example all people living in your street, your village or town, your country, then to all

people on your continent, on other continents . . . You may also radiate these wishes to all women in the world, to all men in the world, to all children . . . or to all people who live in a war zone and are in danger or in an area of natural disaster . . . to all people who are hungry . . . to all people who are ill . . . to all animals . . .

2. *Perhaps more groups come to mind spontaneously . . . and whether the wish affects these people . . . may remain an open question. In any case, the kind and tolerant attitude is already something valuable and worthwhile. So don't hesitate to do this practice. If you feel overwhelmed or helpless in the face of all suffering in the world, allow yourself to return to self-compassion practice. If the exercise becomes rather abstract, you may zoom in on one person whose face you may have seen on a photograph or on the TV news. Imagine this person in front of you as a representative of the group. Also wishing in the 'we-form' may help you feel more connected.*

3. *Then you can extend the practice even more and include all living beings in the flow of kind wishes. People, animals, beings we can't see but that perhaps exist somewhere in the universe, all living beings. 'May all beings be safe.' 'May all beings be healthy.' 'May all beings be happy.' 'May all beings live in peace.' Loving-kindness, compassion, sympathetic joy and equanimity are called the Four Immeasurables or Illimitables because they can be developed without limit to all beings in the universe. When you notice that you have become distracted, you can acknowledge this patiently and with the same gentleness resume the flow of the kind wish . . . on the rhythm of the breath . . . or independently from the breath.*

You may wish to end with the following verse:

> The thought manifests as the word.
> The word manifests as the deed.
> The deed develops into habit.
> And habit hardens into character.
> So watch the thought and its ways with care,
> And let it spring from love
> Born out of concern with all beings.
>
> (Unknown source)

2.6.7 Calendar Exercise: 'Receiving Compassion'

Notice the moments you receive compassion. An example could be that you are visiting a friend in an unfamiliar city and you cannot find his home address. A passer-by kindly decides to help you without being asked. Afterward you can reflect on and take notes as regards the following questions:

• *Were you aware that you were receiving compassion? For example, 'Not at first, but noticed it after some time.'*

- *What physical sensations did you experience? For example, 'pleasant', 'warm', 'soft' or 'relaxed'.*
- *What emotions and thoughts were accompanying this event? For example, 'I felt grateful and thought, fortunately I won't be late for my appointment. How great that she wants to help me.'*
- *What do you feel now, when writing things down or reflecting? For example, 'I feel warm again and happy, now that I am remembering it.'*

Overview of Session 6: Happiness for All

Themes

In Session 6 the theme of common humanity is linked to the Four Friends for Life: loving-kindness, compassion, sympathetic joy and equanimity. We explore the issue of forgiveness and reflect on what brings joy and happiness in life.

Agenda

1. 'Inner Weather' check in and 'What Do You Wish for Yourself?'
2. Guided meditation 'Forgiving Ourselves', followed by sharing experiences (pairs, group).
3. Inquiry about formal and informal home practice done in the week after Session 5.
4. Invitation to 'take in the good' during the break (pleasure walk, what gives joy through the senses).
5. Guided meditation sitting or lying down 'Savouring and Revisiting the Good'. Sharing about the exercise.
6. Theory: the Four Friends for Life; what contributes to happiness.
7. Suggestions for home practice for the week after Session 6 (see below) and information about the additional silent practice session. A few participants are asked to volunteer to bring some refreshments to share during the break.
8. 'Gratitude round': After mindful reflection on the question 'What fills you with gratitude, for example circumstances, other people or personal qualities?' each participant is invited to share a few things that came up. Ending with kindness to the group, other groups and all beings.

Practice Suggestions for the Week After Session 6

Formal

- Regularly connect with the safe place, the compassionate companion and/or the compassion mode.
- Regularly practise kindness meditation or compassionate breathing (2.5.5) and extend to all beings (2.6.6).

- Gently explore the exercise 'Forgiveness' (2.6.2), focussing on one of the three aspects described, respecting your limits.
- Choose one or more of the 'Exercises for Sustainable Happiness' (2.6.5) to practise this week.

Informal

- Practise the breathing spaces with kindness (2.1.2) and compassion (2.2.8) or the self-compassion mantra (2.2.4) as much as you need.
- Calendar exercise: 'Receiving Compassion' (2.6.7).

2.6.8 Additional Silent Practice Session

Between Sessions 6 and 7 we plan an additional silent practice session. This session lasts two and a half hours just like the other sessions and can be seen as an additional opportunity for practice. For logistical reasons we choose the same duration as the other sessions. It is also possible to have a longer silent session, lasting for a day or part of a day, as is customary in the Mindfulness-Based Stress Reduction programme. During the session we offer various mindfulness and compassion practices to deepen and process the exercises that have already been taught. Our choice of the exercises we practise in the silent session depends on the learning process of the group so far. The programme usually includes a longer kindness practice—first towards ourselves, then to a benefactor, a good friend and/or family member, a neutral person, a 'difficult' person, groups and eventually to all beings. Furthermore, we spend time on body-focussed exercises as described in Session 4. We do practices like 'Walking with Kindness' (2.4.8), 'A Compassionate Body Scan' (2.8.2), 'Compassionate Breathing' (2.5.5) or 'The Stream of Awareness' (2.8.3).

Below we have included a sample programme for a silent session. This is just an example; how this session should be done is not set in stone. Trainers can develop a programme themselves depending on the available time, degree of experience of the participants and which exercises they would like to focus on, for example because they have not been practised much so far.

Example of a Programme for the Two-and-a-Half Hour Silent Session

Keep instructions relatively brief and allow for longer periods of silent practice.

1. Short introduction (5 minutes): practical matters, being silent is a gift to each other, the whole period including the break is on-going mindfulness practice. Invite participants to take good care of themselves throughout. The trainer may read a poem for inspiration.

2. Mindful movement exercises with kindness (2.4.7; 20 minutes).
3. Kindness meditation, sitting and walking (45 minutes). For example: oneself and benefactor while sitting; dear and neutral person while walking; difficult person while sitting. If a suffering part in oneself or in another person is met, compassionate breathing (2.5.5) can be suggested as an alternative.
4. Break (20 minutes): 'Savouring', 'Taking in the Good'; eating and drinking what was brought to share by a number of participants.
5. Revisiting the good (10 minutes).
6. Meditation in lying position (30 minutes): 'A Compassionate Body Scan' (2.8.2), 'Kindness for the Body' (2.4.6) or 'The Stream of Awareness' (2.8.3).
7. Ending with kindness meditation to groups and all beings (20 minutes).

2.7 Session 7

Compassion in Daily Life

In this session we revisit the three emotion regulation systems and highlight them from the perspective of motivation to gain a better understanding of what makes us behave as we do in our daily lives.

2.7.1 Exercise: 'Equanimity'

One moment of patience may ward off great disaster.
One moment of impatience may ruin a whole life.
(Chinese proverb)

Before we say more about our drives and motivations, let us begin with an exercise that can help us find calmer waters when our life or that of others is in turmoil. When we lack the clarity to know what to do or where to start, equanimity or openheartedness can be a great companion and support. When we are torn in different directions, equanimity may help us find the eye in the hurricane. When somebody consistently misbehaves and we feel powerless to change that person, equanimity may save us from drowning in reactive emotions. When we are excessively worried about somebody, the practice of equanimity may give us rest and peace. When we notice we are caught by the doing mode and chasing after results, equanimity may help us be open to outcome. Following is an example of how we can formally practise the wise and stabilising power of equanimity.

1. *The exercise may start as described in the introduction in 2.1.7. To get a sense of equanimity you could then reflect as follows: 'All people are heir to their own actions. I can advise people, but their well-being depends on their own choices and actions. Ultimately everyone is responsible for their own choices.'*
2. *Just as in the kindness meditation, you may then bring to mind a person who is relatively neutral: someone you don't know very well or whom you would meet in passing. You can repeat a wish or a phrase that expresses or invites a balanced and harmonious attitude.*
   We can give a few suggestions: 'May you accept things as they are.' 'May you feel calmness and not get thrown off balance by the vicissitudes of life.'

'May you be able to come to terms with how things always change.' 'I wish for you to feel balanced and at ease in joy and sorrow.' 'May you be open to outcome.' If the wish or reflection is short you may let it flow on the in- and out-breath; otherwise you can repeat the wish silently at an easy pace without coinciding the words with the breath.

When thoughts, emotions or other sensations arise, you can greet them as an experience in the present moment. When you feel some space again, you can continue to silently repeat the phrase or wish on the rhythm of the breath or independently of the breath. You may stick to one neutral person or bring to mind a few more.

3. *Then you can return to holding a wish for yourself, or reflect: 'May I stay calm in the midst of the unpredictability and impermanence of life' or 'May I be balanced in the ups and downs of life.' If you know that you are likely to get excessively involved in other people's problems, the following reflection may be helpful: 'I can advise others but can't make choices for them' or 'I can only do what I can.'*

   See what you find suitable and let equanimity resonate in your heart. In this exercise the same applies again: Whatever you experience, you can acknowledge it as it is and note it mindfully as an experience in the present moment.

4. *You may also include in the practice one or more good friends or someone who means a lot to you. You can imagine this person in front of you and then in your mind hold a wish for harmony or ease for this dear person. For example: 'May you accept things the way they are' or 'May you find inner balance in success and adversity.'*

5. *When it is someone who is experiencing a lot of suffering and for whom you are worried or for whom you feel responsible, then you could reflect as follows: 'I care about you but can't prevent your suffering.' Or you can radiate a wish like 'I wish you well-being and wisdom, but I can't make choices for you.' See what feels appropriate.*

   If you wish you could also include one or more people whom you find difficult and let them be the subject of a wish for balance and harmony or for reflection. Perhaps a wish like 'May you have wisdom in dealing with the vicissitudes of life.'

   When you notice that you find it hard to do this you may connect the wish or reflection again with your own attitude. You could wish for yourself, for example, 'May I have inner balance when I'm criticised.' Or you could reflect 'I can't change others but I can be as wise and compassionate as possible in caring for myself.'

6. *Finally, you may let the wish or reflection radiate throughout the whole world. 'May all people and animals be at ease with the vulnerability and finiteness of life.' 'May all be free from worry and have equanimity in dealing with illness and health, old age and death, success and failure, fame and blame, happiness and sadness, wealth and poverty.' 'May all accept the uncertainties in life with an open mind and heart.' 'May all beings find ease in the power of equanimity and open-heartedness.'*

You may continue to sit like this for another few minutes, reflecting on equanimity and openheartedness amidst the miraculous changefulness of life.

2.7.2 Motivation Based on Threat or Drive

We were always on the lookout, reading the omens and judging them fair or dangerous; we lived with nervous noses sniffing the wind so to speak.
(From *Joe Speedboat*, Tommy Wieringa, 2009)

Often we presume we know why we do what we do. We think we are aware of our motivations and are 'sensible' enough not to let ourselves be influenced by reflexes and emotional reactions. Yet the contrary is true: Our motivations are often unconsciously driven by old-brain instincts that carry our new brain along. Often we live with 'nervous noses sniffing the wind', like the narrator in the quoted fragment from Tommy Wieringa's novel *Joe Speedboat*. We judge the signs to be fair or dangerous without being aware of it. Meanwhile we know that mindfulness practice helps us to become aware of our automatic tendencies to follow our likes and dislikes. Insight into how our motivation is influenced by the emotion regulation systems can deepen our understanding and help us in making skilful choices.

We saw in Figure 7 in Session 2 that when the alarm of the threat system goes off, the hare plays it safe rather than risk its life. It is better to miss lunch than to be lunch, so if in doubt: run! This is the same for the fearful hare in us. The threat system easily overrules the drive system. When we still lived close to nature this mechanism was indispensable for our day-to-day survival, and it still tends to be the default setting of our brain. If left on autopilot our mind easily gravitates towards the threat mode. What we do or avoid is motivated by the instinct to protect ourselves. And even if our precious life is not immediately under threat, we are preoccupied with protecting ourselves against imaginary threats.

Once we have been frightened in a certain situation it sticks in our memory so that we are urged to flee, fight or freeze in comparable situations. The *preoccupation with threat* strongly directs our motivation and is very characteristic of people who suffer from anxiety and panic disorders. The preoccupation with what is feared can spread like an oil spill: from remembering and reexperiencing a fearful situation through anxiety about the situation happening again to the focus on the associated physical sensations, feelings and thoughts and all possible stimuli that induce them. In this way fear of the fear itself develops, and what is dreaded begins to include more and more signals that may point to threat. The preoccupation with threat also turns inward: How do we escape from the unpleasant sensations, feelings and thoughts we experience as threatening?

If the threat is external, at least we can physically escape from the situation; this is not possible with perceived internal threats. Yet we often try to do so by looking for distractions, by dissociating or becoming numb to the experience, and also . . . by worrying. This is a kind of 'mentally running away', an escape from the 'life-threatening' phenomena of our inner world. As long as we keep worrying, we are busy in our head and don't need to go down into our body where so many unpleasant things can be felt. The aggressive variety may be that we 'fight' against the part of ourselves we feel threatened by and let the inner bully loose on ourselves with reproachful and punishing comments.

The threat system can also be an important motivator in our relations with others. This may be justified if we are threatened physically, but more often our threat system raises a false alarm because something in the other—appearance, posture, tone or choice of words—triggers what is stored in our memory. In that case no open communication is possible; we avoid contact or keep the other at bay with unkind words or body language. Or it is the other way around: We flee towards the other because the threat comes from somewhere else. We trust the other more than ourselves and constantly look for his or her proximity and reassurance. A dependent relationship develops that may exasperate the person concerned because our clinging behaviour irritates them. There is a good chance that this person will reject us, which activates our threat system even more.

When we feel relatively safe, it is more likely that the drive system becomes our motivator. This will happen as soon as we feel an urge that wants to be satisfied quickly, whether it concerns bodily needs for food, sex and physical comfort or mental needs for success, wealth, status or power. Our instinct is to gratify our needs greedily. The tendency to eat more than we need stems from times when resources were scarce and rivals could steal our precious prey any moment. But greediness leads to overfeeding when supplies are abundant (Goss, 2011). This old-brain greediness easily hijacks our new brain when we pursue desires in whatever direction. Sitting still is not what our drive system is made for, and if we do, feelings of dissatisfaction, disinterest and boredom easily arise. We would rather feel excitement than emptiness and boredom and readily accept the risk of frustration as part of the bargain. If we don't succeed this time, we simply try again. 'Scoring' just once in a while is enough to sustain an addiction. That is why lotteries, gambling, games and expensive stimulants are so addictive. Often the 'pleasure' we seek is merely the discontinuation of an unpleasant state. The use of easily accessible products like alcohol, sedatives, nicotine, cannabis and all kinds of comfort food can increasingly creep into our daily lives as unhealthy habits to dispel dissatisfaction and other unpleasant feelings. Old-brain instincts snare our new brain and feed our *preoccupation with what is desired.* This is characteristic of people with addiction problems but common to many of us because we all have our more or less subtle addictions. Working hard to be admired by others or to do better than our colleagues or constantly looking for new stimuli in relationships can become equally addictive. No authentic communication is possible when we see the other as a rival or as someone to satisfy our needs.

We cannot help these tendencies to avoid sticks or chase carrots because our brain is designed this way; it is the heritage of millions of years of evolution. It is our responsibility, however, to deal with it wisely.

If there is constant danger, real or imagined, and the drive system is continually overruled by the threat system, we may retreat more and more, hiding from all those sticks. We let our behaviour be determined by the fear of failure and the belief carrots are just not for us. A long-lasting overactive threat system and underactive drive system is an unhealthy combination that can lead to severe depression, particularly when our soothing system is difficult to access. This may be because it was never nourished or because we lost someone who was important for our experience of safeness. When we are depressed we are chronically stressed and may either pace up and down in fruitless agitation or passively hide in a corner. We are no longer stimulated by positive expectations and feel incapable of bringing about change. At first we may cling to people for help, but often we may increasingly retreat from social relationships, thinking we are too much of a burden for others. We may end up in a state of helplessness and hopelessness. Our new brain still enables us to busy ourselves with worrying, and *preoccupation with loss and failure* directs our motivation. Worrying becomes mental rumination. Depressed people often spend a lot of time thinking about what went wrong, is wrong or will go wrong. Worrying may give us the impression—at least initially—that we are doing something to find a solution. Or, we engage our inner bully to hold ourselves responsible and bombard ourselves with criticism so that others do not have to do it. However, the longer we continue to worry without finding a way out, the more hopeless it all becomes. We go around in circles and get stuck in ever more negative judgments and views that cause more depressive feelings, which in turn cause more worrying; and so we get caught in a vicious downward spiral. The negative thoughts about ourselves, others and the world around us harden into solid mental constructs with which we identify. We end up in a mental prison that keeps us stuck in one place. We might call that 'mental freezing'.

If we are convinced that change for the better is impossible, is there anything left to motivate us? Many wisdom traditions, myths and fairy tales, but therapists as well, emphasise that we all face periods in our lives where we need to go through a phase of darkness and despair to see the light again. The American psychiatrist James Gordon (2008) described this phase, quoting Joseph Campbell, as 'the dark night of the soul'. When we are really trapped and notice that the old motivations from the threat or drive system no longer help us escape and in fact trap us even more, what is left? This is essentially one of life's main questions, according to Ton Lathouwers (2013), a Dutch Zen teacher: 'When there is nothing left to do, what do you do then?' If you are completely stuck in that place, compassion is the only response that remains.

2.7.3   Motivation Based on Care

Tension is who you think you should be;
relaxation is who you are.
                    (Chinese proverb)

The threat system and drive system are aimed at short-term advantages, quick fixes and a cure for the problem in the shortest possible way. These mechanisms are important for immediate survival and narrow the focus of our mind to avoid the feared or approach the desired. The soothing system is designed to support our motivation for care and social bonding. These changes take place much more slowly and cannot be forced. They come about 'spontaneously' when there is simply time and space for this to happen, and they require an open mind. There is room for playfulness, amazement, new discoveries and creativity. The defending or grasping reactions are not central but rather acceptance and a willingness to let come and go whatever presents itself. Sensitivity to our deeper needs and those of others can make it safe for social connectedness and trust to develop. We could say that the soothing system is designed for sustainability and long-term survival. It requires letting go of our need for control and surrendering to processes we have no power over. Before we can care, we often need to go through discomfort, accept inevitable pain and let go of instant pleasure seeking. We can only fully experience the peace and quiet of the soothing system when the threat and drive systems have stopped raging. Then we can be open to more fulfilling nourishment, rest and digest and be nourished through all our senses. We can quietly enjoy the richness of what we see, hear, feel, smell and taste. If we haven't learned to be open to all this—or if we have 'unlearned' it—then we quickly experience our life as unpleasantly empty when the threat and drive systems are inactive for a while. We won't be able to really enjoy anything, and this makes us more susceptible to depletion, exhaustion and burnout as we keep plunging ourselves into activities in order to escape the void. We would rather let ourselves be motivated from the threat or drive system because it is what we know and where we expect to get solutions instead of coming face to face with emptiness and meaninglessness and becoming depressed.

Yet, paradoxically it can be liberating to realise how it is precisely the attempts that we make to solve our problems that have only caused more problems and that this is how we have become completely stuck. We begin to see that our *striving* for a cure is itself the biggest problem. In this context Acceptance and Commitment Therapy talks about 'creative hopelessness' (Hayes, Strohsal, & Wilson, 1999): Only when we fully acknowledge that our attempts to cure are not working are we prepared to give that up and surrender to a view that allows for new possibilities and opens the way to care. Once we see how we are motivated by automatic reactions of grasping, defending or judging the opportunity dawns of liberating ourselves from the forces that make us ill and we can return to the experience of the present moment, where nothing is fixed and everything is in flux. Then we go back to the awareness of the ever-changing flow of phenomena, of physical sensations, feelings and tendencies that arise and pass away and of thoughts that come and go. Instead of forcefully striving for a cure, we consciously choose care. Thus we let go of the attachment to quick results and open ourselves, with tender and kind attention, to all that comes and goes, with the courage to let ourselves be touched, even by what is painful. Then we can be motivated by compassion.

2.7.4   Freedom of Choice

Do I dare
Disturb the universe?
     (T. S. Eliot, 1917)

We have already established that our emotion regulation systems are not determined by what is morally 'good' or 'bad'. Nor can the motivation mechanisms that we have described be good or bad; they are rooted in our old brain and have developed to enhance our chances of survival. They *can* all be helpful. The question is, how and when do they get activated in the appropriate circumstances, and can we influence that? Motivation based on the soothing system usually happens as unconsciously and automatically as other old-brain reactions, even though this system is, from an evolutionary point of view, part of a younger layer than that in which the threat and drive systems are rooted. A desire for calm, safeness and social connectedness can just as easily motivate us unconsciously as the flight from what threatens us or the chase after what we desire. Here, too, we can only make a conscious choice when we first notice the desire and phenomena that accompany it. When we recognise our driving forces and the automatic reactions we can choose whether to go along with them or not, and conscious motivation can arise.

Thanks to the new-brain functions, we can learn to make conscious choices regarding what motivates us. Because of our innate ability for mindful self-exploration, which can be further developed through practice, we can observe the processes in our body and mind from moment to moment. We can learn to distinguish wholesome and harmful reactions and gain more insight into what would be the best motivator in a given situation. Sometimes this is the threat system, sometimes the drive system and another time—usually more often than we think—the soothing system.

Because we live in relatively safe communities, the threat and drive systems don't need to be active as often as when we were still living in caves. Yet they often are in control so that we are needlessly exposed to stress, with all its long-term harmful consequences for health and well-being, our own as well as that of others and society as a whole. Generally speaking there is a deep need to cultivate the calming influence of the soothing system and free ourselves from compulsive grasping, defending or ruminating, which sustain chronic stress. It could liberate us from the preoccupation with what threatens us, is lacking or went wrong and open us to new possibilities. Whereas overactivation of the threat and drive systems limits our options, a well-functioning soothing system is an important condition for more freedom of choice.

Perhaps the process of change through practising mindfulness and compassion can be compared with changing the position of a stone in a stream. The streambed does not immediately change, but gradually the water takes a different course and sometimes even creates a new channel altogether. Processes of change that are the result of mindfulness and compassion practice operate in a similar manner. Small steps may eventually grow into substantial change, just like the subtle movement of a butterfly's wings through circulation of the air systems can eventually grow into a hurricane at the other side of the world.

Exercise: 'What Motivates Me?'

When you meet dilemmas related to motivation and choices in the next few days, ask yourself the following questions:

- *What emotion regulation system drives my motivation and do I tend to base my choices on? Are they based on the threat, drive or soothing system?*
- *And do I want to follow that tendency or is another choice more wholesome?*

*You can write down what strikes you in the coming weeks as regards your moti-
vations and your choices and actions. Before starting to do so, you could first do
the following exercise.*

2.7.5   Exercise: 'Discovering Compassion in Daily Life'

Many of our activities are carried out on automatic pilot. What follows is an exercise in awareness of the prevalence of a caring attitude in our daily activities.

*Divide a sheet of paper into three columns, with the left column being wide, and
the central and right ones narrower. In the left column you list your daily activities
on an average day. Then in the central column you mark with a number from 1 to
5 to what extent you do that activity out of care for yourself (1 = not at all; 5 =
completely). In the column on the right indicate with a number from 1 to 5 to what
extent you do the activity out of care for one or more other persons (or animals).
When you have completed this, reflect on the list and notice your reactions. What
does it say about your daily life and activities? Perhaps you remember a similar
exercise from Session 7 of the mindfulness training (MBSR/MBCT) where you
were asked to find out to what extent daily activities are 'energy consumers' or
'energy providers'. You can ask yourself now to what extent the score of care for
yourself or for others corresponds to your energy management. Does the activity
in question demand energy or provide energy? What emotion regulation system is
involved? What would you wish for yourself, and what can you do to bring more
kindness and compassion into your daily life? Would it help if your activities
change? Is it about 'what' you do? Or would it help if your intention, motivation
and attitude regarding what you do change? Is it about 'how' you do it? How
would you be able to practise that?*

Our experience does not always confirm what our preconceived ideas tell us
about a certain activity. For example, we might think we are acting compassionately when we do a lot of work for our boss or colleague, while at the same time
we get exhausted and don't experience any self-compassion at all. When we look
more closely we realise that our behaviour towards others is not so compassionate
after all but is motivated by our energy-demanding drive or threat systems. Many
participants notice that being kind to others from the soothing system is also kind
and nourishing to themselves, and being kind to themselves has a positive influence on others. Compassion for ourselves and compassion for others do not exist
independently but are intrinsically connected.

Feedback from participant:

'The exercise "Discovering compassion in daily life" provided insight
into how I do things. I notice how unfriendly I can be to myself when
I am hijacked by the drive system and forget making time for a short
breathing space.'

2.7.6 From Formal to Informal Practice

From the exercises in the previous sessions it will have become clear that practising compassion is not just a formal matter. It can be extended to all aspects of our daily lives. The calendar exercises were an invitation for informal practice. The breathing spaces as we have learned them in the mindfulness course provide a bridge between formal and informal practice. In this course we enriched them with the practice of kindness and compassion. We can wish for ourselves what we need when we pause for a moment. If we are restless, we can wish calmness for ourselves; if we feel threatened there can be the wish for safeness. It is not about a feel-good remedy or about striving for results but about the kind intention towards ourselves or another who is present at that time and the emotional tone that accompanies it. In the MBCT course (Segal, Williams, & Teasdale, 2013) a distinction is made between the breathing space—*regular* (in a chosen, relatively quiet, moment), the breathing space—*coping* (in a stressful situation) and the breathing space—*action* (in a situation that demands a decision or an action). All three of them can be expanded and deepened with kindness and compassion.

There are countless opportunities for informal practice of compassion and the other self-transcending qualities. We can, for example,

- be mindful of resistance, desire, inner patterns or the inner bully and meet those with compassion;
- remind ourselves of the three phrases of the self-compassion mantra;
- let a compassionate wish flow when we witness emotional pain, in ourselves as well as in others;
- imagine how our compassionate companion would approach a certain situation;
- respond to a difficult situation by mindfully connecting to the compassion mode;
- celebrate a moment of sympathetic joy when we see someone who is joyful and happy;
- have a moment of equanimity when we become aware of being swept along in reactions of our threat or drive system in a situation that demands patience;
- treat any passer-by to a wish of loving-kindness (anyone can be included in our practice: those with whom we wait in a queue, fellow passengers on the bus, the postman, the person at the check out, the cows in the field, the guard dog in a yard or the ants on a forest path, and we can consciously embed our words and deeds in tenderness and kindness and express that with our physical posture, our smile, our gaze, our voice);
- during a walk or simple everyday activity, sing or hum to a pleasant melody (one of) the four kind wishes from the kindness meditation.

2.7.7 Practical Ethics

The true value of a human being is determined primarily by the measure and the sense in which he has attained liberation from the self.

(Albert Einstein, 1954, p. 12)

Every thought that we consciously express, every word, every deed, has consequences and is, in effect, an ethical choice. Not in the sense of normatively 'right or wrong' or morally 'good or evil' but in the sense of more or less wholesome, skilful or beneficial. Compassion practice can make us more aware of the consequences of our speech and actions and make us more sensitive to the ethical dimension of our daily lives. Practical ethics is intended to have *as much wholesome effect and as little harmful effect for as many involved as possible.*

An understandable reaction to that definition is 'It is not an easy task to assess that every time we think, say or do something.' However, it does not involve such a rational assessment. The intellect cannot calculate how far-reaching the consequences of a decision are and how much others are affected. Our intellect can help us in making ethical decisions but needs the compass of the intuitive wisdom of our heart. We can only develop that compass when we learn to open our hearts and to *feel* the consequences of our decisions. All qualities of compassion are important in this, and we develop them formally and informally with on-going practice. Practical ethics demand sensitivity to the needs and wants of ourselves and others and sensitivity to the emotional messengers that inform us about the quality of our connectedness with one another.

Self-compassion goes hand in hand with compassion for others. The behavioural expression of compassion to others is altruism. The paradox is that when we do something for others, we become happier and healthier too (Post, 2005). The Dalai Lama therefore calls altruism a form of being wisely selfish (T. Gyatso, 2003). Stefan Klein (2014) provided an extensive overview of scientific arguments from psychology, genetics, neuroscience and even economics that it is not self-centred people who have the best chances of survival but those who are concerned about the welfare of others. In the news media much attention is given to *antisocial* behaviour as well as to people who condemn it. The media show us *prosocial* behaviour less often. Yet human history confirms time and again that hatred creates hatred. Fortunately the opposite is true as well: prosocial behaviour evokes good will in others (Bierhoff, 2005) A striking example is a comment quoted by Norwegian prime minister Jens Stoltenberg shortly after a fellow countryman with extremist views killed 77 people in Oslo and on Utoya island on July 22, 2011. A large number of the victims were young people who had gathered for a summer camp of the Norwegian Labour Party. In his speech at the memorial service, Stoltenberg quoted the words of an eyewitness, a girl who had survived the massacre: 'If one man can show so much hate, consider how much love we can show together' (see www.youtube.com/watch?v=8oPbd9UvZuY, accessed 11 January 2015).

It is hardly possible to make wise ethical decisions when we are controlled by our threat or drive system. That is why people in wars or in an economy that has spun out of control often become unscrupulous and act in cruel ways without consciously choosing to do so. Ethical decisions are made from a caring mentality. Therefore it is so important to let decisions that may have far-reaching consequences arise from calmness and to give ourselves time to open our hearts.

It may be helpful to take a 'breathing space' before acting, before we say or do something. And we can deepen the 'breathing space—action' with compassion.

Whenever we are faced with something challenging it can be helpful to take a compassionate breathing space and remember the Serenity Prayer we quoted in 1.2.1. Sometimes it is wise to take a courageous step to change what we can change, for example to no longer postpone a difficult conversation; sometimes it is wise to accept with serenity what we cannot change, for example to mindfully accept that we feel sad or hurt. And if we unintentionally make a mistake, the advice of Confucius can be helpful and supporting: 'Our greatest glory is not in never falling but in rising every time we fall.'

2.7.8   Exercise: 'A Compassionate Emergency Plan'

If you are vulnerable to relapse in burnout, depression, anxiety or panic attacks, addictions or other problems, it can be supportive to make a relapse prevention or emergency plan when you are in a relatively stable phase. If you have previously made an emergency plan during a mindfulness course or other training, you might have a look at it again. If you lost it or you never made one, you can draw one up. An emergency plan describes the following:

- the **risk situations** or scenarios for relapse, for example, moving house, holiday periods, loss or rejection in your social life, love-sickness, being criticised at work, changing your function or job;
- the **warning signals** (particularly the early ones!) of an imminent relapse, for example, worrying, concentration problems, irritation, gloominess, headaches, low back pain, insomnia or not being able to get up in the morning, loss of appetite or comfort eating, beginning to smoke or drink more, clinging to others or withdraw from social contact;
- the **dos and don'ts**, which means actions that have turned out to be helpful or not helpful in the past. Everything you can think of now that could help you to avoid relapse can be part of your plan— what you can do yourself and how you can continue to take good care of yourself and create space for rest and relaxation. Are there activities you usually enjoy or you are good at that you might do? Which 'energy providers' could you call on and which 'energy consumers' would be better to avoid? What mindfulness or other exercises could help you? What could you ask people in your own network? Whom do you approach first? When and where do you seek professional help?

How would you want to adapt this emergency plan or add to it if you look at it from the compassion mode (or from the perspective of your compassionate companion)?

Remember that stress and crisis situations trigger our threat system. However, reactions caused by these systems are usually less helpful than responding mindfully from the compassion mode. Are there warning signals you would like to add, like the inner bully or old unhealthy patterns being triggered? Are there physical, emotional or mental signals or behaviours you would want to add, now that you are able to notice them sooner? Are there activities, apart from the things you usually like to do or you are good at, that you would want to add from kindness and caring? Are there exercises from the compassion training you want to include in the plan because they could be helpful in a difficult moment? Are there beloved objects, compassionate symbols, texts or perhaps a compassionate letter you would want to keep with the plan so that they can help to remind you of what is so easily forgotten in a difficult moment?

In this way your emergency plan can grow into a compassionate 'survival kit'. Of course you can always adjust, remove or add things.

2.7.9   Calendar Exercise: 'Giving Compassion'

Recognise moments when you are giving compassion. An example of giving can be: 'A friend came to visit me and started to talk about her problems at work. I was able to listen patiently, and when she asked me for advice I could give her some suggestions.' Afterward you can reflect on and take notes using the following questions as a guideline:

- *Were you aware of giving compassion while it was happening?*
- *What physical sensations did you experience? For example, 'pleasant', 'warm', 'soft' or 'relaxed'.*
- *What emotions and thoughts were accompanying this event? For example, when giving compassion, 'I felt moved and calm at the same time and thought, how awful for her, I hope she'll find a solution.'*
- *What do you feel now, when writing things down or reflecting? For example, 'I feel a connection with her. It's great that I could help her by listening and that she felt heard.'*

Overview of Session 7: Compassion in Daily Life

Themes

In Session 7 we discuss how the emotion regulation systems connect with our motivation and how mindful awareness of what motivates us can bring more freedom of choice. How can we continue to develop compassion in daily life, take good care of ourselves and others and come to act wisely and compassionately?

Agenda

1. 'Inner Weather' check in and 'What Do You Wish for Yourself?'
2. Guided meditation 'Equanimity'. Sharing about the exercise.
3. Inquiry about formal and informal home practice done in the weeks after Session 6, including experiences of the silent session.
4. Short break followed by some mindful movement exercises.

5. 'Discovering Compassion in Daily Life'. Exchanging insights and challenges, first in pairs, then sharing in the group.
6. Theory: motivation; practical ethics.
7. Suggestions for home practice for the week after Session 7 (see below).
8. Reminder that the next session is the last; invitation to reflect on what the training has given and to bring a symbol. (A feedback questionnaire can be handed out to be brought back at the final session.)
9. End with a breathing space with kindness when action is required.

Practice Suggestions for the Week after Session 7

Formal

- Choose exercises from previous sessions that you wish to integrate in your personal practice in the future such as the safe space, compassionate companion, compassion mode, compassionate letter writing, kindness meditation, compassionate breathing, kindness for the body, walking in kindness or mindful movement with kindness. If you have used audio devices until now, try to guide yourself without them but do use them if you really need them.
- Alternate the kindness meditation with 'Equanimity' (2.7.1).
- Continue with parts of 'Forgiveness' (2.6.2) and 'Exercises for Sustainable Happiness' (2.6.5).
- Explore further the exercise 'Discovering Compassion in Daily Life' (2.7.5) and make 'A Compassionate Emergency Plan' if you wish (2.7.8).

Informal

- Practise the breathing spaces with kindness (2.1.2) and compassion (2.2.8) or the self-compassion mantra (2.2.4) as much as you need.
- Be aware of what motivates you in moments of decision. Are you deciding from the threat, drive or soothing system (2.7.4)?
- Calendar exercise: 'Giving Compassion' (2.7.9).

If you wish, you can bring a symbol (object, text or poem) to Session 8 that expresses what has been important for you during the training.

2.8 Session 8

The Healing Power of Compassion

I call this transformation 'healing toward the human condition',
and for me it's the deepest healing of all.

(Vidyamala Burch, from *Living Well with*
Pain and Illness, 2008)

2.8.1 Compassion and Self-Healing

Compassion training can have a great effect on our self-healing potential. Healing is not just about reducing complaints and symptoms, removing a sick organ, fixing a broken leg, eliminating harmful bacteria or influencing chemical processes with medication. It is also not just about reducing complaints psychologically by influencing our thoughts and behaviour and by learning to deal differently with emotions and our relationships with others. These may all help, yet we may still not feel 'whole' inside.

Even when we appear healthy and adjusted on the surface, deep down we can be alienated and fragmented because we ignore or resist large parts of ourselves or because we are constantly striving for forms of self-improvement that are out of reach. At a deeper level—that of our common humanity—health and wholeness have a different meaning than in the language of physicians and psychologists. Even when according to them no cure or recovery is possible, we can still experience wholeness. Where cure of the primary suffering turns out to be impossible, care can bring ease from the secondary suffering that arises out of the unhealthy ways in which we deal with the primary suffering. When we no longer try to escape from the relationship with our primary pain or fight against it but instead restore the connection with loving attention, we become whole again in the deepest sense. Accepting that which we cannot change as well as taking responsibility for what we can change helps us to continue our lives in a meaningful direction. We can connect with all of our potential despite limitations, and we can train our new-brain functions to work *for* us.

Feedback from a participant:

'I can get out of a negative thought spiral and approach myself with more tenderness, in thought and in action.'

An example that shows how wholeness can be experienced in spite of serious physical limitations is the following. Vidyamala Burch has been a 'hands-on' expert for years in the field of physical pain after serious trauma to her back. In her book *Living Well with Pain and Illness* (2008) she has described how, while things seemed to be getting 'worse' with more pain and limitations in her functioning, she began to feel 'better' with improved quality of life.

> Fighting and running away from my pain, I was constantly preoccupied with myself and that raised a wall of separation. There was no stillness and hence no inner space that could enable me to gaze over the parapet of myself and glimpse a radically different perspective on life. When that finally happened it was like turning 180 degrees—rather than moving away from life in search of a 'better' existence I turned back toward it. I'd felt like a lonely person in a wilderness, but the view is now full of colour, variety and other people. I call this transformation 'healing toward the human condition', and for me it's the deepest healing of all . . . if you allow life in without resistance or clinging, you can be healthy and whole, no matter what kind of injury or disease process you may be living with. (p. 91)

Burch created a mindfulness-based method in the U.K. for people with chronic pain known as 'Breathworks', developed from her own experience and healing process.

Another example of wholeness at the deepest level despite great psychological pain, is the life of the Austrian neurologist and psychiatrist Viktor Frankl, a survivor of the Holocaust in which nearly all of his closest relatives died. In his now famous book *Man's Search for Meaning* (1946/1985) he described his experiences as a prisoner in a concentration camp and his therapeutic method for discovering value and meaning in all circumstances of life—no matter how difficult. He said, 'Everything can be taken from a man but one thing: the last of the human freedoms—to choose one's attitude in any given set of circumstances, to choose one's own way' (p. 86).

2.8.2 Intimate Connectedness

Mindfulness practice and compassion training heal us at the deeper levels of our being. Mindfulness opens the eye and compassion the heart for the inevitable suffering as it is. Every individual form of suffering is special and unique, but it is a natural law that suffering is unavoidable, and that makes it a shared experience from which nobody is exempt. Mindfulness and compassion are universal qualities, and the more they flourish, the more our mind and heart can open to our suffering and that of others. Instead of shutting it out, criticising or manipulating it, we can lovingly embrace it, like a mother embraces a child in pain. In this way we actively contribute to our self-healing ability. We revitalise again and again the connection with ourselves, others and the world as a whole and intensify our sensitivity for giving and receiving the appropriate care. It is an act of intimacy with ourselves and with others, which leads to healing connectedness.

A very concrete way in which we can develop such intimacy is in relation to our body. The next exercise is an invitation to do just that. Like in the last session of a Mindfulness-Based Stress Reduction or Mindfulness-Based Cognitive Therapy course it can be very fitting to return to the body scan.

Exercise: 'A Compassionate Body Scan'

Together we are going on a compassionate journey of discovery through the body. You don't need to try very hard to experience something; you are allowed to be as you are. You can do the body scan lying down, preferably on a mat or mattress that is neither too hard nor too soft. If you find it difficult to do the exercise lying down because of physical limitations, you can also practise while seated. If you find it helpful you can keep your eyes open, but you can also close them.

If you are doing the exercise while lying down, you can lie on your back (or on your side), loosening your clothes if they are tight around the waist; you can put a small pillow under your head, and if needed, a bigger cushion under your knees so that there is less pressure on your lower back. If you expect to get cold use a blanket . . . take good care of yourself. Let the legs be loose and the feet fall away from each other. The arms loose alongside the body . . . and now you can be aware of lying down. You can also notice how you feel . . . relaxed, tense, tired, peaceful, restless or whatever. And however you feel, it is okay; you don't need to change anything.

You can be aware of the movements of the breath, how the belly goes up and down as you are breathing in and out. You can allow a soothing breathing rhythm and allow the breath to flow freely and find its course . . .

Now bring your attention to the left foot. In your mind say hello . . . and explore the left foot with a relaxed interest. What do you experience? Perhaps your foot feels warm or cold, stiff, soft. Perhaps you feel contact between the toes, or the contact of the skin with your sock . . . or perhaps you feel the pressure that develops from the contact of the heel with the floor. Perhaps you don't feel anything at all, and that's fine too. Whatever you feel, it's okay the way it is. Realise how your foot patiently carries your body weight and see if you can wish something kind for the left foot, as if it is a person. 'May you be at peace' or 'May you be strong' or 'I wish you wholesome rest' or something else that is kind and supportive.

Then you can do the same in relation to the left lower leg . . . the left upper leg . . . breathing in a soothing rhythm and allowing kind wishes to flow with it . . . Then bring your attention to your right foot . . . and wish something kind for this foot. Next to the lower right leg . . . the upper part of the right leg . . . If you notice that you are enjoying the exercise or on the contrary, become impatient, or get distracted or worried whether you're doing it correctly, it is all allowed to be there too. Perhaps you can be mindful of such mind states without needing to change them. Acknowledging what is happening in or around you, and greeting each body part with sensitivity, treating it to a kind wish.

It may well be that you sometimes get pulled away by sleepiness and are not present for a while. If this happens you don't need to condemn or fight it, but perhaps you can be mindful of it. And if sleepiness becomes quite strong and begins to control you, then if you wish you can open your eyes from time to time. However, it doesn't need to turn into a big battle. Being sleepy is completely human and here too you can be kind.

Then you can explore the torso, the arms and finally the head, first being sensitively aware of each part of the body you visit . . . and then letting a kind wish flow to the area you are aware of. You can let yourself be supported by the Friends for Life (see 2.6.3) when you wish something suitable for an area of your body. You can let a compassionate wish flow to the place where you notice pain or discomfort. 'May you be free from pain' or 'May you be able to bear the discomfort.' When you notice a pleasant experience in a certain area, this can be the cause for a wish that expresses sympathetic joy. 'May you celebrate this moment.' Restlessness can inspire a wish for equanimity. 'May you be at peace with what is' or 'May you experience serenity.' An area where you notice predominantly 'emptiness' or 'numbness' can inspire you to a wish expressing loving-kindness. 'May you belong' or 'May you experience vitality.' Continue as long as you feel it benefits you.

In neuropsychology the term 'interoception' describes the sensitivity towards stimuli originating inside of the body. Being more aware of our bodily experiences brings a stronger sense of connectedness and well-being with ourselves and of the ability to resonate with what others feel.

If you like, you can then let the attention go from the top of your head down through the torso and the arms to the legs and into the feet . . . and back up again to the crown of your head. With a relaxed interest feeling the attention flow through you like waves . . . from the crown to the toes . . . and back up again . . . or let the attention flow from the inner centre of the body to the surface and back . . . and if you like, softly letting a kind wish flow through the body as a whole . . . on the rhythm of the breath or independently from the breath.

When you are ready, you can note the intention to move some fingers or toes, to stretch, to massage your face or whatever. And invite yourself to return to your daily activities in the same relaxed, kind and mindful way.

2.8.3 Boundless Openness

Love says, 'I am everything.'
Wisdom says, 'I am nothing.'
Between the two my life flows.
(Sri Nisargadatta, from *I Am That*, 2012, p. 236)

Wholeness connects parts into a whole, and connects the inner and the outer. Wholeness asks for intimacy . . . and for openness, the intimate connection with the smallest details of our experience in the moment . . . and the boundless openness of an awareness that offers space for whatever is possibly there. We started in Session 1 with the visualisation exercise of a 'safe place'. We end in this final session with a visualisation exercise of a 'safe awareness', where there is room for whatever presents itself. Can we feel at home again and again in that spaciousness that extends far beyond our temporary self-constructs? Our mind constantly builds mental constructs, and in order to find stability draws up boundaries, between me and you, us and them, subject and object, inner and outer, good and bad, friend and foe. Our mind seems to want distinctions, and that's an old survival mechanism. It increases our chance of survival when we can distinguish between what is safe and unsafe. So there is nothing wrong with making distinctions between one thing and another. But what happens when 'distinction' changes into 'separation' and we begin to believe in the boundaries our mind creates and become imprisoned in the illusion of duality? We lose sight of the original unity of our experience and the potential to see through and beyond the boundaries.

Exercise: 'The Stream of Awareness'

1. *We invite you to sit comfortably or to lie down as in the body scan. Take your time to feel the connection with your body, and if necessary adjust your posture . . . Feel free to go your own way during this meditation. It's not about straining to stick to the instructions but about noticing from moment to moment what is arising in your awareness. You can choose which field of awareness to focus your attention on. Let the choice be sustained by tenderness and kindness towards yourself. Sometimes you might want to stay with something for longer than the instructions indicate, or sometimes shorter. Both are fine. Later you might decide whether you will go back to the instructions or continue in your own way.*

2. *Imagine . . . there is NOTHING . . . The first experience is yet to come. You don't even know what an experience is. There is nothing and you know nothing . . . And out of nothing the first experience arises, like the first drop of water wells up from a spring. The first experience is the sensation of air that enters via your nostrils . . . the second is the sensation of air that goes out . . . and the moments of awareness of the in- and out-flowing air are linked, like drop after drop into a tiny streamlet of experience that finds its way in the channel of your awareness . . . And the little stream becomes a rivulet growing with the sensations of breathing: in your nose, throat, chest and belly . . . Awareness of the richness of phenomena with each inhalation, each exhalation . . . and the channel of awareness widens when the stream grows in volume.*

3. *The stream becomes a small river when other experiences, too, well up out of nothing and are added to the stream: becoming aware of other bodily sensations . . . warmth or coolness, heaviness or lightness, tension or relaxation, stillness or movement . . . of pleasant or unpleasant feeling tones . . . gross and subtle . . . There is room for all these inner experiences in the channel of awareness that grows effortlessly with the volume of the stream . . . And experiences are added of contact with the space around you through the senses: what touches your skin . . . visual sensations: light, dark, colour, form . . . hearing: silence . . . sounds from nearby or far away . . . And the channel of your awareness broadens and the small river expands into a big river, an ever-increasing stream of experience.*

4. *Besides experiences of the inner space and the space around you, images and memories from your past can arise, and these are added to the stream of awareness: your very first memory . . . memories from early childhood, as a baby, as a toddler . . . memories of your parents or carers . . . perhaps brothers or sisters, pets . . . the house you lived in, the toys you played with . . . memories of the surroundings . . . Pleasant memories, unpleasant memories. Images of that time, now remembered, given space in the channel of your awareness . . . Memories from your time at school, teachers, classmates . . . Primary school . . . joyful or sad experiences, safe or unsafe situations . . . Secondary school . . . memories of puberty, changes in the body, new discoveries, awakening sexuality, the first time you fell in love . . . Memories of fantasies or real experiences you had, of delights or disappointments . . . Space can be offered now to all those images of the past, and the thoughts and feelings that are evoked . . . And the stream becomes an ever-wider river . . . And when there are rapids, waterfalls, obstructions or whirlpools, your awareness can grow, expand and deepen, and in this way whatever pushes forward gets space, whatever is obstructed flows along and finds rest, carried in the ever-widening and deepening channel of your awareness, offering space to whatever needs space.*

5. *More images can join in the stream of experience from your history, of yourself as an adolescent and afterwards . . . Of your further education, of places you lived or worked . . . Of journeys you made . . . Relationships with people important to you . . . intimate or fleeting relationships . . . harmonious or difficult . . . situations that were joyful or painful . . . nourishing or traumatic . . . riches, loss . . . health, illness . . . Memories of the life that lies behind . . . For all those images of the past, arising from nothing, there is space now . . . for all associated thoughts and feelings . . . for everything forgotten or suppressed . . . there is space in your awareness.*

6. *For everything you ever identified with, there is space too, and for everything you are identifying with now or could identify with . . . the qualities and skills, the tasks and roles that are part of you . . . the groups and networks you are involved in . . . the views and opinions about yourself, others and the world . . . political or religious beliefs you may have . . . For every preference and for everything you associate the words 'I', 'me' or 'mine' with, there is space . . . And for everything you associate the words 'not-I', 'not-me', 'not-mine' with, there is space in your awareness as well . . . And the channel deepens and widens . . . and everything with which you identify or don't identify can join the stream.*

7. *For all images of the time ahead of you, there is space too in the channel of your consciousness. For plans, fantasies, dreams, ideals, for all promises the future holds, there is space . . . For visions of bliss and of doom, and for the emotions and thoughts that co-arise, there is space . . . for all hope and all fear . . . for the most subtle intuition and the most heartfelt desire . . . for the deepest longing for happiness and peace . . . And also for all that is still unconscious, for unknown possibilities and never-thought thoughts, even for the unimaginable, there is space . . . in the channel of your awareness.*

8. *The banks of the wide river are so far apart that you can no longer see the other side . . . and the vast river becomes deeper and deeper . . . The river turns into a sea . . . and the sea into an ocean . . . immeasurably vast . . . immeasurably deep . . . a boundless awareness . . . where there is space for whatever . . . boundless space for EVERYTHING.*

Between the wisdom of nothing and the love of everything our life flows.

We often present the previous exercise in the silent session or in the last session. Here, an imagery is used that can help to remind ourselves of the boundless openness of awareness and the healing potential of our mind. Awareness can welcome everything with an open heart, not rejecting anything, not holding onto anything, with equanimity allowing the river of life to flow through the safe holding of our mind and heart, a safe place to all we experience, even the unwanted. A boundless awareness where we are already always home. 'As if you knew this before it had been seen. Had been there before you would arrive.' (Kees Spiering, 1996).

Also in this exercise we can gratefully use our imagination to work for us and be mindful of what emerges moment by moment. Sometimes it is wise and kind to set boundaries; they may give us temporary shelter and support. When the boundaries become prison walls, it becomes more loving to free ourselves and explore what lies beyond them. Then this exercise can offer a helpful metaphor. The boundless openness for the ocean of possibilities and the tender intimacy with the smallest and most vulnerable drop of experience in this moment are both expressions of the healing power of our mind and heart, our heart-mind, in the ancient Pali language simply referred to by the word *citta*. Wisdom and compassion are the healing forces that are lying dormant in us, and that can awaken in every moment when we are mindfully and heartfully present with what is.

2.8.4 How to Continue?

There came a time when the risk to remain tight in the bud
was more painful than the risk it took to blossom.

                                                                (Unknown source)

We can let ourselves be inspired on the path by many well and lesser known examples of human resilience and self-healing ability. But we don't need to imitate them. We can each one of us be our own example for the world by showing how we deal with our suffering—even though that might be very moderate by the standards of our judgmental mind. Yet that is what demands the most courage—to find our own unique answer, from our own vulnerability and from our own strength. This is expressed in words attributed to Lao Tzu:

Always we hope
someone else has the answer.
some other place will be better,

some other time it will all turn out.
This is it.
no one else has the answer.
No other place will be better,
and it has already turned out.
At the center of your being
you have the answer.

If we consciously formulate our own authentic answer to what life asks of us, this is unique to us. We can only displace our own stone, go our own untrodden path, make our own mistakes and discover our own potential. When we realise we are unique evolving and interconnected beings we transcend the temporary edifice of our constructed self and reach out to one another.

We hope that the compassion training journey has been meaningful to you and that you can travel further in your own way. Perhaps you feel it is enough, or have regrets that this is the last session. The work does not need to end here, however. Consider the last session is the beginning of the rest of your life, as trainers often say about the last session of a mindfulness course. It is up to you to integrate the practice of mindfulness and heartfulness into your daily life, with or without the support of others. It is work that never ends because our life is in constant flux, like a river. We can never step into the same river twice, as Heraclitus said.

In the eighth session we usually offer several suggestions. If the programme has been of benefit we advise you to continue. In the further reading section we list a number of books that may inspire and nourish you. Mindfulness centres often organise refresher meetings, or participants of courses form small groups to practise together at home. There are centres and meditation groups in an increasing number of places all over the world where you can continue the practice.

If you have not been practising much but feel inspired after reading the book, we advise you to take part in a compassion training programme.

In any case, now is the start of the rest of your life. Live now; there is no other moment to live. May mindfulness and compassion be your faithful companions, wherever you go. May you arrive home again and again in this moment. May you find wholeness in the imperfection of life. May the sunrays of kindness shine through the raindrops of suffering, and may the rainbow of compassion bring its healing power to you and all beings.

Overview of Session 8: The Healing Power of Compassion

Themes

In Session 8 we discuss the value of compassion for healing processes in our lives, and we look at how we can continue the practice after the training course.

Agenda

1. 'Inner Weather' check in and 'What Do You Wish for Yourself?'
2. An exercise of choice that connects with the need of the participants, such as 'A Compassionate Body Scan' (2.8.2) or 'The Stream of Awareness' (2.8.3). Sharing about the exercise.
3. Inquiry about formal and informal home practice done in the week after Session 7.
4. Short break followed by some mindful movement exercises.
5. A short sitting meditation and reflection on the end of the course.
6. In the group each person is given the opportunity to share what they wish to share in response to the following questions:

    •   What were your expectations and what did you learn?
    •   What did you find difficult in the training?
    •   What can help you to continue to practise?
    •   Is there a symbol (object, text, poem) that expresses what has been valuable for you in the training?

7. Ending with a short (standing) exercise with kindness to oneself, to fellow participants and to all living beings. For example, each participant can in turn mention their names followed by a brief silence during which the others can silently send a kind wish to that person.

Practice Suggestions After Session 8

•   If you have experienced the value of compassion practice, see how you can continue to be nourished by it. This may happen through regular individual practice and self-study or going to a meditation group.
•   If you are interested, you can also discuss and plan how to continue activities with (some) participants from the training group.
•   Above all, let the compass of mindful compassion guide you along your path.

Evaluation

After the eighth session we usually have an individual evaluation meeting with each participant where remaining questions and wishes for continuation can be discussed in more detail. Doing so after a few weeks has the advantage that it is often more obvious how the participant is faring in working with the exercises alone and integrating them in daily life. The whole process can be reviewed using a feedback questionnaire and the desired outcome list that was handed in at the start of the training.

Part 3

The Compassionate Therapist

I thought I knew you,
but it was only me.
The you that you truly are
is not the you I see.
My mind has formed your image
but you have already travelled on.
I want to see only you
but I see you through me.

(Lao Tzu)

The final part of this book offers relevant information specifically for professionals, to support their clients individually or in a group setting.

Various handbooks have been written on the application of mindfulness in the therapeutic process (Germer, Siegel, & Fulton, 2013; Hick & Bien, 2008; Shapiro & Carlson, 2009; D. J. Siegel, 2010a; Wilson, 2008). Germer (2013) described three perspectives on mindfulness and psychotherapy:

- *mindfulness-oriented* therapy, where the therapist practises mindfulness to improve their personal functioning and to enhance their attentiveness and efficacy in the therapeutic process;
- *mindfulness-informed* therapy, where the therapist applies insights into the workings of the mind based on personal practice and theoretical knowledge of mindfulness from Eastern and Western psychology (for example, applying the Buddhist perspective on suffering, impermanence and selflessness);
- *mindfulness-based* therapy, where—unlike in the previous two perspectives—clients are explicitly taught mindfulness skills to support them in dealing with stress more skilfully and to alleviate or prevent suffering. Examples of this therapeutic approach are Mindfulness-Based Stress Reduction (MBSR), Mindfulness-Based Cognitive Therapy (MBCT), Acceptance and Commitment Therapy and Dialectical Behavioural Therapy.

In this section, we will follow up on these three perspectives in the application of compassion practice to the therapeutic process (Germer, 2012). First we will discuss how the therapist can practise compassion to improve their functioning and therapeutic efficacy (3.1). Next we outline how the therapist can use the insights from personal compassion practice and Buddhist and Western psychology to support clients better, without actually encouraging them to engage in formal practice (3.2). Finally we will address how the therapist can teach clients compassion practices as part of individual treatment or in a group setting (3.3). A few points will be mentioned in this respect that are important in deciding which clients would benefit from this and which criteria trainers would need to fulfil.

3.1 The Value of Personal Practice

Paradoxically, the act of helping often leads to burnout in the helpers, suggesting they forget to help themselves whilst helping others. Therapeutic work is often experienced as emotionally demanding (Mann, 2004). 'Compassion fatigue', more correctly called 'empathy fatigue', as argued in 1.6.4, and burnout are related and widespread phenomena in the helping professions (Figley, 2002; Firth-Cozens, 2001; Skovholt & Trotter-Mathison, 2011; Weiss, 2004). A large survey amongst U.S. physicians showed that around 40% experienced symptoms of burnout, which was considerably more than the general population. Those in the frontline of care were the most at risk (Shanafelt et al., 2012). This can result in a drop in both job fulfilment and quality of care. The problem may start during training. A number of studies showed a significant empathy decline during medical school and residency (Chen, Kirshenbaum, Yan, Kirshenbaum, & Aseltine, 2012; Neumann et al., 2011) and also during nursing school (Ward, Cody, Schaal, & Hojat, 2012). It is striking that students do not gain but lose empathic skills during their training, although empathy is generally considered to be a key therapeutic factor. A large American study showed that more than half of medical students met the criteria for burnout, which was associated with more unprofessional conduct and fewer altruistic professional values (Dyrbye et al., 2010). Are our educational systems omitting something crucial when they fail to teach professional caregivers how to care for themselves? Shauna Shapiro offered a fitting metaphor (Shapiro & Carlson, 2009): The heart first pumps blood to itself before it pumps blood to other parts of the body. If this were not the case, the heart would die and subsequently the rest of the body. In the same way professional caregivers can only care well for others after they have learned to care well for themselves. If they are unable to do so, they will suffer as well as their patients. Meanwhile political and economic factors make working in health care organisations increasingly stressful. Mechanistic, bureaucratic organisational systems and neoliberal market ideology increase the risk of dehumanisation and alienation, leaving little room for compassionate practice (Cole-King & Gilbert, 2011; De Zulueta, 2013).

On the positive side, several mindfulness-based programmes that teach health care professionals self-awareness and self-care skills have been evaluated with promising results, both in groups of primary care physicians (Fortney, Luchterhand, Zakletskaja, Zgierska, & Rakel, 2013; Krasner et al., 2009) and medical students (Karpowicz, Harazduk & Haramati, 2009; Saunders et al., 2007). Controlled studies amongst health care professionals and therapists in training showed that Mindfulness-Based Stress Reduction has a beneficial impact on their physical and mental health, quality of life, stress tolerance levels and capacity for self-compassion (Shapiro, Astin, Bishop, & Cordova, 2005; Shapiro, Brown, & Biegel, 2007). Double blind controlled research amongst therapists in training showed that they not only help themselves but also their clients by meditating regularly (Grepmair et al., 2007). The therapists, who were randomly assigned to a meditation programme (so they did not *choose* to do this), achieved better treatment results with their clients than colleagues who just followed the usual training. The clients—who did not know that their therapist meditated (therefore double blind)—had more insights into themselves and showed more improvement in complaints and symptoms than the clients of therapists not practising meditation.

Mindfulness helps therapists to both be in touch with themselves and with clients and cultivates very important skills for the therapeutic process: authentic presence, unconditional regard and the capacity for empathy and holding. These are nonspecific therapeutic factors that offer significant contribution to a good working relationship and to therapeutic success (see also 1.2.2). The more stressful health care organisations become, the more important it is to support health care professionals in regulating their emotions and stress levels, and mindfulness can support that.

It is quite likely—though research has to confirm this—that more explicit compassion practice will have a further positive impact. The score on the self-compassion scale seems to be even more strongly associated with mental well-being, quality of life, wisdom, personal initiative, happiness, optimism, positive emotions and dealing with stress more wisely than the score on the mindfulness scale (Neff, 2008; Van Dam, Sheppard, Forsyth, & Earleywine, 2011). A recent qualitative study amongst therapists in training who received a six-session programme of loving-kindness meditation (after they had completed a Mindfulness-Based Cognitive Therapy course) felt it led to increased self-awareness, compassion for self and others and therapeutic presence and skills (Boellinghaus, Jones, & Hutton, 2013). At the same time, the authors found loving-kindness meditation was experienced as emotionally challenging and recommended it should be taught with care.

We often hear from therapists who formally practise compassion and loving-kindness that it helps them to experience connectedness with their clients and themselves. They feel they are better able to face the clients' pain as well as their own with openness and kindness and are less bothered by feelings of counter-transference. They are less inclined to initiate impulsive interventions or to chase after results and better able to wait patiently until the right response presents itself. The practice supports the sense of common humanity and helps to distinguish between inevitable suffering and suffering that arises from our reactions to it. This helps to normalise existential suffering and prevents unnecessary pathologising of emotional pain. Since we have offered the Mindfulness-Based Compassionate

Living programme to professionals, we have noticed that a fair number of health care employees wish to deepen their practice and carry on with compassion training following a mindfulness training.

A specific form of practice that we would like to mention here is Insight Dialogue, described by Gregory Kramer (2007). He and his team developed a manual for practising meditation in dialogue from a Buddhist perspective, which can be of benefit to psychotherapists as well. A more secular form is called Interpersonal Mindfulness (Kramer, Meleo-Meyer, & Lee Turner, 2008). In psychotherapy trainings a lot of energy is often spent in learning specific techniques and models, although we now know that the nonspecific factors are much more important for good therapeutic outcomes. We still seem to be in need of a proper method that teaches us to develop, sustain and deepen a quality like empathy. Insight Dialogue is a promising method based on formal practice for pairs or larger groups to learn to converse in a wholesome, authentic way by being present with more mindfulness and compassion for themselves and others and listening with more openness and deep alignment. Inspiring examples of meditation teachers who previously worked as therapists are Susan Gillis Chapman (2012) and Rosamund Oliver (2013). They developed secular teaching programmes on interpersonal practice of mindfulness and compassion, each from different Tibetan practice traditions, which are increasingly offered to health care professionals to deepen their communication skills.

Until now it has been the initiative of individual therapists to practise meditation. It is expected formal mindfulness and compassion practices will increasingly be part of training curricula for caregiving professions in the future because they cultivate the skills caregivers need to care for their clients and themselves. Hopefully managers of health care organisations will enable their employees to follow postgraduate trainings in mindfulness and compassion because this will promote health on many levels: that of the employees, that of the clients and that of the organisation itself. In this way it can be shown that good health care needs both cure and care and that compassion for others and self-compassion are interdependent.

3.2 Therapeutic Use of General Insights

No mud, no lotus.
(Buddhist saying)

Whatever model therapists use to work with, insights from inner science and outer science as to how the process of compassion works will always benefit them. There is a growing body of literature on outer science in relation to compassion (see Chapter 1.6). We recommend *Wisdom and Compassion in Psychotherapy*, edited by Germer and Siegel (2012), with many contributions bringing together Western and Eastern perspectives on wisdom and compassion and clinical practice. It is expected that the literature on compassion and self-compassion will expand rapidly, just as the scientific works on mindfulness and meditation have grown exponentially (J. M. G. Williams & Kabat-Zinn, 2011).

Buddhist psychology has produced a wealth of knowledge from inner science in 2,500 years' history, which offers deeper insights in the common roots of human suffering (Mikulas, 2007). It concerns transdiagnostic processes that can be helpful for many clients, irrespective of their symptoms, conditions or disorders. Just like psychoanalytical insights, for example, which are not gained from outer science either, these insights can support the therapeutic work because they offer therapists a richer language for naming mental and emotional processes and for connecting with their clients. And even more important, these insights remind the therapist as well as the client to keep returning to the investigation of their own experience, the 'first person' research where the perception precedes conceptual knowledge.

Many meditation teachers have made Buddhist insights accessible for people in the West in their books. Therapists increasingly read them, verify these insights in their personal practice and weave them into their therapeutic work. The wholesome and unwholesome reactions to suffering have been mapped out and written down systematically in various Buddhist traditions aided by a centuries-long practice of inner science. An elaborate overview of this falls outside the scope of this book; therefore we only mention a few examples of writers who make Buddhist thought accessible for people in the West.

The *Abhidhamma* is a Buddhist study of human existence. It is extremely fascinating and thorough but at the same time not easily accessible. Frits has written an introduction to the *Abhidhamma* entitled *The Web of Buddhist Wisdom* (Koster, 2014). Other guides deal more specifically with the wholesome effects of *metta*, such as *Loving-Kindness* by Sharon Salzberg (1995), who teaches from the *vipassana* tradition. In *The Four Immeasurables* (2010) Alan Wallace describes the practice of the Four Illimitables or Immeasurables (*Brahmaviharas*). Pema Chödrön (2001, 2003) has written accessible books on *tonglen* and the development of courage and compassion from the Tibetan tradition. In *Start Where You Are* (2003), for example, she shows how everything that we encounter on our path—however painful, annoying, fearful, irritating, shameful or devastating it may be—actually can be the beginning of awakening mindfulness and compassion. Also based on ancient Tibetan practice, Tsultrim Allione's (2008) book *Feeding Your Demons* describes a way of dealing with the parts in ourselves we find hard to accept not by fighting our 'inner demons' but by feeding them with loving attention. It can be extremely heartening for therapists to share these insights with their clients, and it gives a completely different meaning to the many forms of suffering and adversity people bring to a health care professional. Our hearts can open and flourish not in spite of but because of adversity.

Buddhist psychology can complement and deepen Western psychology and vice versa, so we give some examples of encounters between Buddhist and Western thinking in different therapeutic schools. The psychiatrist Mark Epstein (1995, 1998) very respectfully has brought the psychoanalytical and Buddhist worlds together. The importance of 'holding' in the therapeutic relationship—a term Donald Winnicott derived from the safe environment a *good enough* mother offers her child—is endorsed by many therapists, whether they work within or outside the psychoanalytical framework. The Buddhist view can help shift the perspective from the holding environment offered by the therapist to developing the capacity for an open and compassionate awareness in the clients themselves—the holding by awareness. This capacity is inherent in everybody, even in those who have a background of insecure attachment.

Therapeutic schools rooted in positive and solution-focussed psychology have quite rightly been pointing out for some time that successful therapy involves more than reducing complaints or symptoms (Carr, 2011; De Jong & Berg, 1998; De Shazer & Dolan, 2007; Seligman, 2002). Since the advent of the humanistic third wave in psychotherapy, the job of the therapist is not just about alleviating suffering; it is also about improving well-being, happiness and quality of life. The therapist who is focussed on what is lacking or not functioning well notices less than the therapist who broadens their perspective to include what strengths are present and what is already functioning well. The pitfall here is that one narrows the focus too much on positive feelings whilst negative emotions are ignored, which was of course never the intention of humanistic psychologists (Lambert & Erekson, 2008). The Four Illimitables of Buddhist psychology offer a way to move towards well-being and to practise kindness and sympathetic joy without excluding inevitable adversity and suffering and to meet the latter with equanimity and compassion (Bien, 2008). Imperfection, however it presents itself, is a key opportunity to awaken our innate healing qualities. Personal growth is perhaps an overemphasised value in many therapeutic schools in Western culture. Ego-strengthening methods have been advocated in mental health care for years, partly driven by the importance our culture places on personal success and self-esteem. From the perspective of Buddhist psychology the question can be asked whether an ego-transcending perspective might not be more beneficial. Forceful striving for a cure and for control over uncontrollable processes only results in more suffering, whereas a kind and nonjudgmental attitude towards the impermanent and uncontrollable can be liberating. Then it is no longer just about 'getting better' and the pursuit of a cure but also about 'being good enough' from an attitude of care. The search for specific remedies can then be imbedded into the care for a healthy way of life with sustainable values.

Modern Western schools, such as the third-generation behaviour therapies (Hayes, Follette, & Linehan, 2004), increasingly emphasise that it can be beneficial to cultivate flexibility in our identification processes. If we take our 'self' more lightly, there is more space for self-transcending and altruistic values, which are more sustainable sources of happiness. In Part 1 (see 1.4.1), Acceptance and Commitment Therapy was mentioned as an example of how a transdiagnostic model was developed in Western psychology by way of outer science that has much in common with Buddhist insights arrived at by way of inner science. Fundamental to both models is acceptance of inevitable pain. It is in this very pain that values and meanings are hidden that can give direction and richness to our lives. And those who devote their lives to values that really matter will inevitably meet—besides happiness—pain. Courage and compassion always go hand in hand. In her book *Radical Acceptance* (2004) Tara Brach widened the term 'exposure' to include a much more radical openness towards our inner pain. Then acceptance is not a superficial acknowledgment but an intimate embrace. This is Step 5 in Germer's stages of acceptance (see 2.2.4). Of course this does not involve a desperate jump from Stage 1 to 5 but an underlying sense—a core value that gives direction to the therapeutic work—that wholeness at the deepest level means that everything may be taken to heart.

3.3 Teaching Compassion Practice to Clients

Compassion Focused Therapy, developed by Paul Gilbert (2010, 2014), is an example of how valuable insights from Cognitive Behaviour Therapy, evolutionary psychology, attachment theory, neuroscience and Buddhist psychology come together in a therapeutic model where the client learns to become more compassionate. Gilbert speaks of Compassionate Mind Training. This can be offered in individual therapy as well as in a group setting and also for the more severely disturbed patients (Gilbert & Irons, 2005; Gilbert & Proctor, 2006). Christopher Germer (2009, 2012) also has described the use of compassion practices in individual therapies. Together with Kristin Neff he developed an 8-week group module called Mindful Self-Compassion Training (Neff & Germer, 2012). Other group trainings have been developed, such as Loving-Kindness Meditation (Fredrickson, Cohn, Coffey, Pek, & Finkel, 2008), Compassion Cultivation Training (Jazaieri et al., 2013, 2014) and Cognitive-Based Compassion Training (Pace et al., 2009, 2010; see also 1.6.2 and 1.6.3). For these programmes no previous experience with meditation or mindfulness is required. The Mindfulness-Based Compassionate Living (MBCL) training that we have developed has a somewhat higher threshold because it is recommended to clients who already are familiar with mindfulness. We see this as an advantage because being familiar with the simpler basic exercises from the mindfulness training makes it easier to work with the more complex practices and visualisations and the backdraft phenomenon in the compassion training. We see this advantage not only in mental health care settings but also in nonclinical settings with participants who have more stable backgrounds.

Daniel Siegel (2010a) uses the metaphor of the 'mindsight lens'. He introduced the word 'mindsight' to refer to the capacity to focus our attention on the processes in the mind. The mindsight lens rests on a support structure with three important legs that are needed to keep the lens stable, namely openness, observation and objectivity. When the lens is insufficiently stabilised by this tripod, processes in our mind cannot be seen clearly and accurately. If we do not have enough skills, keeping the lens stable can become very difficult when it is aimed at the painful content that can surface when we do compassion practices. We particularly notice the prevalence of the backdraft phenomenon in mental health care clients. Old pain triggers the threat system, and automatic defence reactions disturb the potential for openness, observation and objectivity, so that the lens cannot be kept still and the image becomes blurred. A stable mindsight lens, acquired through previous mindfulness practice, broadens the capacity for compassion practice. Then it becomes easier to address the inner attitude of kindness with which the attention is focussed or, to stay with the metaphor, the colour of the lens can become warmer as a result of practice. And even then it may happen that in compassion training the mindsight lens goes off balance. When this happens, we advise the participants to temporarily return to the familiar mindfulness exercises. The simplicity of following the breath attentively or noticing sounds can restabilise the mindsight lens.

If the contents of consciousness are less painful, the practice of mindfulness and self-compassion can go hand in hand much sooner. For some clients a Mindfulness-Based Stress Reduction (MBSR) course can be sufficient for them to continue to cultivate the kind attitude by themselves, or they may start immediately with the practice of loving-kindness and self-compassion, such as in the programme of Neff and Germer. They have more options as to what practices and exercises they can use to support their process of becoming more aware. Others may have fewer options, and the road to more freedom of choice can be longer. In any case, as far as we are concerned it is always a matter of 'and', never of 'or'. Mindfulness and compassion most easily flourish in each other's company, as in the metaphor of the bird who needs both wings to fly.

3.3.1   For Which Clients?

Clients who did not gain sufficient foundation to integrate mindfulness and kindness into their lives from the MBSR/Mindfulness-Based Cognitive Therapy (MBCT) module often have persistently strong self-judgment, shame and unwholesome patterns. To speak in the language of the *Diagnostic and Statistical Manual of Mental Disorders* (American Psychiatric Association, 2000, 2013) there will often be a mixture of Axis I and Axis II problems, which means that there is a combination of long-term or recurring psychiatric phenomena on the one hand, such as depression, anxiety, obsessive–compulsive disorder or addiction problems (Axis I) and on the other hand unhealthy personality patterns (Axis II) that hinder a flexible adaptation to adverse conditions, which in turn make psychiatric problems more likely.

Actual severe depression and suicidal tendencies, manic–depressive disorders, posttraumatic stress disorders, dissociation or psychoses can be reasons for postponing the training until more stability has been gained with the help of first-choice treatment methods. When these problems are part of the client's history, we need to be extra careful. If someone is dependent on alcohol or other substances they will need to reduce their use as much as possible before the training starts. Personality disorders from cluster B (borderline, narcissistic, histrionic) or C (avoidant, dependent, obsessive–compulsive) are not necessarily contraindications. On the contrary, the training offers scope for the recognition and softening of long-term persistent patterns in people with personality problems. As mentioned earlier, the training is transdiagnostic in nature, comparable to the MBSR module, and we do not aim to have groups with homogeneous problems. However, a few remarks are called for.

At the start of Part 2, we described the criteria for participation in the compassion training. It is important that clients have sufficient motivation, time and opportunities to follow the programme and do practices at home. When daily functioning is not stable and when there are indications that a participant is prone to crisis, a therapist needs to be easily accessible during the training, and their agreement on the client's participation is required. Clients are suitable candidates if they have previously done an MBSR/MBCT training or a similar programme without too many complications and found that the exercises were helpful but that the training was too short to integrate the practice into their lives. If the training is offered in a mental health care setting, the levels of distress from complaints or persistent unhealthy patterns in potential participants needs to be sufficiently high to justify participation in the secondary health care. It is advisable that first-choice evidence-based treatments be applied first if that has not yet been done.

Clients with a history of insecure attachment, trauma and/or neglect and a severely underdeveloped soothing system can benefit from the structure of the compassion training, but individual adjustments in the practice programme will be necessary from time to time. We intentionally do not speak of 'homework' but call it 'practice suggestions'. It is important that the participants do the exercises in the order that is feasible for them and at a pace that is manageable. In participants with insecure attachment, the threat system can become easily activated when warm feelings are evoked because these are especially associated with lack of safety. In that case it is important to deal respectfully with emotional boundaries and to gradually introduce exposure to kind and compassionate approaches. The exercise 'The Safe Place' is often less threatening than 'The Compassionate Companion' because a safe place can be imagined without the presence of another person.

Visualisation exercises can be more charged and confusing for other participants, for example because there is a history of psychoses. In that case these exercises can be skipped; the kindness meditation might be more suitable. Expressing wishes of goodwill to oneself and to others demands a careful extension, in small steps, from less to more challenging situations or people. Clients can be invited again and again to return to self-compassion when compassion for others is too difficult.

Participants who are excessively focussed on caring for others and who find it difficult to receive care themselves can take more time with 'The Compassionate Companion' exercise before moving on to the practice of 'The Compassion Mode'. In that case it will be beneficial to primarily focus the attention on the sensations that arise when warmth and security are received and also when the kind wishes are offered to oneself. It is always important to feel connected with the body during the practice and to notice the emotions and feelings in the heart area to prevent the exercises from taking place mainly at the cognitive level.

It may be liberating to reverse the focus from ego-preservation to ego-transcendence. The exercise 'Compassionate Breathing' can help with this. When the inner bully is dominant, acknowledging, naming and lovingly wishing this inner tormentor well can be beneficial. Where there is a persistent striving for success and appreciation from others in an overdeveloped drive system, dealing compassionately with desire ('urge-surfing') and the practice of savouring and being mindful of what kindles gratitude, sympathetic joy and generosity can strengthen the soothing system. If there is aversion to the pain and suffering of others, it can be beneficial to imagine breathing that in and letting kind wishes flow to the other on the out-breath. If there is a tendency to be jealous, sympathetic joy with the other can be practised. If there is *Schadenfreude*, the other can be celebrated with loving wishes. If there is pride or conceit, wishing oneself equanimity can be beneficial.

Participants can spend more or less time with the exercises in this way, depending on their predominant patterns, thus 'tailoring' the training to their own situation. This requires flexibility from the trainer. The programme also allows for flexibility in the frequency of the sessions, depending on the needs of the participants. Although the programme is designed to be taught in weekly sessions, we found it can be advantageous, especially in the second half of the course, to spread out sessions to once every 2 to 4 weeks to enable participants to explore exercises in their home practice in more depth.

Of course MBCL can also be taught in nonclinical settings to participants who live a stressful life and wish to deepen their mindfulness practice with heartfulness. All exercises can be applied in individual therapies, too. What is specific about group training in compassion is a broader spectrum of learning opportunities. Clients hear the other participants' experiences and can recognise and mirror themselves. Furthermore they often realise that they are not the only ones struggling with pain, frustration and sorrow. The common humanity aspect of compassion is more easily accessible in a group. Unfortunately, the influence of group factors has not yet been taken into account much in the research into the effects of mindfulness training; usually only individual outcomes are measured. In one of the few studies where the effect of the group on the outcome was measured, this turned out to be quite significant (Imel, Baldwin, Bonus, & MacCoon, 2008). Learning from each other is emphasised in the book *Teaching Mindfulness* by McCown, Reibel, and Micozzi (2010), in our view with good reason. On the basis of Daniel Siegel's (2007) work, the authors mention a 'resonance circuit' that apparently has a neurobiological basis, too, since the discovery of mirror neurons (special neurons that help us to understand each other and empathise without needing words). The resonance circuit can be strengthened and weakened in accordance with the extent that the participants are connected with themselves and with each other in their practice and in the inquiry afterwards. The intrasubjective alignment reinforces the intersubjective connection, and vice versa. A powerful resonance circuit can be a valuable support in the learning process.

Participants often tell mindfulness trainers that practising in a group is so much more powerful and beneficial than practising at home, and we hear this over and over again from compassion training participants. Practising and experiencing connection with each other in the silence, experiencing the freedom to say something in the inquiry afterward or not, not needing to react to one another, being present just listening and yet feeling accepted, being allowed to respect one's own boundaries and the intention of kindness to oneself and others—all these factors contribute strongly to an atmosphere of safeness and facilitate learning. This seems a wholesome corrective experience, particularly for those participants in mental health care, who did not previously respond well to group therapy or individual counselling. In our view it is important that these aspects are included in future research and that there won't be any hasty conclusions that mindfulness and compassion training can just as easily be learned individually, from books or Internet programmes. Positive effects will undoubtedly be found there, too, but it is likely that the powerful factor of the group process will become lost.

3.3.2   By Which Teachers?

Practising and guiding mindfulness-based methods can seem deceptively simple but require thorough training and personal practice. The same goes for compassion training. In our view, it is important that trainers first have experience in teaching MBSR or MBCT before starting to give MBCL training courses in groups, so that they are familiar with the structure and the alternation between guiding exercises and inquiry in the group afterward as well as being familiar with the basic attitude needed. As in facilitating MBSR/MBCT, personal practice is emphasised so that the teacher is able to convey the exercises authentically and in attunement with themselves and the participants. For a detailed description of the qualities and skills we refer to McCown et al. (2010). The individual experiences of the participants are the main teacher in the compassion training. Just as in MBSR/MBCT, it involves a *training* that is given to a group, and not group *therapy*. In mental health care, the trainer does need to have adequate psychiatric training so they can recognise in the initial interview or subsequently during the course whether problems that arise need a different approach. We notice that old pain can surface in the participants even more so than in MBSR/MBCT, and when this happens, it is desirable that the trainers keep to their role and do not turn into therapists—unless of course it is more compassionate to do so, but then it might be better to do this outside the framework of the training. The underlying message is that as far as possible the participants learn to become their own therapist. They are repeatedly invited to check against their own practice and situation whether reactions to their experiences are wholesome or unwholesome and to make wise choices based on these insights. The exchanges in the group support the individual process of the participants.

The main tasks of the trainers are to organise the external conditions (time, space, means) that enable the training to take place, to ensure a wholesome group atmosphere (resonance circuit), to guide the practices, to weave in appropriate didactics that are suitable for the participants and to discuss the exercises afterward according to the method of inquiry or open mindful dialogue. This does not involve therapeutic exploration but facilitates the process of becoming mindful, through inquiry about what is happening in the present moment to or in the participant. Of course the trainer can practise sympathetic joy when participants share a clarifying insight, just as the trainer can practise compassion when participants share their pain, without being tempted to offer quick suggestions and solutions. 'Practise what you preach' and 'teach from your own practice' are slogans that are usually given to mindfulness trainers in training. They apply just as much to compassion trainers. Offering to be available in between sessions can be valuable for participants who might need this as an extra safety net. In mental health care many participants already see an individual therapist, but nevertheless it can sometimes be helpful to have direct contact with the trainer, for example when a participant meets obstacles in the practice that cannot wait until the next session.

Whether trainers feel capable of teaching MBCL depends on their previous experience with personal practice and the skills in teaching mindfulness. For those who have access to it, the best introduction is to follow an 8-week MBCL training as a participant. We have several offerings that can deepen the personal experience of MBCL and prepare one to work with it and teach it.

Our 3-day MBCL Foundation Course supports becoming familiar with MBCL in an experiential way. It is particularly suitable for teachers of mindfulness-based approaches (such as MBSR and MBCT) and health care professionals. A prerequisite for participation is either being a mindfulness teacher or having completed training in one of the health care professions with additional training in MBSR, MBCT, Breathworks or other mindfulness-based methods such as Acceptance and Commitment Therapy (ACT) or Dialectical Behavior Therapy (DBT). Health care professionals who are not mindfulness teachers are expected to have followed at least one 8-week course in a mindfulness-based training programme and have an established personal mindfulness practice of at least a year.

We have developed a 6-day MBCL teacher-training program consisting of two modules of 3 days each for MBSR/MBCT teachers and health care professionals who are familiar with guiding mindfulness-based methods (in groups or individually). The Foundation Course is a prerequisite to participate. In the first module we highlight the theoretical background, content and practices of the eight MBCL sessions with a mix of experiential work, interpersonal reflection and plenary teaching. In the second module the eight sessions are revisited, but now with the focus on guiding the practices oneself and doing the inquiry that follows.

This teacher-training programme is currently taking place in various countries in Europe. Health care professionals who are not certified MBSR/MBCT teachers can choose to follow the MBCL teacher training for further education to deepen their skills in mindfulness-based and compassion focused therapeutic work with individual clients or groups. Participants who are already certified MBSR/MBCT teachers or who have a comparable teaching background can be certified as MBCL teachers when they have successfully completed both the Foundation Course and the 6-day professional training.

More information about our various offerings can be found at our websites (www. institute-for-mindfulness.eu; www.compassionateliving.info; www.mbcl.org).

Appendix

Guided Mindfulness-Based Compassionate Living Exercises That Can Be Downloaded

The following exercises can be downloaded as audio files at www.routledge.com/9781138022157

1. The Breathing Space With Kindness (2.1.2)
2. The Safe Place (2.1.7)
3. Kindness Meditation—Yourself (2.1.10)
4. Compassionately Dealing With Resistance (2.2.2)
5. The Breathing Space With Compassion—Coping With Emotional Pain (2.2.8)
6. The Compassionate Companion (2.2.11)
7. Compassionately Dealing With Desire (2.3.1)
8. Recognising Inner Patterns (2.3.7)
9. Kindness Meditation—A Benefactor (2.3.9)
10. The Compassion Mode (2.4.2)
11. Kindness Meditation—A Good Friend (2.4.4)
12. Kindness Meditation—A Neutral Person (2.4.5)
13. Kindness for the Body (2.4.6)
14. Walking With Kindness (2.4.8)
15. Kindness Meditation—A Difficult Person or Inner Difficulty (2.5.4)
16. Compassionate Breathing (2.5.5)
17. Forgiving Ourselves (2.6.2)
18. Asking for Forgiveness (2.6.2)
19. Forgiving Others (2.6.2)
20. Savouring and Revisiting the Good (2.6.5)
21. Kindness Meditation—All Beings (2.6.6)
22. Equanimity (2.7.1)
23. A Compassionate Body Scan (2.8.2)
24. The Stream of Awareness (2.8.3)

A pdf-file with examples of movement exercises and eventual addtions to the MBCL programme in the future can be downloaded from www.routledge.com/9781138022157

Further Reading

For those who would like to read more, we can recommend the following books, which are written for the general public. For detailed references for all works cited in the text, see the reference list.

Karen Armstrong, *Twelve Steps to a Compassionate Life*, The Bodley Head, 2011.
James Baraz & Shoshana Alexander, *Awakening Joy*, Bantam, 2010.
Tara Brach, *Radical Acceptance*, Bantam, 2004.
Tara Brach, *True Refuge*, Bantam, 2013.
Brené Brown, *The Gifts of Imperfection*, Hazelden, 2010.
Brené Brown, *Daring Greatly*, Gotham, 2012.
Vidyamala Burch, *Living Well with Pain and Illness*, Piatkus, 2008.
Vidyamala Burch and Danny Penman, *Mindfulness for Health*, Piatkus, 2013.
Pema Chödrön, *Tonglen*, Vajradhatu, 2001.
Pema Chödrön, *Start Where You Are*, Element, 2003.
Christina Feldman, *Compassion: Listening to the Cries of the World*, Rodmell Press, 2005.
Barbara Fredrickson, *Love 2.0*, Penguin Putnam, 2013.
Christopher Germer, *The Mindful Path to Self-Compassion*, Guilford Press, 2009.
Paul Gilbert, *The Compassionate Mind*, Constable & Robinson, 2010.
Paul Gilbert and Choden, *Mindful Compassion*, Constable & Robinson, 2013.
Kenn Goss, *The Compassionate Mind Approach to Beating Overeating*, Constable & Robinson, 2011.
Rick Hanson (with Richard Mendius), *Buddha's Brain*, New Harbinger, 2009.
Rick Hanson, *Hardwiring Happiness*, Ebury Press, 2013.
Lynne Henderson, *Improving Social Confidence and Reducing Shyness Using Compassion Focused Therapy*, Constable & Robinson, 2010.
Jon Kabat-Zinn, *Coming to Our Senses*, Piatkus, 2006.
Frits Koster, *Buddhist Meditation in Stress Management*, Silkworm Books, 2007.
Kristin Neff, *Self-Compassion*, Hodder & Stoughton, 2011.
Sharon Salzberg, *Loving-Kindness*, Shambala, 1995.
Daniel Siegel, *Mindsight*, Bantam, 2010.
Alan Wallace, *The Four Immeasurables*, Shambala, 2010.

References

Adams, C., & Leary, M. R. (2007). Promoting self-compassionate attitudes toward eating among restrictive and guilty eaters. *Journal of Social and Clinical Psychology, 26,* 1120–1144.

Ainsworth, M. D. S., & Bowlby, J. (1991). An ethological approach to personality development. *American Psychologist, 46,* 333–341.

Allione, T. (2008). *Feeding your demons: Ancient wisdom for resolving inner conflict.* New York: Little, Brown.

American Psychiatric Association. (2000). *Diagnostic and statistical manual of mental disorders* (4th ed., text revision). Washington, DC: Author.

American Psychiatric Association. (2013). *Diagnostic and statistical manual of mental disorders* (5th ed.). Arlington, VA: Author.

Appelo, M. (2011). *Het gelaagde brein: Reflectie en discipline bij het werken aan verandering* [The multi-layered brain: Reflection and discipline in working towards change]. Amsterdam, the Netherlands: Boom.

Appelo, M., & Bos, E. (2008). De relatie tussen klachten, veerkracht en welzijn [The relationship between strengths, resilience and well-being]. *Gedragstherapie, 36,* 309–318.

Arch, J. J., Brown, K. W., Dean, D. J., Landy, L. N., Brown, K., & Laudenslager, M. L. (2014). Self-compassion training modulates alpha-amylase, heart rate variability, and subjective responses to social evaluative threat in women. *Psychoneuroendocrinology, 42,* 49–58.

Armstrong, K. (2011). *Twelve steps to a compassionate life.* London: The Bodley Head.

Baer, R. A. (2003). Mindfulness training as a clinical intervention: A conceptual and empirical review. *Clinical Psychology: Science and Practice, 10,* 125–143.

Baer, R. A. (Ed.). (2006). *Mindfulness-based treatment approaches: Clinician's guide to evidence and applications.* London: Academic Press.

Baer, R. A. (2010). Self-compassion as a mechanism of change in mindfulness- and acceptance-based treatments. In R. A. Baer (Ed.), *Assessing mindfulness and acceptance processes in clients: Illuminating the theory and practice of change* (pp. 135–153). Oakland, CA: New Harbinger.

Baker, L. R., & McNulty, J. K. (2011). Self-compassion and relationship maintenance: The moderating roles of conscientiousness and gender. *Journal of Personality and Social Psychology, 100,* 853–873.

Baraz, J., & Alexander, S. (2010). *Awakening joy.* New York: Bantam.

Barks, C. (1996). *The essential Rumi.* San Francisco: HarperCollins.

Barnard, L. K., & Curry, J. F. (2011). Self-compassion: Conceptualizations, correlates, & interventions. *Review of General Psychology, 15,* 289–303.

Barrington, C., Goswami, A., & Jones, A. (2005). *Dru yoga: Stillness in motion.* Bangor, England: Dru Publications.

Bartley, T. (2012). *Mindfulness-based cognitive therapy for cancer.* Chichester, England: Wiley-Blackwell.

Batchelor, S. (1998). *Buddhism without beliefs: A contemporary guide to awakening.* New York: Riverhead.

Baumeister, R. F., Bratslavsky, E., & Finkenauer, C. (2001). Bad is stronger than good. *Review of General Psychology, 5,* 323–370.

Beaumont, E., Galpin, A., & Jenkins, P. (2012). Being kinder to myself: A prospective comparative study, exploring post-trauma therapy outcome measures, for two groups of clients, receiving either Cognitive Behaviour Therapy or Cognitive Behaviour Therapy and Compassionate Mind Training. *Counselling Psychology Review, 27,* 31–43.

Beck, A. T., Rush, A. J., Shaw, B. F., & Emery, G. (1979). *Cognitive therapy of depression.* New York: Guilford Press.

Bennett-Goleman, T. (2003). *Emotional alchemy: How your mind can heal your heart.* London: Rider.

Beutler, L., Malik, M., Alimohamed, S., Harwood, T. M., Talebi, H., Noble, S., & Wong, E. (2005). Therapist variables. In M. Lambert (Ed.), *Bergin and Garfield's handbook of psychotherapy and behavior change* (pp. 227–306). New York: Wiley.

Biegel, G. M., Brown, K. W., Shapiro, S. L., & Schubert, C. M. (2009). Mindfulness-based stress reduction for the treatment of adolescent psychiatric outpatients: A randomized clinical trial. *Journal of Consulting and Clinical Psychology, 77,* 855–866.

Bien, T. (2008). The Four Immeasurable Minds: Preparing to be present in psychotherapy. In S. F. Hick & T. Bien (Eds.), *Mindfulness and the therapeutic relationship* (pp. 37–54). New York: Guilford Press.

Bierhoff, H.-W. (2005). The psychology of compassion and prosocial behavior. In P. Gilbert (Ed.), *Compassion: Conceptualisations, research and use in psychotherapy* (pp. 148–167). London: Routledge.

Boellinghaus, I., Jones, F. W., & Hutton, J. (2013). Cultivating self-care and compassion in psychological therapists in training: The experience of practicing loving-kindness meditation. *Training and Education in Professional Psychology, 7,* 267–277.

Bohlmeijer, E. T., & Hulsbergen, M. L. (2013). *A beginner's guide to mindfulness: Live in the moment.* Maidenhead, England: Open University Press.

Bohlmeijer, E., Prenger, R., Taal, E., & Cuijpers, P. (2010). The effects of mindfulness-based stress reduction therapy on mental health of adults with a chronic medical disease: A meta-analysis. *Journal of Psychosomatic Research, 68,* 539–544.

Bos, E., & Appelo, M. (2009). De focus van psychotherapie: klachten of krachten? [The focus of psychotherapy: Complaints or strengths?]. *De psycholoog, 44,* 318–324.

Bos, E. H., Merea, R., Van den Brink, E., Sanderman, R., & Bartels-Velthuis, A. A. (2014). Mindfulness training in a heterogeneous psychiatric sample: Outcome evaluation and comparison of different diagnostic groups. *Journal of Clinical Psychology, 70,* 60–71.

Bowen, S., Chawla, N., & Marlatt, A. (2011). *Mindfulness-based relapse prevention for addictive behaviors: A clinician's guide.* New York: Guilford Press.

Brach, T. (2004). *Radical acceptance: Embracing your life with the heart of a Buddha.* New York: Bantam.

Braehler, C., Gumley, A., Harper, J., Wallace, S., Norrie, J., & Gilbert, P. (2013). Exploring change processes in compassion focused therapy in psychosis: Results of a feasibility randomized controlled trial. *British Journal of Clinical Psychology, 52,* 199–214.

Breen, W. E., Kashdan, T. B., Lenser, M. L., & Fincham, F. D. (2010). Gratitude and forgiveness: Convergence and divergence on self-report and informant ratings. *Journal of Personality and Individual Differences, 49,* 932–937.

Breines, J. G., & Chen, S. (2012). Self-compassion increases self-improvement motivation. *Personality and Social Psychology Bulletin, 38,* 1133–1143.

Breines, J., Toole, A., Tu, C., & Chen, S. (2014). Self-compassion, body image, and self-reported disordered eating. *Self and Identity, 14,* 432–448.

Brewer, J. A., Worhunsky, P. D., Gray, J. R., Tang, Y., Weber, J., & Kober, H. (2011). Meditation experience is associated with differences in default mode network activity and connectivity. *Proceedings of the National Academy of Sciences, 108,* 20254–20259.

Brewin, C. R. (2006). Understanding cognitive behaviour therapy: A retrieval competition account. *Behaviour Research and Therapy, 44,* 765–784.

Brewin, C. R., Wheatley, J., Patel, T., Fearon, P., Hackmann, A., Wells A, . . . Myers, S. (2009). Imagery rescripting as a brief stand-alone treatment for depressed patients with intrusive memories. *Behaviour Research and Therapy, 47,* 569–576.

Brickman, P., & Campbell, D. T. (1971). Hedonic relativism and planning the good society. In M. H. Appley (Ed.), *Adaptation level theory: A symposium* (pp. 287–302). New York: Academic Press.

Brown, B. (2010). *The gifts of imperfection.* Center City, MN: Hazelden.

Brown, B. (2012). *Daring greatly.* New York: Gotham.

Brown, R. P., & Gerbarg, P. L. (2012). *The healing power of the breath.* Boston: Shambhala.

Bryant, F. B., & Veroff, J. (2007). *Savoring: A new model of positive experiences.* Mahwah, NJ: Erlbaum.

Buber, M. (1937). *I and Thou.* Edinburgh, Scotland: T & T Clark.

Burch, V. (2008). *Living well with pain and illness.* London: Piatkus.

Burch, V., & Penman, D. (2013). *Mindfulness for health: A practical guide to relieving pain, reducing stress and restoring wellbeing.* London: Piatkus.

Calaprice, A. (2005). *The new quotable Einstein.* Princeton, NJ: Princeton University Press.

Canterberry, M., & Gillath, O. (2013). Neural evidence for a multifaceted model of attachment security. *International Journal of Psychophysiology, 88,* 232–240.

Carlson, L. E., Labelle, L. E., Garland, S. N., Hutchins, M. L., & Birnie, K. (2009). Mindfulness-based interventions in oncology. In F. Didonna (Ed.), *Clinical handbook of mindfulness* (pp. 383–404). New York: Springer.

Carr, A. (2011). *Positive psychology: The science of happiness and human strengths.* New York: Routledge.

Carson, J. W., Keefe, F. J., Lynch, T. R., Carson, K. M., Goli, V., Fras, A. M., & Thorp, S. R. (2005). Loving-kindness meditation for chronic low back pain: Results from a pilot trial. *Journal of Holistic Nursing, 23,* 287–304.

Chadwick, P., Newman Taylor, K., & Abba, N. (2005). Mindfulness groups for people with psychosis. *Behavioural and Cognitive Psychotherapy, 33,* 351–359.

Chen, D. C. R., Kirshenbaum, D. S., Yan, J., Kirshenbaum, E., & Aseltine, R. H. (2012). Characterizing changes in student empathy throughout medical school. *Medical Teacher, 34,* 305–311.

Chiesa, A., & Serretti, A. (2011). Mindfulness-based cognitive therapy for psychiatric disorders: A systematic review and meta-analysis. *Psychiatry Research, 187,* 441–453.

Chödrön, P. (2001). *Tonglen: The path of transformation.* Halifax, Nova Scotia, Canada: Vajradhatu.

Chödrön, P. (2003). *Start where you are: How to accept yourself and others.* London: Element.

Cole-King, A., & Gilbert, P. (2011). Compassionate care: The theory and the reality. *Journal of Holistic Healthcare, 8*(3), 29–36.

Cosley, B. J., McCoy, S. K., Saslow, L. R. & Epel, E. S. (2010). Is compassion for others stress buffering? Consequences of compassion and social support for physiological reactivity to stress. *Journal of Experimental Social Psychology, 46*, 816–823.

Costa, J., & Pinto-Gouveia, J. (2011). Acceptance of pain, self-compassion and psychopathology: Using the chronic pain acceptance questionnaire to identify patients' subgroups. *Clinical Psychology and Psychotherapy, 18*, 292–302.

Cozolino, L. (2006). *The neuroscience of human relationships: Attachment and the developing social brain.* New York: Norton.

Crocker, J., & Canevello, A. (2008). Creating and undermining social support in communal relationships: The role of compassionate and self-image goals. *Journal of Personality and Social Psychology, 95*, 555–575.

CVZ. (2011). *College for Health Insurances: The use of antidepressants 2006–2009 in the Netherlands.* Retrieved July 27, 2011 from www.cvz.nl/publicaties/gipeilingen

Czerniak, E., & Davidson, M. (2012). Placebo, a historical perspective. *European Neuropsychopharmacology, 22*, 770–774.

Davidson, R. J. (2012). The neurobiology of compassion. In C. K. Germer & R. D. Siegel (Eds.), *Compassion and wisdom in psychotherapy* (pp. 111–118). New York: Guilford Press.

De Jong, P., & Berg, I. K. (1998). *Interviewing for solutions.* Pacific Grove, CA: Brooks/Cole.

De Saint-Exupéry, A. (1971). *The little prince.* New York: Harcourt, Brace, Jovanovich. (Original work published 1943)

De Shazer, S., & Dolan, Y. (2007). *More than miracles: The state of the art of Solution-Focused Brief Therapy.* New York: Haworth Press.

De Waal, F. (2009). *The age of empathy: Nature's lessons for a kinder society.* New York: Three Rivers Press.

De Wit, H. F. (1991). *Contemplative psychology.* Pittsburgh, PA: Duquesne University Press.

De Wit, H. F. (1999). *The spiritual path: An introduction to the psychology of the spiritual traditions.* Pittsburgh, PA: Duquesne University Press.

De Wit, H. F. (2008). *Het open veld van de ervaring—De Boeddha over inzicht, compassie en levensgeluk* [The open field of experience—The Buddha on insight, compassion and happiness]. Kampen, the Netherlands: Ten Have.

De Zulueta, P. (2013). Compassion in 21st century medicine: Is it sustainable? *Clinical Ethics, 8*, 119–128.

Decety, J. (2011). The neuroevolution of empathy. *Annals of the New York Academy of Sciences, 1231*, 35–45.

Dehue, T. (2008). *De depressie epidemie* [The depression epidemic]. Amsterdam, the Netherlands: Augustus.

Depue, R. A., & Morrone-Strupinsky, J. V. (2005). A neurobehavioral model of affiliative bonding. *Behavioral and Brain Sciences, 28*, 313–395.

Desbordes, G., Negi, L. T., Pace, T. W. W., Wallace, B. A., Raison, C. L., & Schwartz, E. L. (2012). Effects of mindful-attention and compassion meditation training on amygdala response to emotional stimuli in an ordinary, non-meditative state. *Frontiers in Human Neuroscience, 6*, 292.

Dickinson, E. (1891). *Poems by Emily Dickinson: Second series* (T. W. Higginson & M. L. Todd, Eds.). Boston: Roberts Brothers.

Didonna, F. (Ed.) (2009a). *Clinical handbook of mindfulness.* New York: Springer.

Didonna, F. (2009b). Mindfulness and obsessive–compulsive disorder: Developing a way to trust and validate one's internal experience. In F. Didonna (Ed.), *Clinical handbook of mindfulness* (pp. 189–219). New York: Springer.

Dyrbye, L. N., Massie, F. S., Eacker, A., Harper, W., Power, D., Durning, S. J., . . . Shanafelt, T. D. (2010). Relationship between burnout and professional conduct and attitudes among US medical students. *JAMA, 304,* 1173–1180.

Eicher, A. C., Davis, L. W., & Lysaker, P. H. (2013). Self-compassion: A novel link with symptoms in schizophrenia? *The Journal of Nervous and Mental Disease, 201,* 389–393.

Einstein, A. (1954). *Ideas and opinions.* New York: Crown.

Eliot, T. S. (1917). *Prufrock and other observations.* London: The Egoist.

Emmons, R. A., & McCullough, M. E. (2003). Counting blessings versus burdens: An experimental investigation of gratitude and subjective well-being in daily life. *Journal of Personality and Social Psychology, 84,* 377–389.

Engen, H. G., & Singer, T. (2012). Empathy circuits. *Current Opinion in Neurobiology, 23,* 275–282.

Epstein, M. (1995). *Thoughts without a thinker: Psychotherapy from a Buddhist perspective.* New York: Basic Books.

Epstein, M. (1998). *Going to pieces without falling apart: A Buddhist perspective on wholeness.* New York: Broadway Books.

Esch, T., & Stefano, G. B. (2011). The neurobiological link between compassion and love. *Medical Science Monitor, 17,* RA65–75.

Figley, C. R. (2002). Compassion fatigue: Psychotherapists' chronic lack of self care. *Journal of Clinical Psychology, 58*(11, Suppl. 1), 1433–1441.

Firth-Cozens, J. (2001). Interventions to improve physicians' well-being and patient care. *Social Science and Medicine, 52,* 215–222.

Fonagy, P., & Target, M. (2006) The mentalization-focused approach to self pathology. *Journal of Personality Disorders, 20,* 544–76.

Fortney, L., Luchterhand, C., Zakletskaja, L., Zgierska, A., & Rakel, D. (2013). Abbreviated Mindfulness Intervention for job satisfaction, quality of life, and compassion in primary care clinicians: A pilot study. *Annals of Family Medicine, 11,* 412–420.

Frances, A. (2009). Wither *DSM–V? British Journal of Psychiatry, 195,* 391–392.

Frankl, V. E. (1985). *Man's search for meaning: An introduction to logotherapy.* Boston: Beacon Press. (Original work published 1946)

Fredrickson, B. L. (2009). *Positivity.* New York: Crown.

Fredrickson, B. L. (2013). *Love 2.0.* New York: Penguin.

Fredrickson, B. L., Cohn, M. A., Coffey, K. A., Pek, J., & Finkel, S. (2008). Open hearts build lives: Positive emotions, induced through loving-kindness meditation, build consequential personal resources. *Journal of Personality and Social Psychology, 95,* 1045–1062.

Fulford, K. W. M. (2008). Values-based practice: A new partner to evidence-based practice and a first for psychiatry? (Editorial). *Mens Sana Monographs, 6,* 10–21.

Gale, C., Gilbert, P., Read, N., & Goss, K. (2014). An evaluation of the impact of introducing Compassion Focused Therapy to a standard treatment programme for people with eating disorders. *Clinical Psychology and Psychotherapy, 21,* 1–12.

Gardner-Nix, J. (2009). Mindfulness-Based Stress Reduction for chronic pain management. In F. Didonna (Ed.), *Clinical handbook of mindfulness* (pp. 369–381). New York: Springer.

Garland, E. L., Fredrickson, B., Kring, A. M., Johnson, P. E., Meyer, P. S., & Penn, D. L. (2010). Upward spirals of positive emotions counter downward spirals of negativity:

Insights from the broaden-and-build theory and affective neuroscience on the treatment of emotion dysfunctions and deficits in psychopathology. *Clinical Psychology Review, 30*, 849–864.

Geisler, F. C. M., Kubiak, T., Siewert, K., & Weber, H. (2013). Cardiac vagal tone is associated with social engagement and self-regulation. *Biological Psychology, 93*, 279–286.

Germer, C. K. (2009). *The mindful path to self-compassion.* New York: Guilford Press.

Germer, C. K. (2012). Cultivating compassion in psychotherapy. In C. K. Germer & R. D. Siegel (Eds.), *Wisdom and compassion in psychotherapy* (pp. 93–110). New York: Guilford Press.

Germer, C. K. (2013). Mindfulness: What is it? What does it matter? In C. K. Germer, R. D. Siegel, & P. R. Fulton (Eds.), *Mindfulness and psychotherapy* (pp. 3–36). New York: Guilford Press.

Germer, C. K., & Siegel, R. D. (Eds.). (2012). *Wisdom and compassion in psychotherapy.* New York: Guilford Press.

Germer, C. K., Siegel, R. D., & Fulton, P. R. (Eds.). (2013). *Mindfulness and psychotherapy.* New York: Guilford Press.

Gilbert, P. (2000). Social mentalities: Internal 'social' conflicts and the role of inner warmth and compassion in cognitive therapy. In P. Gilbert & K. G. Bailey (Eds.), *Genes on the couch: Explorations in evolutionary psychotherapy* (pp. 118–150). Hove, England: Brunner-Routledge.

Gilbert, P. (2005). Compassion and cruelty: A biopsychosocial approach. In P. Gilbert (Ed.), *Compassion: Conceptualisations, research and use in psychotherapy* (pp. 9–74). London: Routledge.

Gilbert, P. (2009a). *The compassionate mind.* London: Constable & Robinson.

Gilbert, P. (2009b). *Overcoming depression* (3rd ed.). London: Constable & Robinson.

Gilbert, P. (2010). *Compassion focused therapy.* London: Routledge.

Gilbert, P. (2014). The origins and nature of compassion focused therapy. *British Journal of Clinical Psychology, 53*, 6–41.

Gilbert, P., Broomhead, C., Irons, C., McEwan, K., Bellew, R., Mills, A., . . . Knibb, R. (2007). Development of a striving to avoid inferiority scale. *British Journal of Social Psychology, 46*, 633–648.

Gilbert, P., & Choden. (2013). *Mindful compassion.* London: Constable & Robinson.

Gilbert, P., & Irons, C. (2004). A pilot exploration of the use of compassionate images in a group of self-critical people. *Memory, 12*, 507–516.

Gilbert, P., & Irons, C. (2005). Focused therapies and compassionate mind training for shame and self-attacking. In P. Gilbert (Ed.), *Compassion: Conceptualisations, research and use in psychotherapy* (pp. 263–325). London: Routledge.

Gilbert, P., & Proctor, S. (2006). Compassionate mind training for people with high shame and self-criticism: A pilot study of a group therapy approach. *Clinical Psychology and Psychotherapy, 13*, 353–379.

Gillath, O., Shaver, P. R., & Mikulincer, M. (2005). An attachment–theoretical approach to compassion and altruism. In P. Gilbert (Ed.), *Compassion: Conceptualisations, research and use in psychotherapy* (pp. 121–147). London: Routledge.

Gillis Chapman, S. (2012). *The five keys to mindful communication.* Boston & London: Shambala.

Girl, 10, used geography to save lives. (2005, January 1). *Telegraph.* Retrieved January 11, 2015, from www.telegraph.co.uk/news/1480192/Girl-10-used-geography-lesson-to-save-lives.html

Goldstein, J. (2002). *One Dharma: The emerging Western Buddhism.* New York: Harper Collins.

Goleman, D. (1988). *The meditative mind.* New York: Putnam.

Goleman, D. (2002). *Destructive emotions: A scientific dialogue with the Dalai Lama.* New York: Bantam & Mind and Life Institute.

Goleman, D. (2006). *Social intelligence: The new science of human relationships.* New York: Bantam.

Goleman, D. (Ed.). (2003). *Healing emotions: Conversations with the Dalai Lama on mindfulness, emotions and health.* Boston & London: Shambala.

Goodman, T. A., & Kaiser Greenland, S. (2009). Mindfulness with children: Working with difficult emotions. In F. Didonna (Ed.), *Clinical handbook of mindfulness* (pp. 417–429). New York: Springer.

Gordon, J. S. (2008). *Unstuck: Your guide to the seven-stage journey out of depression.* London: Penguin Books.

Goss, K. (2011). *The compassionate mind approach to beating overeating.* London: Constable & Robinson.

Goss, K., & Allan, S. (2010). Compassion focused therapy for eating disorders. *International Journal of Cognitive Therapy, 3,* 141–158.

Green, S. M., & Bieling, P. J. (2012). Expanding the scope for effectiveness of mindfulness-based cognitive therapy: Evidence for effectiveness in a heterogeneous psychiatric sample. *Cognitive and Behavioral Practice, 19,* 174–180.

Grepmair, L., Mitterlehner, F., Loew, T., Bachler, E., Rother, W., & Nickel, M. (2007). Promoting mindfulness in psychotherapists in training influences the treatment results of their patients: A randomized, double-blind, controlled study. *Psychotherapy and Psychosomatics, 76,* 332–338.

Grossman, P., Niemann, L., Schmidt, S., & Walach, H. (2004). Mindfulness-based stress reduction and health benefits: A meta-analysis. *Journal of Psychosomatic Research, 57,* 35–43.

Gumley, A., Braehler , C., Laithwaite , H., MacBeth, A., & Gilbert, P. (2010) A compassion focused model of recovery after psychosis. *International Journal of Cognitive Psychotherapy, 3,* 186–201.

Gyatso, P., & Shakya, T. W. (1998). *Fire under the snow: The testimony of a Tibetan prisoner.* London: Harvill Press.

Gyatso, T. (1984). *Kindness, clarity, and insight.* Ithaca, NY: Snow Lion.

Gyatso, T. (2003). *The compassionate life.* Somerville, MA: Wisdom.

Hall, J. H., & Fincham, F. D. (2005). Self-forgiveness: The stepchild of forgiveness research. *Journal of Social and Clinical Psychology, 24,* 621–637.

Hanson, R. (with Mendius, R.). (2009) *Buddha's brain: The practical neuroscience of happiness, love & wisdom.* Oakland, CA: New Harbinger.

Hanson, R. (2013). *Hardwiring happiness—The new brain science of contentment, calm, and confidence.* New York: Harmony.

Harlow, H. F. (1958). The nature of love. *American Psychologist, 13,* 673–685.

Hartfiel, N., Havenhand, J., Khalsa, S. B., Clarke, G., & Krayer, A. (2011). The effectiveness of yoga for the improvement of well-being and resilience to stress in the workplace. *Scandinavian Journal of Work, Environment & Health, 37,* 70–76.

Hayes, S. C., Follette, V. M., & Linehan, M. M. (Eds.). (2004). *Mindfulness and acceptance: Expanding the cognitive–behavioral tradition.* New York: Guilford Press.

Hayes, S., & Smith, S. (2005). *Get out of your mind and into your life: The new Acceptance and Commitment Therapy.* Oakland, CA: New Harbinger.

Hayes, S., Strohsal, K., & Wilson, K. (1999). *Acceptance and Commitment Therapy: An experiential approach to behavior change.* New York: Guilford Press.

Healy, D. (1997). *The antidepressant era.* Cambridge, MA: Harvard University Press.

Healy, D. (2002). *The creation of psychopharmacology.* Cambridge, MA: Harvard University Press.

Healy, D., & Thase, M. E. (2003). Is academic psychiatry for sale? *The British Journal of Psychiatry 182*, 388–390.

Hebb, D. O. (1949) *The organization of behavior: A neuropsychological theory.* New York: Wiley.

Heffernan, M., Griffin, M., McNulty, S., & Fitzpatrick, J. J. (2010). Self-compassion and emotional intelligence in nurses. *International Journal of Nursing Practice, 16*, 366–373.

Henderson, L. (2010). *Improving social confidence and reducing shyness using Compassion Focused Therapy.* London: Constable & Robinson.

Hick, S. F., & Bien, T. (Eds.). (2008). *Mindfulness and the therapeutic relationship.* New York: Guilford Press.

Hoenders, H. J. R. (2014). *Integrative psychiatry: Conceptual foundation, implementation and effectiveness.* (Doctoral dissertation, University of Groningen, the Netherlands). Available at http://irs.ub.rug.nl/ppn/37073856X

Hoenders, H. J., Appelo, M. T., Van den Brink, H., Hartogs, B. M., & De Jong, J. T. (2011). The Dutch complementary and alternative medicine (CAM) protocol: To ensure the safe and effective use of complementary and alternative medicine within Dutch mental health care. *Journal of Alternative and Complementary Medicine. 17*, 1197–1201.

Hofmann, S. G., Grossman, P., & Hinton, D. E. (2011). Loving-kindness and compassion meditation: Potential for psychological interventions. *Clinical Psychology Review, 31*, 1126–1132.

Hofmann, S. G., Sawyer, A. T., Witt, A. A., & Oh, D. (2010). The effect of mindfulness based therapy on anxiety and depression: A meta-analytic review. *Journal of Consulting and Clinical Psychology, 78*, 169–183.

Hoge, E. A., Hölzel, B. K., Marques, L., Metcalf, C. A., Brach, N., Lazar, S. W., & Simon, N. M. (2013). Mindfulness and self-compassion in generalized anxiety disorder: Examining predictors of disability. *Evidence-Based Complementary and Alternative Medicine.* Online publication. doi:10.1155/2013/576258

Hollis-Walker, L., & Colosimo, K. (2011). Mindfulness, self-compassion and happiness in non-meditators: A theoretical and empirical examination. *Personality and Individual Differences, 50*, 222–227.

Horwitz, A. V., & Wakefield, J. C. (2007). *The loss of sadness: How psychiatry transformed normal sorrow into depressive disorder.* New York: Oxford University Press.

Hsu, D. T., Sandford, B. J., Meyers, K. K., Love, T. M., Hazlett, K. E., Wang, H., . . . Zubieta, J.-K. (2013). Response of the μ-opioid system to social rejection and acceptance. *Molecular Psychiatry, 18*, 1211–1217.

Huta, V., & Ryan, R. M. (2010). Pursuing pleasure or virtue: The differential and overlapping well-being benefits of hedonic and eudaimonic motives. *Journal of Happiness Studies, 11*, 735–762.

Hutcherson, C. A., Seppala, E. M., & Gross, J. J. (2008). Lovingkindness meditation increases social connectedness. *Emotion, 8*, 720–724.

Imel, Z., Baldwin, S., Bonus, K., & MacCoon, D. (2008). Beyond the individual: Group effects in mindfulness-based stress reduction. *Psychotherapy Research, 18*, 735–742.

Jahnke, R., Larkey, L., Rogers, C., Etnier, J., & Lin, F. (2010). A comprehensive review of health benefits of Qigong and Tai Chi. *American Journal of Health Promotion, 24*, e1–e25.

Jazaieri, H., Jinpa, J. T., McGonigal, K., Rosenberg, E. L., Finkelstein, J., Simon-Thomas, E., . . . Goldin, P. R. (2013). Enhancing compassion: A randomized controlled trial of a compassion cultivation training program. *Journal of Happiness Studies, 14*, 1113–1126.

Jazaieri, H., McGonigal, K., Jinpa, T., Doty, J. R., Gross, J. J. & Goldin, P. R. (2014). A randomized controlled trial of compassion cultivation training: Effects on mindfulness, affect, and emotion regulation. *Motivation and Emotion, 38,* 23–35.

Jiménez, J. R. (1973). *Lorca and Jiménez: Selected poems* (R. Bly, Trans.). Boston: Beacon Press.

Johnson, K. J., Penn, D. L., Fredrickson, B. L., Myer, P.S., Kring, A. M., & Brantley, M. (2011). Loving-kindness meditation to enhance recovery from negative symptoms of schizophrenia. *Journal of Clinical Psychology, 65,* 499–509.

Judge, L., Cleghorn, A., McEwan, K., & Gilbert, P. (2012). An exploration of group-based compassion focused therapy for a heterogeneous range of clients presenting to a community mental health team. *International Journal of Cognitive Therapy, 5,* 420–429.

Kabat-Zinn, J. (1991). *Full catastrophe living: How to cope with stress, pain and illness using mindfulness meditation.* New York: Dell.

Kabat-Zinn, J. (1994). *Wherever you go, there you are: Mindfulness meditation in everyday life.* New York: Hyperion.

Kabat-Zinn, J. (2005). *Coming to our senses: Healing ourselves and the world through mindfulness.* London: Piatkus.

Kannan, D., & Levitt, H. M. (2013). A review of client self-criticism in psychotherapy. *Journal of Psychotherapy Integration, 23,* 166–178.

Karpowicz, S., Harazduk, N., & Haramati, A. (2009). Using mind–body medicine for self-awareness and self-care in medical school. *Journal of Holistic Healthcare, 6,* 19–22.

Kashdan, T. B., Barrios, V., Forsyth, J. P., & Steger, M. F. (2006). Experiential avoidance as a generalized psychological vulnerability: Comparisons with coping and emotion regulation strategies. *Behaviour Research and Therapy, 44,* 1301–1320.

Kearney, D. J., Malte, C. A., McManus, C., Martinez, M. E., Felleman, B., & Simpson, T. L. (2013). Loving-kindness meditation for posttraumatic stress disorder: A pilot study. *Journal of Traumatic Stress, 26,* 426–434.

Kelly, A. C., Zuroff, D. C., Foa, C. L., & Gilbert, P. (2010). Who benefits from training in self-compassionate self-regulation? A study of smoking reduction. *Journal of Social and Clinical Psychology, 29,* 727–755.

Kelly, A. C., Zuroff, D. C., & Shapira, L. B. (2009). Soothing oneself and resisting self-attacks: The treatment of two intrapersonal deficits in depression vulnerability. *Cognitive Therapy Research, 33,* 301–313.

Keltner, D. (2009). *Born to be good: The science of a meaningful life.* New York: Norton.

Kemp, A. H., Quintana, D. S., Kuhnert, R.-L., Griffiths, K., Hickie, I. B., & Guastella, A. J. (2012). Oxytocin increases heart rate variability in humans at rest: Implications for social approach-related motivation and capacity for social engagement. *PLoS ONE, 7*(8), e44014. doi:10.1371/journal.pone.0044014

Kim, S., Thibodeau, R., & Jorgensen, R. S. (2011). Shame, guilt and depressive symptoms: A meta-analytic review. *Psychological Bulletin, 137,* 68–96.

Kirsch, I., Deacon, B. J., Huedo-Medina, T. B., Scoboria, A., Moore, T. J., & Johnson, B. T. (2008). Initial severity and antidepressant benefits: A meta-analysis of data submitted to the Food and Drug Administration. *PLoS Med, 5,* e45, doi:10.1371/journal.pmed.0050045

Klein, S. (2014). *Survival of the nicest: How altruism made us human and why it pays to get along.* New York: The Experiment.

Klimecki, O. M., Leiberg, S., Lamm, C., & Singer, T. (2013). Functional neural plasticity and associated changes in positive affect after compassion training. *Cerebral Cortex, 23,* 1552–1561.

Klimecki, O. M., Leiberg, S., Ricard, M., & Singer, T. (2013). Differential pattern of functional brain plasticity after compassion and empathy training. *Social Cognitive and Affective Neuroscience, 9*, 873–879.

Kok, B. E., & Fredrickson, B. L. (2010). Upward spirals of the heart: Autonomic flexibility, as indexed by vagal tone, reciprocally and prospectively predicts positive emotions and social connectedness. *Biological Psychology, 85*, 432–436.

Kok, B. E., Coffey, K. A., Cohn, M. A., Catalino, L. I., Vacharkulksemsuk, T., Algoe, S. B., . . . Fredrickson, B. L. (2013). How positive emotions build physical health: Perceived positive social connections account for the upward spiral between positive emotions and vagal tone. *Psychological Science, 24*, 1123–1132.

Kosfeld, M., Heinrichs, M., Zak, P. J., Fischbacher, U., & Fehr, E. (2005). Oxytocin increases trust in humans. *Nature, 435*, 673–676.

Koster, F. (2004). *Liberating insight.* Chiang Mai, Thailand: Silkworm Books.

Koster, F. (2014). *The web of Buddhist wisdom: Introduction to the Abhidhamma.* Retrieved January 10, 2015 from www.silkwormbooks.com

Kramer, G. (2007). *Insight dialogue: The interpersonal path to freedom.* Boston: Shambala.

Kramer, G., Meleo-Meyer, F., & Lee Turner, M. (2008). Cultivating mindfulness in relationship: Insight dialogue and the Interpersonal Mindfulness Program. In S. F. Hick & T. Bien (Eds.), *Mindfulness and the therapeutic relationship* (pp. 195–214). New York: Guilford Press.

Krasner, M. S., Epstein, R. M., Beckman, H., Suchman, A. L., Chapman, B., Mooney, C. J., & Quill, T. E. (2009). Association of an educational program in mindful communication with burnout, empathy, and attitudes among primary care physicians. *JAMA, 302*, 1284–1293.

Kuyken, W., Watkins, E., Holden, E., White, K., Taylor, R. S., Byford, S., Evans, A., . . . Dalgleish, T. (2010). How does mindfulness-based cognitive therapy work? *Behavior Research and Therapy, 48*, 1105–1112.

Laithwaite, H., Gumley, A., O'Hanlon, M., Doyle, P., Abraham, L., & Porter, S. (2009). Recovery After Psychosis (RAP): A compassion focused programme for individuals in high security settings. *Behavioural and Cognitive Psychotherapy, 37*, 511–526.

Lambert, M. J., & Erekson, D. M. (2008). Positive psychology and the humanistic tradition. *Journal of Psychotherapy Integration, 18*, 222–232.

Langer, E. J. (1989). *Mindfulness.* Reading, MA: Addison-Wesley.

Lathouwers, T. (2013). *More than anyone can do—Zen talks.* Amsterdam, the Netherlands: VU University Press.

Lawrence, V. E., & Lee, D. (2014). An exploration of people's experiences of Compassion-Focused Therapy for trauma, using interpretative phenomenological analysis. *Clinical Psychology and Psychotherapy, 21*, 495–507.

Leary, M. R., Tate, E. B., Adams, C. E., Allen, A. B., & Hancock, J. (2007). Self-compassion and reactions to unpleasant self-relevant events: The implications of treating oneself kindly. *Journal of Personality and Social Psychology, 92*, 887–904.

LeDoux, J. (1998). *The emotional brain.* London: Weidenfeld & Nicolson.

Lee, D. A. (2005). The perfect nurturer: A model to develop a compassionate mind within the context of cognitive therapy. In P. Gilbert (Ed.), *Compassion: Conceptualisations, research and use in psychotherapy* (pp. 326–351). London: Routledge.

Lee, D., & James, S. (2012). *The compassionate mind approach to recovering from trauma.* London: Constable & Robinson.

Lee, T. M. C., Leung, M.-K., Hou, W.-K., Tang, J. C. Y., Yin, J., So, K.-F., . . . Chan, C. C. H. (2012). Distinct neural activity associated with focused-attention meditation and loving-kindness meditation. *PLoS ONE 7*(8), e40054. doi:10.1371/journal.pone.0040054

Leiberg, S., Klimecki, O., & Singer, T. (2011). Short-term compassion training increases prosocial behavior in a newly developed prosocial game. *PLoS ONE 6*(3), e17798. doi:10.1371/journal.pone.0017798

Léon, I., Hernández, J. A., Rodríguez, S., & Vila, J. (2009). When head is tempered by heart: Heart rate variability modulates perception of other-blame reducing anger. *Motivation and Emotion, 33*, 1–9.

Lewis, S. E. (2013). Trauma and the making of flexible minds in the Tibetan exile community. *Ethos, 41*, 313–336.

Liotti, G., & Gilbert, P. (2011). Mentalizing, motivation, and social mentalities: Theoretical considerations and implications for psychotherapy. *Psychology and Psychotherapy: Theory, Research and Practice, 84*, 9–25.

Lincoln, T. M., Hohenhaus, F., & Hartmann, M. (2013). Can paranoid thoughts be reduced by targeting negative emotions and self-esteem? An experimental investigation of a brief compassion-focused intervention. *Cognitive Therapy and Research, 37*, 390–402.

Linehan, M. (1993). *Cognitive behavioral treatment of borderline personality disorder.* New York: Guilford Press.

Longe, O., Maratos, F. A., Gilbert, P., Evans, G., Volker, F., Rockliff, H., & Rippon, G. (2010). Having a word with yourself: Neural correlates of self-criticism and self-reassurance. *NeuroImage, 49*, 1849–1856.

Lowens, I. (2010). Compassion focused therapy for people with bipolar disorder. *International Journal of Cognitive Therapy, 3*, 172–185.

Lucre, K. M., & Corton, N. (2013). An exploration of group compassion-focused therapy for personality disorder. *Psychology and Psychotherapy: Theory, Research, and Practice, 86*, 387–400.

Luskin, F. (2003). *Forgive for good: A proven prescription for health and happiness.* San Francisco: HarperCollins.

Lutz, A., Brefczynski-Lewis, J., Johnstone, T., & Davidson, R. J. (2008). Regulation of the neural circuitry of emotion by compassion meditation: Effects of meditative expertise. *PLoS ONE, 3*(3), e1897. doi:10.1371/journal.pone.0001897

Lutz, A., Greischar, L., Rawlings, N., Ricard, M., & Davidson, R. J. (2004). Long-term meditators self-induce high amplitude gamma synchrony during mental practice. *Proceedings of the National Academy of Sciences, 101*, 16369–16373.

Lyubomirsky, S. (2007). *The how of happiness: A practical guide to getting the life you want.* London: Sphere.

MacBeth, A., & Gumley, A. (2012). Exploring compassion: a meta-analysis of the association between self-compassion and psychopathology. *Clinical Psychology Review, 32*, 545–552.

Machado, A. (1983). *Times Alone: Selected poems of Antonio Machado* (R. Bly, Trans.). Middletown, CT: Wesleyan University Press.

MacLean, P. D. (1990). *The triune brain in evolution: Role in paleocerebral functions.* New York: Springer.

Maex, E. (2006). *Mindfulness: In de maalstroom van je leven* [Mindfulness: In the whirlpool of your life]. Tielt, Belgium: Lannoo.

Magnus, C. M. R., Kowalski, K. C., & McHugh, T.-L. F. (2010). The role of self-compassion in women's self-determined motives to exercise and exercise-related outcomes. *Self and Identity, 9*, 363–382.

Mann, S. (2004). 'People-work': Emotion management, stress and coping. *British Journal of Guidance & Counselling, 32*, 205–221.

Mascaro, J. S., Rilling, J. K., Tenzin Negi, L., & Raison, C. L. (2013). Compassion meditation enhances empathic accuracy and related neural activity. *Social Cognitive and Affective Neuroscience, 8*, 48–55.

Matos, M., & Pinto-Gouveia, J. (2010). Shame as traumatic memory. *Clinical Psychology and Psychotherapy, 17*, 299–312.

Matos, M., Pinto-Gouveia, J., & Gilbert, P. (2013). The effect of shame and shame memories on paranoid ideation and social anxiety. *Clinical Psychology and Psychotherapy, 20*, 334–349.

Mayhew, S., & Gilbert, P. (2008). Compassionate mind training with people who hear malevolent voices: A case series report. *Clinical Psychology and Psychotherapy, 15*, 113–138.

McCown, D., Reibel, D., & Micozzi, M.S. (2010). *Teaching mindfulness: A practical guide for clinicians and educators.* New York: Springer.

McCullough, M. E., & Witvliet, C. V. O. (2001). The psychology of forgiveness. In C. R. Snyder and S. Lopez (Eds.), *Handbook of positive psychology* (pp. 446–458). New York: Oxford University Press.

McKay, K. M., Imel, Z. E., & Wampold, B. E. (2006). Psychiatrist effects in the psychopharmacological treatment of depression. *Journal of Affective Disorders, 92*, 287–290.

McKay, M., Wood, J. C., & Brantley, J. (2007). *Dialectical Behavior Therapy workbook: Practical DBT exercises for learning mindfulness, interpersonal effectiveness, emotion regulation and distress tolerance.* Oakland, CA: New Harbinger.

Meevissen, Y. M. C., Peters, M. L., & Alberts, H. J. M. E. (2011). Become more optimistic by imagining a best possible self: Effects of a two week intervention. *Journal of Behavior Therapy and Experimental Psychiatry, 42*, 371–378.

Megginson, L. (1963), Lessons from Europe for American business. *Southwestern Social Science Quarterly, 44*, 3–13.

Mikulas, W. L. (2007). Buddhism & Western Psychology: Fundamentals of integration. *Journal of Consciousness Studies, 14*, 4–49.

Moncrieff, J. (2003). *Is psychiatry for sale? An examination of the influence of the pharmaceutical industry on academic and practical psychiatry* (Maudsley Discussion Paper No. 13). London: Institute of Psychiatry.

Mosewich, A. D., Kowalsky, K. C., Sabiston, C. M., Sedgwick, W. A., & Tracy, J. L. (2011). Self-compassion: A potential resource for young women athletes. *Journal of Sport & Exercise Psychology, 33*, 103–123.

Neely, M. E., Schallert, D. L., Mohammed, S., Roberts, R. M., & Chen, Y.-J. (2009). Self-kindness when facing stress: The role of self-compassion, goal regulation, and support in college students' well-being. *Motivation and Emotion, 33*, 88–97.

Neff, K. D. (2003a). Development and validation of a scale to measure self-compassion. *Self and Identity, 2*, 223–250.

Neff, K. D. (2003b). Self-compassion: An alternative conceptualization of a healthy attitude toward oneself. *Self and Identity, 2*, 85–102.

Neff, K. D. (2008). Self-compassion: Moving beyond the pitfalls of a separate self-concept. In J. Bauer & H. A. Wayment (Eds.), *Transcending self-interest: Psychological explorations of the quiet ego* (pp. 95–106). Washington, DC: American Psychological Association.

Neff, K. (2011). *Self-compassion: Stop beating yourself up and leave insecurity behind.* New York: HarperCollins.

Neff, K. D. (2012). The science of self-compassion. In C. K. Germer & R. D. Siegel (Eds.), *Compassion and wisdom in psychotherapy* (pp. 79–92). New York: Guilford Press.

Neff, K. D., & Beretvas, S. N. (2012). The role of self-compassion in romantic relationships. *Self and Identity, 12*, 78–98.

Neff, K. D., & Germer, C. K. (2012). A pilot study and randomized controlled trial of the mindful self-compassion program. *Journal of Clinical Psychology, 69*, 28–44.

Neff, K. D., Hsieh, Y., & Dejitterat, K. (2005). Self-compassion, achievement goals and coping with academic failure. *Self and Identity, 4*, 263–287.

Neff, K. D., Kirkpatrick, K. L., & Rude, S. S. (2007). Self-compassion and adaptive psychological functioning. *Journal of Research in Personality, 41*, 139–154.

Neff, K. D., & Pommier, E. (2012). The relationship between self-compassion and other-focused concern among college undergraduates, community adults, and practicing meditators. *Self and Identity, 12*, 160–176.

Neff, K. D., Rude, S. S., & Kirkpatrick, K. (2007). An examination of self-compassion in relation to positive psychological functioning and personality traits. *Journal of Research in Personality, 41*, 908–916.

Neff, K. D., & Vonk, R. (2009). Self-compassion versus global self-esteem: Two different ways of relating to oneself. *Journal of Personality, 77*, 23–50.

Neumann, M., Edelhäuser, F., Tauschel, D., Fischer, M. R., Wirtz, M., Woopen, C., . . . Scheffer, C. (2011). Empathy decline and its reasons: A systematic review of studies with medical students and residents. *Academic Medicine, 86*, 996–1009.

Olff, M. (2012). Bonding after trauma: On the role of social support and the oxytocin system in traumatic stress. *European Journal of Psychotraumatology, 3*. Online publication. doi:10.3402/ejpt.v3i0.18597

Olff, M., Frijling, J. L., Kubzansky, L. D., Bradley, B., Ellenbogen, M. A., Cardoso, C., . . . & Van Zuiden, M. (2013). The role of oxytocin in social bonding, stress regulation and mental health: An update on the moderating effects of context and interindividual differences. *Psychoneuroendocrinology, 38*, 1883–1894.

Oliver, R. (2013). Being present when we care. In A. Fraser (Ed.), *The healing power of meditation: Leading experts on Buddhism, psychology, and medicine explore the health benefits of contemplative practice* (pp. 176–193). Boston & London: Shambala.

Orsillo, S. M., & Roemer, L. A. (Eds.). (2005). *Acceptance and mindfulness-based approaches to anxiety: Conceptualization and treatment.* New York: Springer.

Pace, T. W. W., Negi, L. T., Adame, D. D., Cole, S. P., Sivilli, T. I., Brown, T. D., . . . Raison, C. L. (2009). Effect of compassion meditation on neuroendocrine, innate immune and behavioral responses to psychosocial stress. *Psychoneuroendocrinology, 34*, 87–98.

Pace, T. W. W., Negi, L. T., Sivilli, T. I., Issa, M. J., Cole, S. P., Adame, D. D., & Raison, C. L. (2010). Innate immune, neuroendocrine and behavioral responses to psychosocial stress do not predict subsequent compassion meditation practice time. *Psychoneuroendocrinology, 35*, 310–315.

Pascal, B. (1995). *Pensées* (A. J. Krailsheimer, Trans.) London: Penguin Classics. (Original work published 1669)

Pauley, G., & McPherson, S. (2010). The experience and meaning of compassion and self-compassion for individuals with depression or anxiety. *Psychology and Psychotherapy: Theory, Research, and Practice, 83*, 129–143.

Piet, J., & Hougaard, E. (2011). The effect of mindfulness-based cognitive therapy for prevention of relapse in recurrent major depressive disorder: A systematic review and meta-analysis. *Clinical Psychology Review, 31*, 1032–1040.

Pinto-Gouveia, J., Duarte, C., Matos, M., & Fráguas, S. (2013). The protective role of self-compassion in relation to psychopathology symptoms and quality of life in chronic and in cancer patients. *Clinical Psychology & Psychotherapy, 21*, 311–323.

Porges, S. W. (2003). Social engagement and attachment—A phylogenetic perspective. *Annals of the New York Academy of Sciences, 1008*, 31–47.

Porges, S. W. (2007). The polyvagal perspective. *Biological Psychology, 74*, 116–143.

Post, S. G. (2005). Altruism, happiness, and health: It's good to be good. *International Journal of Behavioral Medicine, 12*, 66–77.

Przezdziecki, A., Sherman, K. A., Baillie, A., Taylor, A., Foley, E., & Stalgis-Bilinski, K. (2013). My changed body: Breast cancer, body image, distress and self-compassion. *Psychooncology, 22*, 1872–1879.

Raichle, M. E., MacLeod, A. M., Snyder, A. Z., Powers, W. J., Gusnard, D. A., & Shulman, G. L. (2001). A default mode of brain function. *Proceedings of the National Academy of Sciences of the United States of America, 98*, 676–682.

Reddy, S. D., Tenzin Negi, L., Dodson-Lavelle, B., Ozawa-de Silva, B., Pace, T. W. W., Cole, S. P., Raison, C. L., . . . Craighead, L. W. (2013). Cognitive-Based Compassion Training: A promising prevention strategy for at-risk adolescents. *Journal of Child and Family Studies, 22*, 219–230.

Rein, G., Atkinson, M., & McCraty, R. (1995). The physiological and psychological effects of compassion and anger. *Journal of Clinical Neuropsychiatry, 5*, 132–139.

Ricard, M. (2010). Is compassion meditation the key to better caregiving? *HuffPost Healthy Living.* Retrieved March 2, 2014 from www.huffingtonpost.com/matthieu-ricard/could-compassion-meditati_b_751566.html

Riemersma, T. (1973). *Teksten fwar ien hear* [Texts for a gentleman]. Bolsward, the Netherlands: Koperative Utjowerij.

Rilke, R. M. (2002). *Letters to a young poet* (R. Snell, Trans.). New York: Dover. (Original work published 1929)

Ringpu, T. R., & Mullen, K. (2005). The Buddhist use of compassionate imagery in mind healing. In P. Gilbert (Ed.), *Compassion: Conceptualisations, research and use in psychotherapy* (pp. 263–325). London: Routledge.

Rizvi, S. L., Welch, S. S., & Dimidjian, S. (2009). Mindfulness and borderline personality disorder. In F. Didonna (Ed.), *Clinical handbook of mindfulness* (pp. 245–257). New York: Springer.

Rockliff, H., Gilbert, P., McEwan, K., Lightman, S., & Glover, D. (2008). A pilot exploration of heart rate variability and salivary cortisol responses to compassion-focused imagery. *Journal of Clinical Neuropsychiatry, 5*, 132–139.

Rockliff, H., Karl, A., McEwan, K., Gilbert, J., Matos, M., & Gilbert, P. (2011). Effects of intranasal oxytocin on 'Compassion Focused Imagery'. *Emotion, 11*, 1388–1396.

Rogers, C. (1995). *On becoming a person: A therapist's view of psychotherapy.* New York: Mariner.

Rossman, M. L. (2000). *Guided imagery for self-healing.* Tiburon, CA: Kramer.

Rozin, P., & Royzman, E. B. (2001). Negativity bias, negativity dominance, and contagion. *Personality and Social Psychology Review, 5*, 296–320.

Rutter, M., Anderson-Wood, L., Beckett, C., Bredenkamp, D., Castle, J., Groothues, C., . . . O'Connor, T. G. (1999). Quasi-autistic patterns following severe early global privation. *Journal of Child Psychology and Psychiatry, 40*, 537–549.

Sackett, D. L., Straus, S. E., Richardson, W. S., Rosenberg, W., & Haynes, R. B. (2000). *Evidence based medicine.* Edinburgh, Scotland: Churchill Livingstone.

Salzberg, S. (1995). *Loving-kindness: The revolutionary art of happiness.* Boston: Shambala.

Sapolsky, R. M. (1994). *Why zebras don't get ulcers.* New York: St Martin's Press.

Saunders, P., Tractenberg, R., Chaterji, R., Amri, H., Harazduk, N., Gordon, J. S., . . . Haramati, A. (2007). Promoting self-awareness and reflection through an experiential mind-body skills course for first year medical students. *Medical Teacher, 29*, 778–784.

Sbarra, D. A., Smith, H. L., & Mehl, M. R. (2012). When leaving your ex, love yourself: Observational ratings of self-compassion predict the course of emotional recovery following marital separation. *Psychological Science, 23*, 261–269.

Segal, Z., Williams, J. M. G., & Teasdale, J. D. (2002). *Mindfulness-Based Cognitive Therapy for depression: A new approach to preventing relapse.* New York: Guilford Press.

Segal, Z., Williams, J. M. G., & Teasdale, J. D. (2013). *Mindfulness-Based Cognitive Therapy for depression* (2nd ed.). New York: Guilford Press.

Seligman, M. (2002). *Authentic happiness: Using the new positive psychology to realize your potential for lasting fulfillment.* New York: Free Press.

Selye, H. (1976). *Stress in health and disease.* Woburn, MA: Butterworth.

Servan-Schreiber, D. (2005). *The instinct to heal: Curing depression, anxiety and stress without drugs and without talk therapy.* New York: Rodale.

Shanafelt, T. D., Boone, S., Tan, L., Dyrbye, L. N., Sotile, W., Satele, D., . . . Oreskovich, M. R. (2012). Burnout and satisfaction with work-life balance among US physicians relative to the general US population. *Archives of Internal Medicine, 172*, 1377–1385.

Shapira, L. B., & Mograin, M. (2010). The benefits of self-compassion and optimism exercises for individuals vulnerable to depression. *The Journal of Positive Psychology, 5*, 377–389.

Shapiro, F. R. (2008). Who wrote the Serenity Prayer? *Yale Alumni Magazine, July/August.* Retrieved February 28, 2014 from http://archives.yalealumnimagazine.com/issues/2008_07/serenity.html

Shapiro, S. L., Astin, J. A., Bishop, S. R., & Cordova, M. (2005). Mindfulness-based stress reduction for health care professionals: Results from a randomized trial. *International Journal of Stress Management, 12*, 164–176.

Shapiro, S. L., Brown, K. W., & Biegel, G. M. (2007). Teaching self-care to care-givers: Effects of mindfulness-based stress reduction on the mental health of therapists in training. *Training and Education in Professional Psychology, 1*, 105–115.

Shapiro, S. L., & Carlson, L. E. (2009). *The art and science of mindfulness: Integrating mindfulness into psychology and the helping professions.* Washington, DC: American Psychological Association.

Shihab Nye, N. (1995). *Words under the words: Selected poems.* Portland, OR: Far Corner Books.

Siegel, D. J. (2007). *The mindful brain: Reflection and attunement in the cultivation of well-being.* New York: Norton.

Siegel, D. J. (2010a). *The mindful therapist: A clinician's guide to mindsight and neural integration.* New York: W.W. Norton.

Siegel, D. J. (2010b). *Mindsight: The new science of personal transformation.* New York: Bantam.

Siegel, R. D., & Germer, C. K. (2012). Wisdom and compassion: Two wings of a bird. In C. K. Germer & R. D. Siegel (Eds.), *Wisdom and compassion in psychotherapy* (pp. 7–35). New York: Guilford Press.

Singer, J. L. (2006). *Imagery in psychotherapy.* Washington, DC: American Psychological Association.

Sister Stan (Kennedy, S.). (2013). *Day by day—A treasure of meditations on mindfulness to comfort and inspire.* London: Random House.

Skovholt, T. M., & Trotter-Mathison, M. (2011). *The resilient practitioner: Burnout prevention and self-care strategies for counselors, therapists, teachers, and health professionals.* New York: Routledge.

Smith, A. (2004). Clinical uses of mindfulness training for older people. *Behavioural and Cognitive Psychotherapy, 32*, 423–430.

Spek, A. A., Van Ham, N. C., & Nyklicek, I. (2013). Mindfulness-based therapy in adults with an autism spectrum disorder: A randomized controlled trial. *Research in Developmental Disabilities, 34*, 246–253.

Spiering, K. (1996). *Een prachtige tuin* [A beautiful garden]. Middelburg, the Netherlands: CBK Zeeland, Slibreeks.

Sri Nisargadatta. (2012). *I am that: Talks with Sri Nisargadatta Maharaj* (S. S. Dikshit, Ed., & M. Frydman, Trans.). Durham, NC: Acorn Press.

Stahl, B., & Goldstein, E. (2010). *A mindfulness-based stress reduction workbook.* Oakland, CA: New Harbinger.

Tai, K., Zheng, X., & Narayanan, J. (2011). Touching a teddy bear mitigates negative effects of social exclusion to increase prosocial behaviour. *Social Psychological and Personality Science, 2*, 618–626.

Taylor, S. (2006). Tend and befriend: Biobehavioral bases of affiliation under stress. *Current Directions in Psychological Science, 15*, 273–277.

Terry, M. L., Leary, M. R., & Mehta, S. (2013). Self-compassion as a buffer against homesickness, depression, and dissatisfaction in the transition to college. *Self and Identity, 12*, 278–290.

Thompson, B., & Waltz, J. (2008). Self-compassion and PTSD symptom severity. *Journal of Traumatic Stress, 21*, 556–558.

Tirch, D. (2012). *The compassionate mind guide to overcoming anxiety: Using compassion-focused therapy to calm panic, worry and fear.* Oakland, CA: New Harbinger.

Toussaint, L., & Friedman, P. (2008). Forgiveness, gratitude, and well-being: The mediating role of affect and beliefs. *Journal of Happiness Studies, 10*, 635–654.

Tracy, J. L., Robins, R. W., & Tangney, J. P. (Eds.). (2007). *The self-conscious emotions: Theory and research.* New York: Guilford Press.

Turner, E. H., Matthews, A. M., Linardatos, E., Tell, R. A., & Rosenthal, R. (2008). Selective publication of antidepressant trials and its influence on apparent efficacy. *New England Journal of Medicine, 358*, 252–260.

Tutu, D. (2009). *No future without forgiveness.* New York: Doubleday.

Van Dam, N. T., Sheppard, S. C., Forsyth, J. P., & Earleywine, M. (2011). Self-compassion is a better predictor than mindfulness of symptom severity and quality of life in mixed anxiety and depression. *Journal of Anxiety Disorders, 25*, 123–130.

Van den Brink, E. (2006a). Naar een integrale benadering van stemmingsstoornissen: Voorbij regulier of alternatief [Towards an integrative approach of mood disorders]. *GGzet Wetenschappelijk, 10*(1), 4–26.

Van den Brink, E. (2006b). Zoek geen problemen, maar oplossingen: Een model voor een gezondheidsgerichte GGz [Seek no problems but solutions: A model for a health-orientated mental health service]. *GGzet Wetenschappelijk, 10*(2), 4–18.

Van Ravesteijn, H., Lucassen, P., Bor, H., Van Weel, C., & Speckens, A. (2013). Mindfulness-Based Cognitive Therapy for patients with medically unexplained symptoms: A randomized controlled trial. *Psychotherapy and Psychosomatics, 82*, 299–310.

Van Vliet, K. J., & Kalnins, G.R.C. (2011). A compassion-focused approach to nonsuicidal self-injury. *Journal of Mental Health Counseling, 33* (4,) 295–311.

Van Vreeswijk, M., Broersen, J., & Schurink, G. (2009). *Mindfulness en schematherapie: Praktische training bij persoonlijkheidsproblematiek* [Mindfulness and schema therapy: Practical training for those with personality problems]. Houten, the Netherlands: Bohn Stafleu van Loghum.

Vandereycken, W. & Van Deth, R. (2006). *Psychiaters te koop?* [Psychiatrists for sale?]. Antwerp, Belgium: Cyclus.

Vetesse, L. C., Dyer, C. E., Li, W. L., & Wekerle, C. (2011). Does self-compassion mitigate the association between childhood maltreatment and later emotional regulation difficulties? *International Journal of Mental Health and Addiction, 9*, 480–491.

Vrticka, P., & Vuilleumier, P. (2012). Neuroscience of human social interactions and adult attachment style. *Frontiers in Human Neuroscience, 6*(212), 1–17.

Wallace, B. A. (2010). *The four immeasurables: Practices to open the heart*. Boston: Shambala.

Wallace, B. A., & Hodel, B. (2008). *Embracing mind: The common ground of science and spirituality*. Boston: Shambala.

Wallmark, E., Safarzadeh, K., Daukantaitė, D., & Maddux, R. E. (2013). Promoting altruism through meditation: An 8-week randomized controlled pilot study. *Mindfulness, 4*, 223–234.

Walsh, R. (2011). Lifestyle and mental health. *American Psychologist, 66*, 579–592.

Wampold, B. E. (2001). *The great psychotherapy debate: Models, methods and findings*. Hillsdale, NJ: Erlbaum.

Wang, S. (2005). A conceptual framework for integrating research related to the physiology of compassion and the wisdom of Buddhist teachings. In P. Gilbert (Ed.), *Compassion: Conceptualisations, research and use in psychotherapy* (pp. 75–120). London: Routledge.

Ward, J., Cody, J., Schaal, M., & Hojat, M. (2012). The empathy enigma: An empirical study of decline in empathy among undergraduate nursing students. *Journal of Professional Nursing, 28*, 34–40.

Weiss, L. (2004). *Therapist's guide to self-care*. New York: Routledge.

Welford, M. (2010). A compassion-focused approach to anxiety disorders. *International Journal of Cognitive Therapy, 3*, 124–140.

Weng, H. Y., Fox, A. S., Shackman, A. J., Stodola, D. E., Caldwell, J. Z. K., Olson, M. C.,. . . Davidson, R. J. (2013). Compassion training alters altruism and neural responses to suffering. *Psychological Science, 24*, 1171–1180.

Werner, K. H., Jazaieri, H., Goldin, P. R., Ziv, M., Heimberg, R. G., & Gross, J. J. (2012). Self-compassion and social anxiety disorder. *Anxiety, Stress, & Coping, 25*, 543–558.

Westerhof, G., & Bohlmeijer, E. (2011). *Psychologie van de levenskunst* [Psychology of the art of living]. Amsterdam, the Netherlands: Boom.

Wieringa, T. (2009). *Joe Speedboat* (S. Garrett, Trans.). London: Portobello Books.

Wilde, O. (1899). *An ideal husband*. London: Leonard Smithers.

Williams, J. M. G., & Kabat-Zinn, J. (2011). Mindfulness: diverse perspectives on its meaning, origins, and multiple applications at the intersection of science and dharma. *Contemporary Buddhism, 12*(1), 1–18.

Williams, M., Teasdale, J., Segal, Z., & Kabat-Zinn, J. (2007). *The mindful way through depression: Freeing yourself from chronic unhappiness*. New York: Guilford Press.

Wilson, K. G. (with Dufrene, T.). (2008). *Mindfulness for two: An acceptance and commitment therapy approach to mindfulness in psychotherapy*. Oakland, CA: New Harbinger.

Wolever, R. Q., & Best, J. L. (2009). Mindfulness-based approaches to eating disorders. In F. Didonna (Ed.), *Clinical handbook of mindfulness* (pp. 259–287). New York: Springer.

World Health Organization. (1978). *Declaration of Alma-Ata*. International Conference on Primary Health Care, Alma Ata, USSR: Author.

World Health Organization. (1979). *Formulating strategies for health for all by 2000*. Geneva, Switzerland: Author.

Wren, A. A., Somers, T. J., Wright, M. A., Goetz, M. C., Leary, M. R., Fras, A. M., . . . Keefe, F. J. (2012). Self-compassion in patients with persistent musculoskeletal pain:

relationship of self-compassion to adjustment to persistent pain. *Journal of Pain and Symptom Management, 43,* 759–770.

Young, J. E., Klosko, J. S., & Weishaar, M. E. (2003). *Schema therapy: A practitioner's guide.* New York: Guilford Press.

Zabelina, D. L., & Robinson, M. D. (2010). Don't be so hard on yourself: Self-compassion facilitates creative originality among self-judgmental individuals. *Creative Research Journal, 22,* 288–293.

Zellner Keller, B., Singh, N. N., & Winton, A. S. (2013). Mindfulness-Based Cognitive Approach for Seniors (MBCAS): Program development and implementation. *Mindfulness, 5,* 453–459.

Zylowska, L., Smalley, S. L., & Schwartz, J. M. (2009). Mindful awareness and ADHD. In F. Didonna (Ed.), *Clinical handbook of mindfulness* (pp. 319–338). New York: Springer.

About the Authors

Erik van den Brink is a psychiatrist/psychotherapist and qualified mindfulness teacher. He studied medicine in Amsterdam, the Netherlands, and trained and worked in psychiatry in West Yorkshire districts in the U.K. He has been practising meditation (*vipassana* and Zen) for over 20 years and trained in Mindfulness-Based Stress Reduction and Mindfulness-Based Cognitive Therapy, Acceptance and Commitment Therapy, Compassion Focused Therapy and Interpersonal Mindfulness (Insight Dialogue) with founding teachers from these areas. He works at the Center for Integrative Psychiatry, an innovative mental health clinic in the Dutch city of Groningen, where he is one of the cofounders, and at *Het Behouden Huys*, a psycho-oncological centre in Haren, near Groningen. He has specialised in mindfulness-based and compassion-focused approaches in mental health care and is a frequently asked guest teacher at training institutes in the Netherlands and across Europe.

See www.mbcl.org

Frits Koster is a *vipassana* meditation teacher and qualified mindfulness teacher. He has also trained and worked as a psychiatric nurse. He has taught mindfulness in mental health settings, including clinics and hospitals for many years. He has been practicing Theravada Buddhism for 35 years and was a Buddhist monk for 6 years in the 1980s. He has been leading *vipassana* retreats and courses since then. While he was a monk he studied Buddhist psychology at various monasteries in Southeast Asia. He is a teacher and member of the faculty of the Institute for Mindfulness-Based Approaches, the Institute for Mindfulness in the Netherlands as well as various training institutes across Europe. He is the author of several books, of which the following have been translated and published (by Silkworm Books) into English: *Liberating Insight* (2004), *Buddhist Meditation in Stress Management* (2007) and *The Web of Wisdom* (2014).

See www.fritskoster.com or www.compassionateliving.info

Index